D1560023

BEHIND
THE
BADGE

BEHIND THE BADGE

REAL STORIES FROM THE POLICE BEAT

ROCKY WARREN

VARRO PRESS
Kansas City

BEHIND THE BADGE

REAL STORIES FROM THE POLICE BEAT

ROCKY WARREN

VARRO PRESS
P.O. Box 8413 - Shawnee Mission, Kansas 66208 USA

Copyright 1998 by Rocky Warren

All rights reserved. No part of this book may be reproduced or transmitted in any form or by any means electronic or mechanical including photocopying, recording, of any information storage or retrieval system without permission in writing from the publisher, Varro Group, Inc.

Publisher's Cataloging-In-Publication
(Provided by Quality Books, Inc.)
Warren, Rocky.
    Behind the badge: real stories from the police beat/ Rocky Warren. - 1st ed.
    p.cm.
    Preassigned LCCN: 97-62353
    ISBN: 1-888644-49-4

    1. Police--Anecdotes. 2. Law enforcement--Anecdotes.
    3. Police officers' writings. I. Title.

HV7914.W37 1998   363.2'3
                                  QBI98-37

Printed and bound in the United States of America

DEDICATION

This book is dedicated to my patient wife, my kids, family, and friends. Without their positive outlook and help, this book would not have been written. Without them, there would be no reason to keep trying so hard.

Also to Mom and Dad, who tell me that being a cop is positive proof of brain damage. I claim I was disadvantaged by heredity.

A special thank you to Dave Rose and Don Cameron. Their training has saved this "pig's" bacon more than once.

Rocky Warren

TABLE OF CONTENTS

PREFACE

This book involves true cases, real victims, and actual suspects. I can attest to the vast majority of the cases...I was there. In the remainder of the cases, I have worked with the officers involved.

Because of the confidentiality of criminal records, I have not fictionalized names. Any name I made up would correspond to someone in the United States. Where necessary, I have used only the first or last names of suspects. Only my partners and myself know the personalities involved. No one should assume they know the people involved. With 260 million people in the U.S., that would be highly unlikely.

When other officers deserve credit, and gave me permission to be named, I have used their full names. They deserve the recognition and thanks of all of us.

This book started as a series of articles for training use in a Reserve Officer Program. In writing them, I found the articles gave insight into how cops think, act, and react. They also offer the civilian insight into matters routinely confronted by working cops.

This book will probably make you laugh, make you angry, and give you something to think about. Another point to note regarding these stories is they are "success" stories. Police are successful thousands of times a day; when they talk down a suspect without force; or take someone into custody through a simple arrest. These things are *not* news.

My co-workers and I have been frustrated about the media-bashing of our profession for many years. We have gone ahead and done the job the right way regardless. It's time the media, liberals, and politicians know their efforts to undermine the police are counter-productive.

They benefit from the protection of police service in this country. They better hope the murderer, rapist, robber, or deviate who attacks them or theirs is willing to sit down and reason. If they expect to dial 911 and get help without having a policeman arrive, they should think again. If they are successful in negating public support and compliance, they will find the true meaning of the following:

A society which makes enemies of its police,
had better make friends of its criminals.

For the average citizen, enjoy. For the young cop just starting out, I hope this book will give you some options. For the working cops across the nation, my thanks and admiration.

Rocky Warren

BEHIND
THE
BADGE

A REASON TO TRAIN

The seventeen year old arose from his chair at Chana High and walked toward the door. The boy, about 5'9" tall and 160 pounds, was obviously drunk. His mom and the school principal had called me. He snarled, "I'm getting out of here." I was standing in the door, but he was ready to walk right through me.

I turned my body into a bladed stance, and as he reached out to grab my arms I twisted my forearms and re-grabbed his wrists. The thought occurred to me, "this kid's arms feel like oak trees, and I don't want to have to fight him."

I looked directly in his eyes and told him, "You **don't** want to do this. Sit down!" He started back toward his chair, then launched himself at what looked like a plate-glass window. After smashing though the glass (thank God it was plexi-glass), he ran across the quad in front of the office. A teacher slowed him down, and I caught up, swinging him to the ground from behind with a chin-cup takedown. Another deputy joined in (thank you Deputy Hadley!) and our suspect was in handcuffs with nothing more than minor scrapes.

I let go of the restraining chin-cup and the young man promptly began beating his head against the pavement. I re-grabbed the chin-cup to keep him from hurting himself. A crowd of about 20-25 students had gathered. Hadley went to the car to get the off-side door unlocked so we could move the prisoner into the car. There were grumbles from the student crowd, "Fuckin' pigs, come on our campus." "He didn't do anything." I could also hear a couple of young people trying to be peacemakers, "Man, you know he was twisted." "He hit Jules for nothing dude."

A sixteen year old girl stepped forward and screamed, "You don't have to treat him like a dog, you fucking pig." I told her, over the rising crowd noise, I was keeping him from hurting himself. "You lying pig," she shouted. I looked up at her with a wide smile and said, "Okay, have it your way." I released the chin-cup and rocked back on my heels. The young prisoner obligingly began battering his head against the pavement again. I let him have two solid thumps, then replaced the restraining chin-cup.

A young man stepped forward and said, "We oughta kick your ass man." I stood up, newly rejoined by Hadley, and told the young man, "Unless you want to end up alongside him in handcuffs, I suggest you go back to class." Several teachers were working the back of the crowd and the students began filtering away. Hadley and I moved our prisoner, and the situation was defused.

When I first became a cop, I could run miles and miles, lift much more than my own body weight, and felt slightly less than indestructible. I was in several scrapes over the years, but as I became older, I found small twinges took longer to go away, and some things just didn't heal.

I determined many years ago I was **not** going to lose on the street, **to anyone!** The only remedy was training. I personally signed up for almost a year of hands-on training, which taught me impact weapon, carotid, and defensive tactics. Through that training I learned something which is now the basis for this book.

As I trained, I spent less and less time in physical encounters. The encounters either didn't occur, or were over quickly, in my favor. I found my injuries, and even injuries to the suspect, were less frequent. I didn't have to get dirty and wrestle with the person I was taking into custody. This resulted in fewer injuries to myself and other officers, and allowed for a quickly controlled situation.

As I get older, the average age of the suspects I encounter stays the same. They are predominantly in the 16 to 30 year age range. They feel good, are physically fit on average, and feel like I used to. It behooves me and every person who puts on a uniform to be well trained. I owe that to my co-workers, my family, and more importantly, to myself.

Another contributing factor to my training is my attitude and mindset. I don't underestimate the intelligence, determination, ability, or aggressiveness of any suspect. If we underestimate them, we leave room to be surprised.

Another trap officers often fall into is a mindset called "elitism." This is as old as time. "Myself, my wife, my brother John and his wife...we four and no more." Limiting your group, and not talking freely with everyone gives a slanted view of reality. If we exclude someone, we may exclude a wealth of knowledge or a valuable bit of training. The next person I talk to may give me a piece of necessary knowledge. He might be a person on the street, a shopkeeper, schoolteacher, co-worker, or family member.

The best reason to train and keep a healthy mindset is I'm getting a little older and the next technique or bit of knowledge I learn may save my "bacon."

You will certainly not be able to take the lead
in all things yourself.
For to one man the gods have given deeds of war,
and to another the dance,
to another the lyre and song,
and in another wide-sounding Zeus puts a good mind.

Homer
The Iliad

A MATTER OF COURAGE

People in hazardous occupations, and people in general, often wonder...when I get threatened by a critical incident, will I be up to it? Will I react quickly, precisely, and efficiently?

Some people care only for themselves. Criminals seem to do only what feels best or satisfies their immediate desires. Their responsibility is only to themselves, and they are sorry they got caught because it's going to cost them. They have to face themselves and their actions in the uncomfortable, hard, reflected light of societies' judgment.

The policeman has a higher standard. They are responsible for themselves, their co-workers, and the general public's safety. Our level of responsibility rises much higher than just a personal self-interest. No one can say how many lives we've saved by the service we perform. It's impossible to say how many times our mere presence, or the possibility of our presence, has made some budding criminal stop and turn away from a crime.

We may well wonder...when the balloon goes up, will I have the personal courage to meet the challenge?

The answer is yes...to the best of your ability at the time. Will you be afraid? If you are sane, you bet! I'm scared pea-green every time. But we go on and overcome the fear; that's the proof of the measure.

Police and enforcement ability can be damned impressive when considered overall. There are 600,000 police to work the crimes occurring among 260 million people. Many of those police are in support roles, and don't work actively in direct enforcement functions. All in all...not bad.

The fact remains that it often comes down to an individual officer's personal courage and tenacity...searching a building when it's dark and quiet, and the suspect may be there; and a thousand other situations. We train, to a greater or lesser degree, to prepare for the test. We expand our comfort zones so we can respond to emergencies.

We all know hindsight is 20/20. It is repugnant to "Monday Morning Quarterback" an officer after the fact. Situations can be learned from, options and alternative actions discussed, but the statement can never begin, "They should have..." or "I would have..." or worse yet, "Why didn't you...?" That is inexcusable. The critique should not be critical of the persons involved, nor contain anything demeaning or critical of their performance.

No one but the officer(s) involved can know all the factors in a situation. We all do the best we can with what we have, at the time of the critical incident. Then we prepare and train for the next one. That's the tough one, the one ahead, the one that's an unknown.

Expand your "comfort zone" through realistic situational training, hone your skills through practice, and be confident you can and will be able to do what is necessary when things go sour.

You gain strength, courage and confidence
by every experience in which you really stop to look
fear in the face.
You are able to say to yourself, I lived through this.
I can take the next thing that comes along.
You must do the thing you think you cannot do.

Eleanor Roosevelt

A QUESTION OF AUTHORITY

I asked the man to step back into the other room of his apartment. He was about 5'10" and probably 20 pounds heavier than me, and he was also quite drunk. This was a danger factor since his judgment was impaired, but a possible advantage since his reactions were visibly slowed and sloppy. That advantage was partly nullified as his tolerance for pain might be greater.

All this flashed through my mind while the man suggested I perform a physically impossible act, then refused to go into the living room. I attempted to separate him from his wife, with whom he had been arguing. The man snarled his follow-up, "What are you going to do if I toss your ass out of this house?" I fixed him with a steady stare while standing in a bladed stance, and told him in a low, level voice, "I have asked you to go in the other room to allow me to talk to your wife for a minute. I will come talk to you in a little while. You've threatened me and I won't allow you to endanger my, or anyone else's, safety. I'm about ten years younger than you. I'm a member of the Special Enforcement Team. I'm well trained in defensive tactics and all the tools of my trade. I can also give you some very tough lessons in Karate. I hope you won't make that necessary." The belligerent man's wife broke in, "Stop being an ass, Karl."

After this little "Jack Webb" type tirade, I succeeded in getting him to comply with the request. The wife later agreed to leave for the night for a "cool down period," her idea, her choice. The bare truth is the closest I had been to a Karate dojo was a Bruce Lee movie. The rest of my speech was true. I was also scared stiff. I could have been punched out or hurt in a fight. What caused the husband to comply? I ran a bluff, and it worked.

We as policemen need several things. We have the authority given to us by law to request compliance from citizens, and the right to arrest in the proper circumstances. We also have the power to use "that minimum amount of force necessary to overcome resistance." What else do we need here?

With the number of people living in the country today, versus the number of police in the nation, it's important to remember that we *need the consent of the people.* If we lose the consent of the majority to enforce the law, we might as well throw in our uniforms. Without massive, *voluntary* compliance with the law, we would never be able to keep up.

Police are not an armed soldiery, with the citizenry being the "enemy." The main danger with the public's perception of "excessive force" is we will lose that consent from the citizenry. It is important to note the vast majority of "excessive force" cases arise from the underlying cause of "failure to train."

The other thing we need is within ourselves. We need to insure there is never any twinge of revenge, personal animosity, prejudice, or self-aggrandizement motive for our words or actions.

If you have any of these motives on your mind, you will slip sooner or later. Go through a mental housecleaning, if necessary, **but get rid of them**. The proper amount of force, directed in the proper way, at the right time, is a matter of personal judgment, training, experience, and ability.

If we know the laws that *allow* us to use force, we more quickly recognize those situations requiring force, and *which level* of force is appropriate. Our response to a threat will be faster because *we will know we are right.* But above all, the following should stick in our minds:

For an action to be just, three things are necessary...
Public Authority, Just Cause, Right Motive.

Saint Thomas Aquinas
1225-1274

THE MECHANICS
OF CONFRONTATION

The struggle had been going on for more than ten minutes. For anyone who's never been in a physical confrontation, that adds up to a total of about three lifetimes. This guy was drunk, 6'2", 190 pounds, and I later learned he threw firewood for a living. I told him, "You don't want to break loose, because if you do, I'll take you with a stick." His response was not totally rational, but predictable, "Let me loose and bring it on!" My first thought was, "Well damn! That didn't work."

I had a handcuff on his right wrist, and every time I put pressure on the wristlock applied to his left wrist, I would catch the right and try to bring it down to complete the handcuffing. His shirt-tail was loose and he twisted his wrist and fought, so I always caught the cuff-ratchet in his shirt-tail. My arms were totally worn out from the fight, and he kept trying to kick and swing at me wildly. At one point, I tried to disable him and take him to the ground, but I didn't have enough strength left.

The suspect finally succeeded in raising his elbow and twisting his way out of the wristlock. I had stopped him for drunk driving, and he was definitely that. I was near the out-skirts of Wheatland, and this guy figured once he got across the county line, it would be "King's X." It doesn't work that way, even though I work for a Northern California Sheriff's Department. I had been in hot pursuit and the seal in the center of the badge reads "State of California."

I drew my baton and dropped into a strike position. My suspect responded with kicks and the fight went on. I struck with the baton, he retreated, then kicked with his right foot. I blocked that with my left hand. I struck with the baton again and just as I made contact with the suspect's left knee, his right foot connected with my hand. My baton slipped out of my hand and landed 75 yards down the street. I raised my fists in a boxing stance and got ready to fight. The suspect decided he didn't want any of that and retreated to his 4x4 pickup. He then tried to evade by driving toward Yuba City and turning onto Beale Air Force Base Road. I followed, wondering, "what's going to happen when he runs the gate to a Strategic Air Command Base?"

This guy obviously had not thought this out because I still had his driver's license with me and had informed dispatch who he was. Later with help from Yuba County and Security Police from Beale (no, he didn't get onto the base), we took him into custody.

I've related all this to point out that should you get into a long, drawn out struggle, expect several things to happen physiologically:

1. The popular press has done plenty of writing on the speeding up or slowing down of our sense of time. Expect this in any critical incident. Good physical conditioning will help overcome most of the "adrenaline shock" in these situations and allow us to function better.

2. Auditory suppression. Don't expect that your partner will hear and follow shouted directions. He may...but don't rely on it. Auditory suppression may very well prevent him from hearing a shout at a distance of mere feet. Even gunfire may sound muted.

3. Tunnel vision. Pick up your side-to-side and up-and-down scanning to make up for the loss of peripheral vision. This helps locate any other possible threats and helps clear your vision.

4. If the confrontation is physical, you may find yourself holding your breath. **This is a trap!** You will go like gangbusters for ten or fifteen seconds, then find yourself running out of gas. You will begin weakening and finally breathe. But from that point on, you are trying to make up ground. You have starved your muscles of oxygen, established an oxygen deficit, and are now fighting with one foot in a barrel. Be conscious of your breathing.

5. Adrenaline dump. This causes or contributes to all the above situations. The by-product is strength for fight or flight, an increased tolerance for pain, and less likelihood of shock. Adrenaline burns off quickly, so you need to beware.

6. The side effect of all this is muscle tremors. These can be small tremors which can degrade small muscle coordination, or *gale-sized*, which I've personally experienced and they aren't much fun.

The more you are aware of your personal reactions under stress, the more sure you can be of your ability to function under such stress. The better you know your abilities and limitations, the more sure you will be of your reactions in crisis.

A hero is no braver than an ordinary man,
but he is braver five minutes longer.

Ralph Waldo Emerson

HUMOR...
THE LAST LINE OF DEFENSE

I was sitting at the counter at Denny's Restaurant in Train Village trying to wrap myself around a hot roast-beef sandwich when I was approached by a man, possibly 60 years old. This was about 1982 and this distinguished grey-haired citizen approached me very boisterously. "Officer, are you aware your sidearm is cocked?" At the time I was carrying a Government Model .45. I looked at the man and said, "Yes, it's very safe that way." The man looked skeptical and said, "That's not true. Surely you don't have a round in the chamber!" I told him I did not normally discuss the condition of my service sidearm. He persisted. I patiently explained I had the thumb-strap locked under the hammer, the grip-safety engaged, the thumb-safety engaged, and the trigger covered by the holster. This guy was simply going to bull his way through, and several other patrons were beginning to pay attention to the exchange. He told me, "You should lower the hammer on that weapon and make it safe. Who do you think you are?"

He really shouldn't have made that last remark. I removed the magazine from my belt pouch, flipped a round off the top, and offered a 185 grain aluminum coated Silvertip bullet to him, smiling all the time. I told my antagonist, "Here...this silver bullet should identify me." He obviously remembered the Lone Ranger, because his faced turned red and he stomped out of the restaurant amid the laughter of the crowd at nearby tables. I had gone through a very tough week and was very tired. All I wanted was to eat my meal, drink my coffee, and be left in peace. I did not receive any complaints, although I certainly expected some.

Police humor is often termed "black or dark humor." We too often see the dark side of life. This type of humor is often inappropriate to people who have not experienced the things seen by emergency workers, police, and the military. Humor is often our last line of defense. Sometimes we have to joke about a situation in an effort to find some way to make it hurt less. It's a very common and very human reaction.

A little humor can be a useful tool. When I'm frisking someone for weapons, I often ask them if they have any flamethrowers, machetes, hand-grenades, bazookas, machine guns or other hardware. The most common reaction I get from the person I'm frisking is a laugh. This frequently relieves a tense situation where someone objects to being searched. It seems to distract them from what I'm doing. I judge very carefully to whom I make the remark, and wouldn't dream of using it on a hardened ex-con. But if I don't get a laugh, a smile, or some appropriate reaction, I search very carefully and my officer safety awareness climbs a notch. I almost always find some type of weapon under those circumstances.

The thing to remember is humor is a defense, a tool, and can also be taken too far. I've been guilty of this and it's cost me dearly at times. We need to watch our reactions, especially around civilians, as they cannot be expected to understand our attempt at humor is a defense mechanism.

To talk without thinking...is to shoot without aiming.

Author Unknown

TRAPS, LURES, AND SUCKER PUNCHES

The suspect had just kicked the side of our victim's car. We were after him because he had about $10,000.00 worth of arrest warrants, and had been terrorizing his girlfriend. He had already fled on foot from us once. This guy was very brazen, because my trainee and I were sitting only 40 yards away when he kicked his girlfriend's car.

My trainee and I unloaded from the car. The trainee went around the east of the house and I stayed on the west, walking into some brush toward a neighbor's house where the suspect had last been seen. At a shout from my trainee, I saw the suspect hot-footing it toward me. I broke from cover and took an angle on the suspect. My trainee got caught up in the lower limbs of a tree, and, I later found out, caught a branch in the eye. I had my side-handle baton in my left hand and used it as a guard, laying the long shaft along my forearm as I crashed through a dense thicket of brush.

The suspect was doing his best imitation of a jack rabbit down a driveway to another house. He then slipped and fell and I gained more ground. He got up and ran into a gully which was steep and densely wooded. My trainee arrived very quickly, despite the injuries (scrapes, scratches, and not being able to see from one eye), and I had to keep him from pursuing the suspect into the draw. I told him, and I still believe I was right, "Don't let the suspect lure you in!" All of us, at one time or another, let our ego get in the way of our better judgment. The result can range from success to disaster. If someone has evil intentions toward you, he may lure you into a trap, using your own persistence as the bait.

The officer who gets in a vehicle pursuit, then unloads into a foot pursuit, running past an uncleared car, is taking a dangerous gamble. The suspect left in the car may be the most dangerous one, and now *he's* behind *you.*

I know of a case locally where a suspect ran from officers while verbally baiting them. Thankfully, one of the officers knew the suspect and how violent he was. The suspect was trying to bait the officers into an extended foot pursuit, into an area where he could turn on the officers when they were exhausted. The suspect was know to be ex-military and in extremely good physical condition, in addition to being violent. The officers wisely declined to fall into the trap.

External clues may tell you when a suspect is trying to lure you. If the suspect is doing "the ex-con pace," that should be a clue to you to get more help. If you stop adjusting your bladed stance and expose your center body mass to the suspect, you may come under attack.

Action is faster than reaction. How many times have we heard this? The question is, do you really believe it? Does it sink in that if you lock onto a suspect and get into a stare-down the suspect starts, you may be playing his game? You may be allowing the suspect to sucker punch you without warning.

When confronted with a suspect, don't lock onto his face or eyes. Watch his hands and let your peripheral vision take in the shoulders. Some amateurs will have a "give-away" of the eyes before they strike at you, some won't. A much larger majority will have a give-away in the shoulder area. A bunching of the shoulder muscles or a sudden drop, "setting the shoulders" for a punch.

The clenching of fists or repetitive closing and opening of the hands is a dead give away. Occasionally, amateurs will draw back an arm, giving you clear warning and time to close in or back off and give yourself reaction distance.

At any rate, visualize situations before they occur. Then think your way out of them. If you don't, you may be setting yourself up for a trap, lure, or sucker punch.

By the way, my trainee who got a branch in the eye received an outstanding rating that day for her performance. She also found herself in another foot pursuit a week later and ran a 16 year old burglary suspect into the ground. Both the suspects mentioned in this story were later taken into custody without problems.

A fool must learn by his own experience.
I prefer to learn by the experiences of others.

Otto Von Bismarck

THE BOUNDARIES OF ARMED CONFRONTATION

The patrol car came up over the rise and around a slight curve which had brush obstructing the view. The call had been a suspicious circumstance call, a possible drug deal along the railroad right of way. My partner, a reserve officer in training, stopped with his patrol car door 12 feet away from the rear of the suspect vehicle. The rear window of the suspect vehicle was partially fogged, but two heads popped up and there was fast and furious motion inside the car.

From our vantage, we didn't know if the suspects were simply stashing their dope, arming themselves, or exactly what we had driven into. The suspects were both males. My trainee and I pulled our service weapons and took positions behind the doors of the patrol car. My trainee began shouting identification and orders. I could barely hear him, and I wasn't sure the suspects could, so I added my voice I.D. My voice at full volume has been known to stop freeway traffic. The driver was taken from the car and secured without incident. That's when things went sour.

I directed the passenger out of the vehicle, and he stepped out into ankle high grass. His hands were raised per our directions. He suddenly stooped down from the knees and reached into the grass at his feet, picking up a black object.

My finger was on the trigger instantly. As both officers commanded "Drop it," I saw a flash of blue color in the suspect's right hand. The suspect complied, dropping the black bristled, blue handled hairbrush from his hand. He was very slow and resistive to verbal direction, but was taken into custody with no more than bio-mechanical control. After a search, he and his companion were released. They had nothing illegal.

The guy's reason for reaching into the grass and picking up the hairbrush? Your guess is as good as mine, but during the remainder of the contact he seemed to find the whole thing immensely funny. I told him how close he had come to being shot and he still found it amusing.

A suspect who is armed can draw and fire before you can respond. We have to be prepared to answer a lethal threat, but my trainee's performance evaluation that day was "excellent." He had exercised the highest judgment a peace officer is called on to make. He had been provoked by a foolish act, and had reacted properly making the right decision within the second it took for the act. Someone lived that day, when it could easily have ended otherwise. Had the shooting occurred, would it have been justified? Yes.

That may be controversial to some factions in our society. The fact remains, the suspect took provocative action despite direction. He knew he was facing two armed officers and his actions, and those of his partner, had caused us to fear for our safety. The point remains that the circumstances, and only those factors known to us at the time, may be used to justify that incident. The Supreme Court, jurisprudence in general, and the department specifically, do not want to excessively limit the use of force by police to defend themselves or others. They are all well aware if they overly limit our right to defend, we would have to be crazy to put on a uniform. As a result, society would suffer.

They don't expect us to be perfect. They don't expect us to wait to be shot before we defend ourselves. Federal, state, local, and case law give us the power to defend ourselves, or others, if the situation warrants.

In this situation, the suspect walked away. Our discretionary decision-making was tested that day, and was most decidedly found **not** wanting. Our quote here is very appropriate:

"Detached reflection is not expected in the presence of an upraised knife (much less a gun)."

Justice Oliver Wendell Holmes (paraphrased)

THE FIRST ROUND

It was a hot July day and my countersniper/observer class was going well. Students had been subjected to extreme heat and what seemed like interminable waiting in the sun. They were tired and lax by the middle of day two. The 4-wheel drive Suburban belonging to the SWAT Team had high ground clearance and they had taken shelter under it from the hot sun.

I was on the voice activated radio to my co-instructor. After a couple of words, the sharp crack of a Mini-14 sounded and the dust began to rise from the backstop on the firing line. This produced a muffled thump and a groan from below the truck, then an awful lot of scrambling to get 360 degree security back. After it was over, one of my students came to me and smiled, all the while calling me graphic names. He was the primary countersniper and when the first round went off, he had been startled and bumped the underside of the truck with the back of his head. He quickly decided to change his position to get better cover once his vision cleared. There is an old adage about, "No plan survives past the first shot without change."

After being shot at, you tend to view things differently, do things differently, and react differently. What you would have considered cover before, now seems flimsy, even transparent. A cinder block wall? A .22 caliber cuts through one like hot butter. A telephone pole? Any center fire rifle makes neat holes at entry and bigger holes on the other side. Driver's door of a car? Not if I can help it.

What's the point here? If at all possible, don't be where the suspect expects you to be.

Quite some time ago, I pulled up to the Emergency Entrance of our local hospital. I shined a spotlight into the eyes of a friend of mine who was the ambulance passenger. He cussed a little and reached for his 200,000 candlepower spotlight. He trained the spotlight on the patrol car and overpowered the spotlight I had trained on him. About the time he said, "Where did he go?" I flashed a 30,000 candlepower streamlight into his eyes from where I was standing...four feet from the front bumper of his ambulance. He accused me of having an evil, devious mind. Guilty as charged, sir...

Whenever possible, I'll be somewhere else, anywhere the suspect doesn't expect me to be...or behind the best cover I can find.

There is no better feeling than when your enemy shoots at you...without result.

Winston Churchill

"INSTINCT SHOOTING" ... BEG PARDON?

Running the firearms range is an educational experience. We learn from our own mistakes when firing, but we also learn from the various mistakes made by students. These can run the entire spectrum...from improper grip, to grip induced malfunctions, poor use of cover, poor reloading skills, and more outrageous safety violations.

It is my job to make sure no one gets hurt, and stop the action when necessary. It is also my job to correct the problem the shooter is having. I have sometimes recognized a problem with another person's shooting from correcting a different shooter. Anyone who doesn't learn from his students, both good and bad points, as well as remedies, is not utilizing the full potential of the training experience.

I have to respect the people who are watching the action during a training scenario. They are trying to use all the information they can find. Teaching them seems to be somewhat easier. They have a positive mindset toward the training and will be receptive to constructive criticism. I do my best to ensure that *constructive* criticism is what I offer.

There are some problems with some techniques taught. People who are taught to hold the gun down close to their strong side when firing at close range, to "point shoot," have been somewhat of a problem.

Since I teach cops, their usual stance is a bladed one, body at an angle to the center of the suspect's body. This is an effort to keep the firearm as far from the suspect's reach as possible. It's a very common police tactic widely taught throughout the country. The problem comes in when the gun is drawn, held close to the side and fired. The body must be twisted, the wrist bent, or both, in order to bring the weapon to bear. Especially when practicing Failure Drill; I have seen students bring the weapon straight up about 10 inches in front of their face, with the wrists bent at a radical angle, and pull the trigger. Besides endangering dental work with a semi-auto slide, all these acute bends in elbow and wrists are *not* easily reproducible. They require much more training to become proficient.

Some folks say they keep the weapon tight against their body to keep it less available to the suspect. If you are grappling with the suspect over control of your weapon, you are fighting for your life. Promptly disable the suspect, or fire!

In any case, you should be confronting the suspect from behind cover, or the justification for lethal force should be imminent before you try to use a firearm at close range. Even then, a locked position such as Weaver or Isosceles would be more appropriate. No angles and bends at wrist and elbow to compensate for and remember at close range under stress. No small muscle movements to work from, therefore, less misses.

Training takes work. Mental and physical work. When I see people who are very smooth, fast and accurate under stress courses, I dig into their background during conversations with them. The methods they use may appear instinctive, but it's a cinch they're a trainer, interested in training, or very interested in keeping their hide intact. Bottom line, they work at it.

If the method is one you can perform well, and you are comfortable with it's validity, then train...**hard**! It may well save your skin.

The term "instinct shooting" is very inaccurate...
instincts are inborn...
and shooting is not one of them.

Ken Hackathorn

HANDCUFFS AND DRUNKS

The woman looked like someone's grandmother, with one small difference. No grandmother I had ever seen was that drunk! This woman staggered out the back door of the bar into the parking lot and toward a Chrysler New Yorker with her car keys in hand. She could hardly walk, but was going to drive home. This wasn't going to happen.

My partner tried to get her to give us her keys and call someone to come get her, but she wasn't having any of it. She swayed so much on her feet she had to reach out and grab my partner to keep from falling. Grandma slid her fingers down into the front of my partner's belt. When she reached for me, I took hold of her hand since I have this aversion to someone getting a hold of me in a place where they can pull me around. Grandma certainly "washn't gonna give up my car keys. They are my freedum and I have conn... conn... conshtatushnul rights by gawd!." My partner looked at me and shrugged. I took the keys from her left hand and began to place her in handcuffs. She resisted very little and I completed the handcuffing with no more than minor struggles. As I completed the handcuffing, I decided this woman must have been a sailor prior to being a grandmother. She did have quite a diverse gutter vocabulary. All the way to jail, grandma called me every name in the book and sang the praises of my partner. It always seems someone who is drunk will like one partner, and immensely despise the other. If you are a single patrol, you get the hatred, period.

People who are drunk must be handled with extra care. Their reactions are impaired, inhibitions lowered, and pain tolerance can be incredibly high. Because of these factors, they could be seriously injured and never react. We must not let any remark, slander, or even a wild swing make us treat them any differently than we would any other situation. Use the minimum of force to contain and secure them, then let it go. We must be aware and wary whenever handling drunks. There are some folks who are very drunk, but become red-eyed, fast, pain-tolerant, back alley scrappers when they get a charge of adrenaline from their impending arrest. All cops who have some time on the job have seen people who are habitual drinkers; people who wake up drunk and function long after others would have passed out. These are the ones we have to look out for. Youth also makes for real unpredictability. Good physical conditioning and alcohol's effect, coupled with an immature judgment system, make for some really bizarre reactions.

Any time you suspect a tandem effect from drugs and alcohol, be on your toes. I'm sure most, if not all, officers have run into the drunk who waits until nearly, or fully, in handcuffs before becoming resistive and obnoxious. It's like the suspect is shouting to friends or family, "If you love me, hold me back," all the while outwardly threatening violence. The drunk then regales us with threats or vilification all the way to jail. We leave the jail quickly... the drunk doesn't. We have to be satisfied with that.

I have taken a punch from a drunk, and seen other officers do so. But in each case, the force used by police at that point was minimal, getting the suspect in handcuffs and leaving it at that. Sometimes it's tough to do. Take the insults, the physical attack, and continue to have restraint and do the job the right way. All you need is self-protection, firmness, discipline, training, and a touch of compassion.

The following quote is very old. Be assured that I recognize women in law enforcement and their contribution. Any time the masculine term is used, it is as a generic for humankind. These stories are directed to people who wear the uniform or bear the credentials of police, regardless of any other predilection, preference or status. That having been said...

God give us men!
A time like this demands strong minds, great hearts,
true faith and ready hands; men whom the lust of office
does not kill; men whom the spoils of office cannot buy;
men who possess opinions and a will;
men who have honor, men who will not lie.

Josiah Gilbert Holland

THE TRUTH,
THE WHOLE TRUTH...

The defense attorney stood facing me and made a bald-faced statement about the truth of a cop who testified on the stand. "He doesn't do anything wrong, but under cross-examination, he makes it easy for me...he's so adversarial and so reluctant to give **any** information even on the things he's done right. He leaves the jury feeling he **did** do something wrong. He's so shifty in front of a jury, it works in my favor."

I knew the case we were on was making this defense attorney unhappy. I had clearly documented the entire case, all leads, and all elements. This left the defense attorney nothing to hang his hat on. I had even documented the mistake I made during the course of the investigation. When it was time for court, I told the D.A. about the mistake and ensured that he would bring it out on direct examination. I could then tell my side of the story, explain how the mistake had been made, and **not** let the D.A. get surprised by it in front of the jury. The mistake was a procedural one, not likely to be fatal to the case.

If, on the other hand, I had not documented it, not told the D.A., and he found it through other means, the defense attorney gets to bring it up in front of the jury, casting his own particular light on it. You can bet it wouldn't be favorable to me or my case. My credibility would diminish with the court, the D.A., my peers, and most importantly, myself. I refuse to lie. I learned long ago I have no talent for it, and invariably get caught. I have been involved in a couple internal affairs investigations, and didn't lie then, and won't lie now.

Even if the mistake had been an error which was fatal to the case, I would tell the D.A. immediately. It is better to acknowledge the mistake, tell the D.A. how you learned about it, pertinent case law, and how it happened. The D.A. can tell you if your case law is outdated, whether it is in fact a fatal error, or if the case is salvageable. In the worst case, the D.A. can then go into chambers in the pre-trial conference and dismiss the case. Better to do that than try to bull it through and put your career and credibility on the line.

A co-worker of mine once put it very clearly, "I'm in law enforcement as a profession, a career, and for the long haul. I won't jeopardize everything I've worked for, my job, my family, and my self-respect, to put someone away temporarily, or to keep someone out of trouble who should have avoided it."

To that, I can add nothing. I can't put it any better.

Truth has no special time of it's own.
It's hour is now; always.

Albert Schweitzer

MINDSET:
POSITIVE AND NEGATIVE

The suspect was obviously on PCP. The people with him told us he had just run 13 miles. He was dressed in a pair of tennis shoes, levi's and no shirt, even though it was jacket weather. A classic looking case of PCP. When approached by the first unit, the suspect climbed a bank beside the road and stood challenging the officers to fight.

Several other officers responded, myself and my trainee among them. I took one look at the suspect, 6'3", 190 pounds, and decided this situation was going to be anything but fun. Another deputy and I flanked the suspect who eventually retreated about 40 yards into an orchard. His movements indicated he had some measure of martial arts training, or was making a very good show of being a "TV Bruce Lee."

Four deputies surrounded the suspect in a semi-circle on the south side, and I was on the north blocking further retreat into the orchard. I saw more evidence of martial arts training as the suspect was in a bladed stance with his head tilted forward so he could see me and the other deputies without turning his head. His hands were up in a classic "hand sword" position. Scratch the "TV Bruce Lee" idea, this was looking worse every minute.

After twenty minutes of talking to the suspect, he lowered his hands to waist level. About that time, the flashlights of responding California Highway Patrol officers began flashing near the top of the bank. The suspect screamed, "You lied to me" and raised his hands. A deputy on his left pulled on a pair of gloves and the suspect turned his head for a half second. That was all I needed. I hit him from behind with my best tackle.

It was immediate melee, with five deputies on the suspect. A set of handcuffs went on one hand and the hand was moved by main force behind the suspect's back. One deputy on the scene screamed at me to get my jacket out of the way of the cuffs. I pulled a shock of field grass out of the way of the cuff ratchets, but that deputy swears to this day that *I* was getting in the way.

The handcuffs went on and everyone stood up panting, swearing and well scraped up. I didn't have the level of training then that I do now, so control holds didn't come to me instinctively. One deputy handed me the side-handle baton I had been wearing, which evidently had been thrown from the ring on my belt when I hit the suspect. It had sailed about12 feet over the knee high grass. Thank God, it hadn't hit one of my co-workers.

Later at the hospital, the doctor examined my shoulder and forearm. Although not broken, it was badly wrenched and bruised. The suspect was also examined, and we waited for a blood toxicology panel to make sure he wouldn't die from drug toxicity while in custody.

The suspect looked at me and said, "That was a pretty good hit out there in the field. I do a lot of karate training. Think we might workout some time?" I assured him I had more than enough workout time as it was. Thanks, but no thanks.

The whole point here is mindset. There was no referee at the scene. There was no director to yell "cut" when things got nasty. After the confrontation, the actors didn't get up and walk away laughing, and wiping away fake blood. This is life, this is police work, and it's **real**.

Your mindset when going into a fight should be, "I'm going to get hurt." If a suspect closes in with a knife, "I'm going to get cut." If up against a gun, "I'm going to get shot." In all these cases, the statement should continue..

"I'm Not Going To Stop! I Will Win. I Will Survive!"

The negative part of the mindset is expecting to get hurt. If it happens, you won't be shocked into immobility because this has never occurred to you. It won't freeze you. You can and will continue to function. If it doesn't happen, you can walk away thinking, "Damn that was close." The positive mindset is that portion which says you will win and survive.

There is also a mindset which says we should not use force against someone who has their back turned to us, even though that person may be presenting a very real danger to another person. Sweep that out of your mind. There are no Marquis of Queensbury rules here. You need to resolve the situation at hand, with the proper level of force, quickly and without great bodily injury or loss of an innocent life.

Realign your mindset to be realistic. Don't expect a bullet to do all the things you've read in horror stories. Don't expect a suspect to "fall like a pole-axed ox" if hit with a baton or even with lethal force. When justified, continue to use the appropriate level of force until the situation is resolved.

Expect to get hurt and know if you do, you will keep on functioning. Train for and expect the worst, then if something better happens...that's positive.

To get profit without risk, experience without danger,
and reward without work,
is as impossible as it is to live without being born.

A. P. Gouthey

WEAPONS:
ON AND OFF DUTY

The Pontiac Bonneville came southbound on Yosemite Street in Roseville, and turned eastbound onto Atlantic Street. I could hear the woman's screams long before I saw the right passenger door flapping open and her legs sticking out, shoes hitting the pavement at times. I went after the suspect, even though my wife and I were in our own car.

The car went east at 50 miles an hour on Atlantic, then slammed to a stop about two blocks later. I could see the male driver hitting the woman passenger in the face repeatedly.

I went after the car onto Interstate 80 where the suspect accelerated to 90 miles an hour then took the next off-ramp. My old car was left behind, since it didn't have the legs to come anywhere near the suspect. I had the license number of the car memorized, but didn't want to see the woman continue to be beaten. I approached the stop light at the end of the off-ramp and saw the suspect's car sitting nearly sideways at the limit line. The light turned green and the car peeled away from the light, when suddenly its engine went dead and headlights went out.

Good, my turn! I went to the driver's door and shoved my badge in front of the man's face. I pulled him out the driver's door with a twist-lock and handcuffed him.

I had the woman get out the passenger door, took a wrist-lock on the suspect and sat him down on the curb behind the car. The woman had a split lip, bruises, and was justifiably hysterical. I sent my wife to call 911 and get a patrol unit on the scene. The suspect told me, "If I had known you were a cop, I'd have fucked you up good!"

The carrying of weapons on and off duty (or as a legally armed citizen) brings with it it's own set of responsibilities and priorities. I could not stop the habit of intervention, and I don't think any person with a well-developed conscience could look the other way when someone is being hurt. With the current conditions on our streets, you can never tell when you will be involved in a confrontation.

I carry a weapon, two magazines, impact tool (collapsible baton or Kubaton), and flex-cuffs both off duty and when I'm working detectives. The reason is simple. When you are off duty or working in plain clothes, you don't have great access to communications. In the majority of cases, we can't get on a radio or telephone and holler for help. This makes the critical incident last longer. We may need access to all levels of force, and we will need it **now**. We can't say, "Time out" while we get the needed items from our car, briefcase, or purse. Without this access, we have only those options available to the average citizen: look, report, witness, or try to survive if you become a victim yourself. Not a very good scenario if you don't have the training, equipment, or knowledge to meet, defuse, or defeat the threat.

Carry enough equipment to do the job the right way, with access to all levels of force. Increased security for myself and all those around me, especially my family, is all the reward I need to pack a little extra weight.

He who goes unarmed in paradise...
better make sure that is where he is!

James Thurber

THE TACTICAL ENVIRONMENT: A LOCAL HISTORY

The recent history of armed confrontations within my Northern California Sheriff's Dept. goes back to 1982, with one officer using a rifle, one a shotgun, one an HK MP5 submachine gun, and the remainder using handguns. This includes only the primary shooters, not other officers on the scene, of which there were many. One officer was involved in no less than four officer-involved shootings,

The suspects in these situations were all lone offenders armed with the following: a .45 semi-auto handgun, two with high-powered rifles, a sawed-off .22 rifle, a shotgun, a sawed-off shotgun, and various other weaponry. The situations leading to the use of lethal force were anywhere from seconds to hours in length, and from seconds to hours in heightened awareness and warning to the officers. The distances encountered covered six feet to 80 yards. The conditions encountered were predominantly hours of darkness with two situations encountered in full daylight.

Only one officer was on scene by himself at the time of the shooting. The other situations involved multiple officers on scene, some where all officers fired at the suspect, and other's where accompanying officers never got off a shot.

Several things have been highlighted by the preceding situations:

1. Don't count on a suspect falling down when hit by any level of force. Continue to apply force until the suspect's illegal activities are stopped.

2. The situations have predominantly occurred at night or in poor lighting conditions. We need to do low light/night training.

3. The situations have often lasted for hours. But once the matter came down to use of force, actions accelerated at an incredibly fast pace.

4. The officers involved were most often accompanied by other officers. There was only one incident where the officer was on scene by himself.

5. The use of cover was crucial in several incidents. According to use-of-force incidents across the nation, good use of cover is the most critical factor in insuring officer survival.

6. The next factor is also critical. You must hit where you are aiming. A miss is not acceptable in a tactical situation. The more actively you train under stress, the better equipped you will be to act in a tactical environment.

Remember...

The history of gunfighting fails to record a single fatality resulting from a quick noise.

Bill Jordan

THE CASE FOR
BEING TACTICAL

It was the first day of training for my female trainee. Over the past six hours, we had a battery call, a couple of "hot" calls, and were now rolling toward our next call, one that would turn out to be attempted murder.

The trainee's eyes were a little glazed as the "victim" was loaded aboard the ambulance, shouting at me to get the bad guy. The suspect had shot him in the leg with a rifle and he wanted us to do it...**now!**

We hadn't time to think about anything other than the calls we had just completed, and were now on our way up the freeway to the area of the suspect's house. I told the trainee the suspect's history. I was a little worried about this trainee. Sitting there on the other side of the car, she had a small smile on her face, and hadn't said a word for a minute or two. She then looked me straight in the eye and said, "You sure know how to show a girl a good time!"

Other comments I've heard include, "He sleeps with his bulletproof vest on." "Oh, he's your training officer...you'll learn how to low-crawl." "You carry so many guns, if you fell down you would explode." "Hey killer, how's it going today?" I've heard all these and many more. They have become back-handed compliments of sorts.

I haven't carried a second weapon since the early eighties, but would not hesitate to do so if I saw the necessity. As for the rest of the comments, I'll call them what they are...attempts at humor meant in fun, or just nonsense.

The tactical necessities of the job can be ignored at peril to yourself and those around you. Perhaps you feel that's a little over dramatic. I am glad my department's use-of-force incidents have all been favorably resolved. Our department hasn't provided a name for the Peace Officer's Memorial for a few years now. But the next case is the one we have to look out for. An unbroken streak of luck cannot last, and with that in mind, we need to be alert, aware of danger signs, and have plenty of tactical tools with us. Some of those tools may look pretty silly to someone who doesn't see the need for them.

A bladed stance, knocking on a door from the side, keeping your car far enough back from other traffic so you can do a turnout without being boxed in, "watching six o'clock" on a traffic stop or citizen contact, frisking someone properly with a control-hold applied, even wearing a ballistic vest are just a few tools we have at our disposal.

Going into a building search with a low, soundless profile, rushing through a door to get out of the "fatal funnel," a peek around a corner, then looking again at a different level, carrying a mirror and using it around corners, all these things look paranoid to those who don't believe them necessary. Some of us do these things regularly, others do them with a lesser degree of regularity or attention. We all hope for the best.

A ballistic vest is like an insurance policy...you have it and hope you never have to use it. You should take the tactical advantage whenever and wherever you can. Think and work tactically.

Be tactical and careful. The life you save may be your's...or mine.

There is no forgiveness in this world or the next,
for being caught by surprise.
I would rather look foolish than be damned!

U.S. Marine Commandant

THE PROGRESS OF POLICE SERVICE

The progress of police service in America is a story that should not be told without the proper aura of mystery, intrigue, violence, and danger. The pure fact is police service in this country has progressed from the posse looking to "lynch" the criminal, to today's scientific criminology. We have graduated to the era of DNA technology, computer technology, highly trained SWAT teams, officer credentials, state standards for training, and myriad technological benefits. This "scientific criminology" will probably look primitive to us in 20 years.

The technology of the Persian Gulf War astounded me. The use of "smart bombs," and missile and computer technology, allowed us to win, in a minimum amount of time, with the lowest possible casualties to both our soldiers and civilians.

A police officer talks a suspect down instead of using force. A cop takes his time putting together a particularly good case to submit to the D.A. Another cop risks himself to save someone, or puts himself in danger to prevent someone from injuring others. There is no "smart weapon" that can do all this. A person in uniform, thinking, reacting, and intervening as trained, is the only solution. Cops and other first responders regularly become casualties to these situations.

The media is not a participant in this, much as they might think otherwise. They put themselves in jeopardy, by choice, to feed off "the story." But they do not cure it, stop it, or delay it. Contrary to what you might hear, media personnel have no expertise in police procedures or tactics.

Police service has no parallel in history. Every so often, cops provide another name for the Peace Officer's Memorial. A name to be etched on our professional wailing wall. This has been going on during the history of this country and before.

There are no "time outs" during a crisis situation. There are myriad solutions to the crisis, but the most frequent call made is "dial 911." This is not limited to cops. The jeopardy extends to firefighters, ambulance attendants, and medical personnel.

It actually covers the entire "emergency responder" network. Take a look at who is liable, or who gets sued if something goes wrong. Does a judge? How about a District Attorney or defense attorney? A Child Protective Services worker? None of these can be sued for decisions which injure others.

Only cops, firemen and medical responders are held vicariously, civilly, and sometimes personally liable. Is there any sense to this set-up? Not from where I sit. Those who most frequently risk their own safety, those who are most likely to save your life, are the ones who are sued for mistakes, bad luck, or just a "no win" situation. This must change.

Stress retirements are simply another name for "battle fatigue." Every stress added by the media, public, courts, departmental administration, and "instant experts," makes the situation that much worse. Police want to work, raise their families and do some good in their community.

The reward we get? Look at the above and wonder if things are going to change for the better any time soon.

A man who is good enough to shed his blood
for his country is good enough to be given a
square deal afterward. More than that, no man is
entitled to; and less than that no man shall have.

Theodore Roosevelt

THE QUESTION
OF REWARDS

I put the apartment pass key in the door, then knocked and shouted," Sheriff's Department, Search Warrant!" The suspect didn't answer, so I opened the door and entered. When I walked into the apartment, I was greeted by the sight of the suspect standing at the breakfast bar fiddling with a video camera which was one of the items named as stolen property on my search warrant. All Right!!

Across the living room was a bag of video cam accessories stolen during a second burglary. I later found keys to the laundry room, also stolen property. The suspect had a bindle of methamphetamine sitting on the breakfast bar. My sergeant, who was upstairs, yelled down the stairway, "He's growing dope up here." The suspect lied, denied, and demanded proof. I put the surveillance video tape I brought with me in the apartment's VCR and played the tape which showed the suspect committing two burglaries.

The suspect was taken to jail. That was my sum total of satisfaction in that case. The suspect was arrested again, about two months later, with methamphetamine, packaging, scales, and cash . The deputy D.A., in his infinite wisdom, said the suspect had no prior record, and plead all seven of my counts, and the second drug arrest, as misdemeanors.

This isn't the first time this has happened to me. I have often been asked by civilians, "Why do you keep doing this thankless job? Why do you bother? Why do you try so hard?" The question is not the D.A.'s, nor the judge's to answer. It isn't the department's administration who has to answer, it's me .. my answer to myself that's important. As long as I know my reasons for doing this job, I will keep going and will stay motivated.

I help my community every time I go on duty. Every cop who goes on duty helps make the difference between the society we have with all its faults, and the rules of the human predators. When I lock up a suspect, I may have saved other victims. When I talk with a kid headed for trouble, I've made a difference once or twice. When I've caught someone and shut the cell door on him, I know I've done my part.

If the remainder of the system can't get it's act together, I can't be responsible for that. It's their mess to clean up. I can't really help if the suspect is released after I do my best and put together a good case. I've done my job and I can look at my next paycheck knowing I've earned it, and feel pride in going that extra mile. That makes a difference when I face my family, and when a small child comes up to me during a school presentation, I can meet that open stare and startling curiosity with openness and honesty.

The working conditions may not be the greatest. It may be a negative service job for the most part. But the bottom line is, during the course of my career, I know there are at least ten people still breathing because of me and my partners. That alone is worth the doing...and doing well.

I did my best to give the nation everything I had in me.
I always quote an epitaph on a tombstone
in a cemetery in Tombstone, Arizona;
"Here lies Jack Williams, he done his damndest."

President Harry Truman
(paraphrased)

THE SMALL THINGS AREN'T IMPORTANT...?

The suspect stood with his fists clenched, refused all verbal directions, and said in no uncertain terms he was not going to go without a fight. I stood about 10 feet away with baton in hand. After 20 minutes of talking, the suspect was handcuffed and in the back of my car without force. My partner looked at me with more than a little curiosity, "I've been told you would take people on when they challenged you. Why did you talk to that guy so long?" I sighed and told him, "The guy's in the car. We did what we came to do. We don't have to justify use of force, and we don't have to take him to the hospital because he's hurt. We don't have to cut extra paper on this, and most importantly, **we're not hurt.**"

I don't want to give the wrong impression through these stories. Over a 17 year period as a full-time cop, I've had to use a baton six times and a firearm once. That's over the course of a long and active career. If I've had to use force, I have used my hands and defensive tactics in every other situation.

How many times have you heard the phrase, "Take care of the small things and the big things will turn out okay." We need to do that in our profession. We study law and case law, defensive tactics, impact weapons, and physical discipline of all kinds in order to prepare for our job.

We can never forget the details. Those are the ones that can trip you up. Not listing a critical comment in a report, or not having all elements of the crime present in a report, can make you look very bad. Being aware your credibility in court is riding on every report you make is absolutely essential.

Don't skip procedures. There should be a mental checklist to ensure we've taken care of the small details necessary in any case we handle. If we train exclusively in one small area, we are used as "specialists." But once we are out of our field of knowledge and expertise, we may flounder because we haven't looked at the entire problem and our knowledge or techniques may be rusty or out of date.

We all need to be "general practitioners of law enforcement." This doesn't mean we shouldn't develop expertise. We should, for many reasons. But we shouldn't focus on one area to the exclusion of all others. If we focus on physical skills without review of case law, we may be plenty of help on the street, but in court, our documentation or courtroom demeanor may be embarrassing or cost us or our department credibility.

We need to look at the small details and stay abreast of all new developments and case requirements or we may end up like this warrior:

But he, mighty man,
lay mightily in the whirl of dust,
forgetful of his horsemanship.

Homer
The Iliad

THE PROPOSITION OF JUSTIFICATION FOR POLICE USE OF FORCE

That video tape. It's been played over and over again. The image of Rodney King rolling around on the ground to repeated baton blows by members of the LAPD. The entire nation has seen it, and the media made sure that image stayed in front of the public throughout the trials.

Most of the public have seen only 10 or 15 seconds of the tape which has been replayed on every news channel. I saw the entire tape on the late news the night after it occurred. What a revelation!

The times I've witnessed the use of a baton on a suspect, where the power generation and targeting were correct, the suspect was down after two blows were struck, unable to resist, rise, or fight. The times I've used a baton have been successful for the most part, but how do we justify the police use of force?

It is stated in the penal code that a civilian has **no right to resist a peace officer**. Be aware this is California State Law and may not be applicable in your jurisdiction. Most states have something similar.

834a PC: Resistance To Arrest

If a person has knowledge, or by the exercise of reasonable care should have knowledge, that he is being arrested by a peace officer, it is the duty of such person to refrain from using force or any weapon to resist such arrest.

Rodney King charged the officers in an aggressive manner and was hit repeatedly with batons. The scene included several attempts to reach toward officers. But not enough force was used to disable Mr. King, put him on the ground, and keep him on the ground without further application of force. On the other hand, it is the officers' responsibility to take people into custody in a manner prescribed by law.

835a PC: Use of Force To Effect Arrest, Prevent Escape, Or Overcome Resistance

Any peace officer who has reasonable cause to believe that the person to be arrested has committed a public offense may use reasonable force to effect the arrest, to prevent escape or to overcome resistance. A peace officer who makes or attempts to make an arrest need not retreat or desist from his efforts by reason of the resistance or threatened resistance of the person being arrested; nor shall such officer be deemed the aggressor or lose his right of self-defense by the use of reasonable force to effect the arrest or to prevent the escape or to overcome resistance.

We do have to balance this with what's "reasonable." The penal code also makes the distinction of "the minimum amount of force necessary to overcome the suspects' force."

The people who tried the King case, especially those who sat on the jury, and most assuredly those in the media, have never fought with a determined adversary who was really *trying* to kill them - a situation which happens all too frequently to police, and even more frequently to our big city counterparts.

In this type of scenario, the amount of force used is very controversial. Citizens think the amount of force used was excessive. A few of the very best trainers agree, but for a different reason. The force used was not targeted accurately enough, nor with enough power to end the resistance. In other words, the force used was not enough in the beginning or the situation would not have continued to play to the grinding camera.

Let's make another change in the scenario. The sergeant on the scene picked the officer whom he knew to be the best at defensive tactics and handcuffing. The sergeant designates that officer as the "capture officer." The other officers are using impact weapon force against the suspect. The sergeant calls a halt. The "capture officer" then directs the suspect to a prone control position. Failure to comply, or reaching for an officer is still resistance, and force is again used. The attempt to de-escalate is made repeatedly. Is this a valid technique? Yes.

By the same token, when responding patrol officers form an inner perimeter to contain a barricaded suspect or hostage situation, the supervisor would be well-advised to pick out several officers on the perimeter as "designated officers." The rest of the officers are told they are in "defensive mode only." The "designated officers" are placed under the supervisor's direct orders, and on the supervisor's command, are to employ force against designated targets.

This supervisor has now established a controlled scene instead of a free-fire zone. The supervisor should know his officers' capabilities and stability. But with this one move, he has established some control over the situation.

These situations are both a matter of allowable time on scene and training. Lack of training is the single most common failure that brings problems to police work.

There are factions in this country which decry any use of force by police. They have tried to ban control holds, pain compliance holds, possession or use of firearms and generally have decided they "ain't gonna study war no more." They believe that violence "never solved anything" in any way, shape, or form.

We live in an imperfect world and deal with people. There is no way criminal suspects are always going to listen and comply with a "pretty please." And as long as there are criminals, we must not indulge in wishful thinking - it tends to get police and citizens killed or injured needlessly.

It is useless for sheep to pass resolutions
in favor of vegetarianism,
while wolves remain of a different opinion.

William Ralph Inge, D.D.
1860-1954

THE SCIENCE OF MISDIRECTION

It had been a hot, sweaty, boring, day topped off by a burst of frustration. We had been on a stake-out nearly all day, sitting in camouflage clothes on a marijuana plantation. One suspect had been caught, but the other escaped because of a blunder on my part. The other detectives on this case were otherwise involved, and the task of interviewing the suspect fell to me.

I Mirandized the suspect and got a waiver. The suspect denied planting the dope, saying he and his friend "found it" about three weeks ago. He admitted tending and watering it after that, but he never planted it. In an attempt to get a lever on the interview, I pointed out to him that the escaped suspect hadn't even told his friend the cops were there, even though they had been standing two feet apart.

The suspect continued to dance around the fringe of the story trying to push it back into shape whenever I found a hole. I knew the suspect and his partner had planted and tended the marijuana but... your assignment Rocky...should you decide to accept it...getting an admission from this guy was looking like it wasn't in the cards. One more thing to try.

I threw down my notebook, "Okay, I tried. The interview's over. Your buddy sure didn't do you any favors. I know you and he planted that dope, didn't you," I said with a smile. The suspect smiled back at me. He said, "Yeah, we planted it. I'd blame in all on him if I could get away with it."

BINGO!! The suspect's face fell when I picked up my notebook and wrote down the statement. I don't think he liked me very much by the time we left the interview room at the jail.

The science of misdirection worked in my favor. Did I tell the suspect the truth? Yes. This is something I have done on occasion with some varying degree of success. One of the other notable successes I had was in saving a life.

A woman had walked away from Placer Mental Health and was standing about four feet away from traffic passing by her at 40 miles per hour or better. As we approached, I heard the woman mention babies. When she turned and saw me and my partner, she backed within a foot of the curb and said, "Stay away! I don't like you. I only like babies." She accused me of being a baby-raper among other foul things, and looked like she was about to run across the road - a sure and certain death. I had an inspiration.

"Betty, don't you recognize me? I'm Rocky. You used to baby sit me a long time ago. I lived next door to you and you baby sat for me all the time." The woman moved closer and looking curiously, tried to make out the baby behind the grown up face.

About that time, my partner grabbed her and her colorful prose once again began to flow. We saved her life, so she could cuss at us some more...oh well. It was worth doing.

The point to these cases? Keep your mind functioning and look for opportunities to apply the science of misdirection. It can be a tool limited only by your ability to think fast on your feet, an ability very common in police work.

Danger: the spur of all great minds.

George Chapman

THE ELEMENT OF SURPRISE

The suspect was sitting in a pickup with his head slumped forward. The smell of booze was nearly strangling me and this guy was not reacting to the flashlight beam I had trained on his face. I shouted twice and got no response. I reached in the open window and touched his shoulder. I wish I hadn't.

It was like touching a tornado. The door came flying open and I jumped back to keep from being hit by it. The suspect swayed to his feet, put his hands in his pants pockets and kept mumbling something I couldn't understand. I kept the flashlight pointed at his feet and told him to put his hands on top of his head. He took his left hand out of his pants pocket and put it on top of his head. I told him, both hands on his head. He kept the left hand on top of his head but pulled a knife from his right pocket. He opened the knife with his thumb and held it point up in his right hand. I backed up and told him to put the knife away. He put the knife away.

Again I told him to put his hands on his head. The left hand went up...okay now, both hands...right hand out...open knife...put knife away... we did this two more times. Backup was some minutes away, and we didn't have reliable portable radios - naturally mine didn't work. The suspect finally pulled his empty right hand out of his pocket. He must have been confused about when to draw the knife in this little choreography. I closed quickly, charging right at him. I saw his eyes widen as I took hold of his right arm in a wrist-lock. After a few minor struggles, he was handcuffed and in the back of the car for some time before backup got there.

The point here is the last thing the suspect expected was for me to close in on him. He expected me to back off, or to have time to take a swing at me. I went at him like a freight train and had him under control in a couple of seconds. Had I approached slowly and cautiously, he would have had his chance. Had I backed away, I'm not sure I could have gotten into my car. I was too young and inexperienced to do something sensible like **retreat** - so I did something I was trained to do, and did it fast!

I was lucky. I know it. Had the guy been a trained knife-fighter, I could have been slashed or skewered. Had he been that dangerous brand of drunk who can get completely wiped out and adrenaline makes them mean, I might not be writing this. But I got lucky.

Everyone thinks about having to face poor odds, and then we hope for a chance to keep pushing air in and out of our lungs after things finish up. The hope may not be in vain if we do things in a way that's unexpected. It's only a tool, and frequently retreat may be a much better option. If your opponent is 10 feet or more away from you, you can't act fast enough to close the distance before your opponent prepares, or reacts with a nasty surprise.

Taking cover is a better option in many situations. But when you must close with the suspect, do it **fast**, and with a trained response. It may save your bacon.

Our quote:

> *We are so outnumbered,*
> *there's only one thing to do,*
> *we must attack.*

Sir Andrew Browne Cunningham

A REAL ROCKET SCIENTIST

We've all heard the "Stupid Crook of the Month" awards frequently given out when the media stumbles across the antics of some notorious citizen. Many years ago, in Placer County Jail, a break was made by two criminals with a sense of humor. They left notes pinned to their pillow, "Help, we're being kidnapped!"

Every cop has his favorite stupid suspect story. "He couldn't have known it was me, I was wearing a mask!" Or, "Those can't be my fingerprints 'cause we wore gloves!" Probably one of the better ones I've been involved with was telling a man he was under arrest and his reply, "I didn't do no 211 man!" He had prior convictions for...you guessed it...armed robbery, Section 211 of the California Penal Code.

One trap we cannot fall into is believing our opponents are always stupid. They make mistakes the same as we do. But they learn from each encounter. During the course of my career, I have seen many suspects start off really dumb, then continue to become somewhat competent criminals. We cannot become complacent about our personal safety, physical proficiency, knowledge, investigative procedure, or any of the myriad smaller things which go into the successful solution of a case.

Recently I went to a call of people skydiving off a 740' tall bridge in my jurisdiction. This was not the crime of the century. Another deputy questioned people standing on the bridge, who denied any knowledge of parachutists. The deputy then looked down and saw two men hot-footing it away from the bridge toward the road and a waiting van. Somehow, the van had eluded my partner that day.

As I pulled up to the bridge, I saw the van and two people getting into it. I walked to the van and asked the driver for his driver's license, which he didn't have. The passenger got mouthy about the reason for the stop, and I asked him for his I.D. He gave me his U.S. Passport. When I opened the passport, I found a business card inside that said:

*"99% of all skydivers are decent, law abiding citizens
dedicated to jumping out of aircraft...and then there's us!"*

Like the FBI is fond of saying, "This might be a clue!" On
the card was a cute little logo of a skydiver falling between a
building, a bridge, and a cliff. The nasty smile on my face
must have said it all as the accomplished thrill-seeker sunk
down in his seat.

I found out Yosemite National Park Police had two warrants out for the suspect's arrest for...yes, basejumping.

The U.S. Marshal's Service arrived later in the day with
three more warrants, and the parachutist resides in our local
walled hotel. The parachutist's gear resides snugly in our evidence locker.

Stupid suspect? Yes, but we can't count on it lasting. We
can't keep doing the same job, the same way, in the same rut,
year after year. If we don't innovate, learn, train, and adapt...we
are asking for trouble.

*You must not fight too often with one enemy,
or you will teach him all your art of war.*

Napoleon Bonaparte

THE FIGHT IS ON

The night was cold and the rain had made a mud-slide out of the driveway leading down to the house trailer. A neighbor heard what he thought was automatic weapon fire. It was now just before 10 p.m. and we were here to serve an arrest warrant on the trailer's owner.

The suspect and his friend met me and my partner at the front of the house trailer. The police ride-along from another agency stayed near the 4x4 patrol unit. The suspect gave a false name and, as so often happens, the false name came back with warrants. The suspect then gave another bogus name. My partner came forward and said, "I think we have the right guy here." The suspect refused to comply with any verbal direction, then crouched and balled up his fists. My partner took hold of him by the scruff of his jacket, getting some of his hair in the hold, and told the suspect to give it up...now! The suspect began to tremble and shout repeatedly, "I've got to think." I took out my side-handle baton and stood in a modified stance telling the suspect to put his hands atop his head. The suspect turned, swung at my partner, then began to run. I struck for his legs, striking the shins. Results...not much.

My partner was left holding a small hank of hair in his left hand as the suspect rocketed past him across the yard. I struck again and hit the thigh muscle on the left leg. The suspect climbed a woodpile and turned, setting his feet where he had a height advantage.

With both his fists raised in front of his face, I struck again. This strike landed on the point of the right elbow. Net result: again not what I expected. The suspect raised his fists again and charged my partner. I pivoted, ran, and caught up with the suspect, landing a solid strike to the outside of the left knee. The only reason I knew my strikes were having any effect was he was slowing and stiffening up, and I hoped would be giving up soon. My partner jumped past me and took hold of the guy by the shoulders, spinning him to the ground.

The mud then became a factor, causing my partner to lose his footing, ending up under the suspect. The suspect was back on his knees instantly, fighting, with my partner struggling under him. The only thing I could think about was the security of my partner's gun. I launched a rib strike to the suspect's right side. At the same time, my partner got his feet under the suspect like a kid on a playground and pushed. The suspect fell down and back to my right. My intended rib strike had suddenly turned into a head strike!

I had already begun the strike, but before the blow landed, I was able to take plenty of power off it. There was nothing I could do to stop the strike, and so land it did. The suspect's immediate reaction was an astonished, "You hit me in the head. That really takes something out of ya when you get hit in the head. You have to hit people in the head to make that thing work?"

I put my baton away and arm-barred the suspect onto the ground. We handcuffed him as my partner squirmed out from under him. The transport to the hospital was uneventful. Eleven stitches to the suspect and he was ready to go to jail.

During the fracas, my partner had been hit in the thumb with the tip of my baton, had damaged a shoulder in the tumble with the suspect, and I messed up my knee and ankle in the chase and fight over uneven ground.

The suspect was very willing to talk about the fight. The reason he gave for fighting was he didn't want to go to jail. He also said, "It felt like the fight was in slow motion. I knew I wasn't going to get away, but I had to try. It was like one of those nightmares where you're wading through quicksand and can't get away." He also said the reason he kept charging my partner was because he wasn't using a baton (he had left his baton in the car).

The next morning detectives served a search warrant on the residence and found a couple pounds of marijuana and 61 marijuana plants in the woods near the trailer. No wonder he fought so hard.

The impact weapon instructor for my agency was briefed immediately and ruled the strikes all justifiable. The report was done and recuperation started for my partner and me.

The reason I tell all of this is to make some points to the reader.

1. What will the suspect do when you use an impact weapon or even lethal force against him? Answer: Most likely exactly what he was doing before the application of force. Don't expect the suspect to stop anything he's doing. Keep applying

justifiable force until such time as he stops his actions and ceases to be a threat.

2. It is not uncommon to be hit by your co-workers. More than one cop in my agency has had this experience, and I've taken a good shot or two from a fellow officer in my career as well. Expect it. You're working in close quarters, adrenaline flowing, with bio-mechanical force or impact weapon force being used. It's going to happen occasionally.

3. Most frequently I've been tagged by co-workers when everybody piles onto a suspect. The infamous "pig pile." If you can help it, don't do this, folks. The cops are the ones who get hurt, and the suspect gets up, flexes his muscles and brags to his fellow inmates, "It took **six** of them this time!" I'm not saying don't come to a fellow cop's aid when it's needed! Train and work together, and know what your partner is going to do so you're not working against or injuring each other.

4. The best method seems to be for two trained officers to use the proper level of force to control the suspect. When appropriate, de-escalate, restrain and treat or transport as needed. Officers will be hurt less often, suspects are controlled more quickly and effectively, and the suspect doesn't get bragging rights.

5. Another consideration is that officers will frequently use conflicting techniques. A properly applied wrist-lock on one arm keeps the suspect's heels on the ground because the elbow is restrained by the applying officer. If your partner has a twist-lock on the opposite arm, that makes the suspect want to elevate onto his toes. Result? The conflict hurts, and he's likely to fight.

The best resolution to this is to train. Train frequently in techniques that are well taught and proven street effective. If the training doesn't meet one of these criteria, you will have problems. Our big advantage is training...constantly.

Winning!
That is the whole secret of successful fighting.
Get your enemy at a disadvantage,
and never, on any account,
fight him on equal terms.

George Bernard Shaw

THE PROBLEM
WITH ANIMATION

The problem with animation ... sounds like something out of a Disney studio script, doesn't it? The problem with animation is the tendency to forget the human factor in police work. That ornery, cussedness that makes human beings so contrary, and even vicious, under the right set of circumstances. Despite our most careful preparation and calculation, despite the best training and execution, "Murphy's Law" can rear it's ugly head.

A friend of mine recently told me about an engineering student in our area who was given a study project. The problem: Calculate the sail area necessary for a parachute to drift a payload to a soft landing within a two minute time frame from atop a certain high bridge.

The student carefully calculated the sail area and shroud line length for a payload of six pounds, calculated the drag factors, and all necessary elements for the parachute drop. He forgot the animation factor...the payload was alive. The big day arrived and the payload was strapped onto the parachute. The parachute and payload were set over the side and dropped on it's leisurely way to the ground.

The family cat looked down between it's paws at the ground 740 feet below and the animation in this animal was terrific. Instinct took over, and kitty climbed the shroud lines trying to get atop the solid-looking canopy, with predictable results.

The student forgot to include the animal's reactions, and the fact that the animation factor could change the situation for the worse, despite it being under control ...temporarily.

Most peace officer training is static. Targets don't move on the firing line. The bag we hit in baton training has a large surface area and doesn't duck and dodge like the surfaces we strike on the street. Police training needs to be as realistic as possible, within safety limits.

Since "the animation factor" and it's unpredictability can change any situation for the better (if we are prepared to respond to the change in conditions), or the worse (if we get caught by surprise), we need broad range, live training.

Targets which move, targets which react unpredictably, or disappear altogether to pop up and recommence hostilities from unexpected quarters, is quality live training. Role players who are suited with protective gear and are willing to absorb some impact, definitely help to make training more realistic. This helps train us to accept the large range of changing conditions which make up "the animation factor."

There are also tactical situations where the animation factor has the jump on you. Something the suspect does makes the situation completely uncontrollable.

Two officers, a few years ago, came upon an accident scene on the freeway where a young woman had apparently fallen from a speeding car. The officers were on-scene and the woman was being attended to by a paramedic, when the young woman's "fatal attraction-type" lover came up, pulled a firearm from beneath his jacket, and shot her. The animation factor had the jump on these officers and what they did was try to race and catch up to get control of the situation.

This is easier if you have trained reactions, have a wide selection of trained responses to different situations, and have visualized the cussedness people can cause. The officer later told me that everything happened so fast, he was racing to catch up, but couldn't. The suspect destroyed himself before either officer on scene could take any action. Had the suspect wanted to harm both officers, he could have done so. Thankfully, the young woman survived her injuries.

Train yourself, train your responses, visualize situations and responses beforehand, think and react properly to situations...and expect the "animation factor."

Despise the enemy strategically,
but take him seriously tactically.

Mao Tse-Tung

IF YOU NEED TO BE LIKED...
BE A FIREMAN

Policemen are not the favorite people of many factions in society. I recently came across an article in a radical publication which advocated the raping of cops' wives. There is a small cross section of society which is radical enough to consider this an appropriate response to the "crimes" (their term) committed by police, for merely enforcing the law.

The pure fact of the matter is that proactive police work is, for the most part, a negative service job. The unjustified attacks on families of police cannot and will not be tolerated by any portion of the legal or political system. But if you intend to be in police work, understand you are going to catch some heat.

I was a back-up officer on a domestic violence call some time ago. A fellow officer and her trainee went to the house and were confronted with a man who said in no uncertain terms they were to "get the #*#* off his property." The officers stayed until they could confirm the wife was still standing, apparently relatively undamaged. When the wife made the same demand, stated in the same language, they left.

Hubby, in the meantime, called 911 demanding they send someone to get these cops out of his house. I thought that was a novel approach, and we all surmised we hadn't heard the last of this charming couple.

Some time later, the worm turned. The woman who so adamantly wanted "those pigs" out of her house, went to a local hospital. When examined, the doctor found she had been bruised by her potty-mouthed husband on virtually every plane of her body. The first people she called were, you guessed it, the police.

We went to the house to arrest the husband. Hubby fought, was subdued, and booked. He was adamant the arrest was unjustified and was defiant to everyone. You can bet he will be even harder to handle the next time.

There are many folks who don't like me personally, because of the job I do. It's part of the territory. Even the people who don't like cops, will be the first to call when something ugly happens. They will also be the ones screaming in your face that they pay your salary if things don't go exactly the way they think they should. We need to keep doing the job the right way, despite their attitude.

The bottom line is, if you have a high need for approval...be a fireman.

The following quote is from England where a "tommy" was a foot soldier. It could apply to police service.

"For it's 'tommy this' and 'tommy that'
and 'chuck him out, the brute!'
But it's 'savior of his country'
when the guns begin to shoot!"

Rudyard Kipling

A BAD SEARCH

As a young Military Policeman, I completed the search of a 12 year old Panama citizen I found on base. These children came onto the base and sometimes burglarized the officers' houses near the frontier. We had orders to take them to the nearest gate and show them the way back to the frontier. Since the kid was only 12 years old, I didn't think handcuffs were necessary, and I had done this transport many times without trouble.

I frisked, then began to move the kid toward the back of the patrol car for the trip to the gate. That's when he dropped a four-inch knife and kicked it under the car. It sank in real fast that if this kid had wanted to plant the knife in me, it would have been possible. For a long time, I paid much closer attention to my searches.

After seven years as a civilian policeman I arrested a convicted felon on parole for possession of drugs and drug paraphernalia. I had obviously become complacent about my security. I made two mistakes.

I searched the suspect, handcuffed him behind his back and put him in the rear of the patrol car. I searched the suspect's car thoroughly. I found all the drugs, packaging, needles, and bindles I could find and went back to the patrol car.

Without checking my suspect, I got in and began to take him to jail. My suspect was very quiet in the back seat. I had my rear view mirror angled to be able to watch him. As I drove up a major county road, I heard the suspect say very quietly, "You didn't search me very well." Suddenly I saw a flash in my rear view mirror. The suspect was sitting forward and had his hands and an object near the cage separating me from him. My first thought was "I'm dead. I'll feel the pain any second." My foot reacted on it's own, slamming on the brake and sliding the car into a dry skid to the shoulder.

When I got out and looked in the rear passenger window with my flashlight, I saw the suspect sitting with his hands cuffed in front of him and a butane lighter in his hand. I called another patrol car and had them handle the suspect, again handcuffing him in the rear. When I took the lighter from the suspect, I found the flame had been turned to blow-torch level. This made me decidedly unhappy with my suspect. The suspect was returned to prison and the district attorney refused to charge the suspect with trying to burn me.

I've made my share of mistakes. You can bet I now make thorough and frequent searches. But still, I don't have all the answers.

The same man cannot be well skilled in everything;
Each has his own special excellence.

Euripides (480-406 BC)

P.S. Frisking and searching however, are skills we all must cultivate.

A TEACHER...OR A TECHNICIAN?

The course had been going on for a day and a half. It wasn't bad, but I had been trained in more advanced and effective methods of impact weapon use. I asked a question about the method being taught, and the instructor went off into a diatribe about throwing the baton away, and added the inevitable statement..."Because I said so!"

I have found when an instructor is not totally comfortable and confident with his instructional material or techniques, he is apt to lash out in this manner. When I first began teaching, I made this mistake. I have tried not to repeat it, with greater or lesser success over the years.

When I first begin teaching a class, I try to locate all the training records of the classes I have taken on the subject matter, include all the up-to-date techniques, refresher instructor training, and compile a complete training outline.

This has several advantages as it helps me to later document the course, document my expertise to teach the course, introduce alternate techniques, and answer the students' questions with a solid answer. If I don't have the answer, I can then say, "Whoa, you asked a question I can't answer, but this instructor can." Or, "I don't have an immediate answer for you, but I know where to look for the answer and I'll research it and get the answer for you."

This is much preferred to handling student's questions as challenges, or worse yet as personal affronts. Be sure of your curriculum, be sure of your skills with it, and take the time to do it the right way. You have something to give, and taking the "high road" of instruction will get it across much faster. I never take, nor teach a class, where I don't learn something.

I have been given some instructors who have been very gifted. They all seem to adhere to this principle:

The true teacher defends his pupils against
his own personal influence.
He inspires self trust.
He guides their eyes from himself
to the spirit that quickens him.
He will have no disciple.

(Amos) Bronson Alcott

THE CAKE FIGHTERS

Three-fifths of military personnel don't work in armed combat occupations. They work in supply, maintenance, and a hundred other occupations. I am not saying they are not necessary. Quite the opposite, they are crucial. Statistics during the Vietnam war era indicated that for each person who saw combat, there were 10 keeping him alive, fed, and supplied.

During the Desert Storm conflict, the numbers were probably hundreds of technicians, tacticians, engineers, supply and logistics personnel for each person who heard a bullet crack overhead, or locked on "incoming bandits."

In police service, there are no "R&R" periods when you can stand down and breathe easier. There is no clearly defined enemy uniform. There is no faceless enemy. Your every action is scrutinized and subject to analysis by people, some of whom are, "The Cake Fighters."

They may include members of the following: media, courts, attorneys, judges, department administration, investigators, internal affairs, middle managers, line supervisors, peers, defense attorneys, plaintiff's counsel, "instant experts," special interest groups, and all the other alphabet soup groups who oversee police actions. In some cases, this group of Monday Morning Quarterbacks may also include: federal prosecutors, federal investigators, and federal courts.

In this process of existence under the microscope of scrutiny, police find out who their suspect is. What the suspect does for a living, his prior criminal record, where he lives, what kind of friends he has, mother, father, sisters, brothers, and what his life is like. This is a major difference from the military. We find out personal information about the suspect who causes the critical incident. All this follows a critical incident which may have taken only seconds from beginning to end.

The Monday Morning Quarterbacks will render their decisions after thinking about the situation, analyzing it in depth, photographing it, diagramming it, re-enacting it, talking with other investigators, compiling notes and reports on it, talking with witnesses who may or may not carry a bias, sleeping on it, and finally making their pronouncement, days, months, or years after the fact.

This is the system we have. It is no different than a criminal investigation and may conclude in one. When a policeman is the subject of the investigation, he deserves to be trained to the highest possible degree, experienced in handling his job, and have the best documentation skills and legal expertise available.

It is important to remember that police have the protection of the public in mind. If the system unjustifiably rolls over and flattens police, we're going to have problems. The highest quality people will quit, leave, or retire. This will leave the field to the criminals because effective enforcement of laws will be less commonplace.

By the same token, useless laws lessen respect for the law, and compliance of the populace is what we must have to make enforcement practical. It makes law enforcement less efficient to be forced to waste effort, time, and money on bad law.

Police as a whole, in my experience, seem to practice the following attitude frequently in regard to their job performance. Officers spend very little time defending themselves against the barbs thrown by others. Their attitude seems to be:

I think that saving a little child,
and fetching him to his own,
is a darn sight better business
than loafing around the throne.

John Milton Hay

THE VERY BRAVE...

The divorce rate for police officers is among the highest of any profession. So is the rate of alcoholism, heart disease, hyper-tension, and suicide. The root of these problems is stress.

Police and other emergency service workers sacrifice themselves. Look at how many people in today's society have never seen a dead person, unless one is properly "presented" in a funeral setting. They don't see the immediate situations.

Citizens don't commonly see first hand, the brutality of criminals toward their victims. They don't see the hard cases involving good people, the accidents without reason, or the gut-wrenching finality of the death or brutalization of children. Civilians don't have these things repeatedly thrust in their faces. What sane person would do this for wages lower than that of a refuse worker? Why?

The answer for myself is the opposite side of the coin... when you catch the brutalizer and finally shut the cell door on a nice, long, long term of imprisonment...when you save a life, or prevent brutality...when you can help ease the pain of someone who has lost a loved one, or endured the seemingly unendurable. If it weren't for first responders, of all types...this wouldn't get done.

Hey folks...hooray for us! We do a very necessary job! The job does take its toll on us, but we are stronger for it.

The superior person acts before they speak, and afterwards speaks according to their actions.

The Confucian Analects

WHEN IT COUNTS...

The call came out, "possible mentally disturbed person with a rifle." The suspect could be seen by several neighbors standing in his driveway, shooting, reloading, and shooting again, at his mailbox. Several units began moving in that direction. The first unit on scene included a veteran deputy and a dispatcher riding with him for familiarization. The dispatcher got much, much more than she bargained for.

As the deputy took cover on the far side of his car, the suspect directed the 30-06 bolt action rifle at the patrol unit and bullets and glass began flying. The deputy pulled the dispatcher from the car to behind the wheel at the front fender.

The suspect directed accurate fire at the front of the car and the deputy pulled the dispatcher to the rear of the car. The suspect stepped back inside the house, reloaded, and stepped back out directing accurate fire at the rear of the car.

The deputy again moved the dispatcher to the front of the patrol car, and the suspect again fired at the front of the car. The suspect stopped firing, and there was a lull for a second or two.

Our rifle toting suspect was standing outside the house, 30 yards away from the deputy, when the officer figured he'd had enough, bounced up to the hood and fired two rounds at the suspect. The suspect disappeared inside the house. A public address system was used to tell him to come out and surrender.

The suspect reappeared at the door, walked out onto the lawn, and collapsed. The deputies' rounds had done their job. One round had hit the suspect in the left shoulder and the second hit the door frame, shoulder-high, one foot away from the suspect's left shoulder.

The suspect was handcuffed and began laughing. He said, "Ralph's still inside and he's got a gun too." This caused a distinct anal pucker among the restraining deputies who had entered the area in front of the house rather quickly due to the adrenaline inherent to the situation.

Turns out, thankfully, that "Ralph" was the suspect's dog. Our deputies secured and transported the suspect to the hospital and turned to the business of investigating the officer-involved shooting.

What's the point here? Make your fire accurate in any tactical scenario. The 30 yard range was extreme for the situation, coupled with adrenaline, speed of the incident, and the handgun the deputy was using. He later told me that what he remembered seeing was the front site superimposed on his suspect, but he held his fire and made sure it was accurate. The deputy involved was later awarded the Gold Medal of Valor for police service.

If you don't have time to aim,
you certainly don't have time to miss.

Sgt. Dennis Tueller
Salt Lake City Police Department

A CAPSULE
HISTORY OF VIOLENCE

Cain slew Abel and started the horrors of homicide. Wandering gangs burned, looted, raped, and killed while preying on hunter-gatherer tribes and farmers. The invading Celts and Saxons swept across Europe and England, and were absorbed into the populace. Hitler caused the deaths of millions, and an entire populace chanted "never again" 50-plus years later, justifiably so.

The United States has tried to become more non-violent. We have factions within our society which use political pressure, economic pressure, censure, public opinion, and a complete symphony of tactics to try to stop any violence by any political system, especially our own. We no longer need be too concerned about wholesale slaughter by invading armies. We have made our borders somewhat secure against a direct frontal assault by an occupying force. Unfortunately the slaughter goes on, in diminishing numbers, but continues. Retail instead of wholesale slaughter. It is called crime.

Here are a few indicators. Murder is broken into many categories under the lights of law and publicity. Mass murderers are a distinct category apart from serial killers. Gang related killing may also be drug related. Yet drug related murder can also be a separate and distinct category of it's own. Then you have murder itself. Is it premeditated? First degree murder? A result of "hot blood?" Voluntary manslaughter? A result of something which went wrong on a grand scale? Involuntary manslaughter? Then there is justifiable homicide...the result of a citizen or the police defending themselves or another from the actions of a criminal predator. Whew!

The media coins terms for rape, murder, beatings, knifings, drive-by shootings, and executions which include: "gang related activities" and "wilding." Why not be honest about these things and not euphemize them? If it's murder, call them murders. If it's rape or drug dealing, don't soften the impact by calling it "gang activities."

The popular press and television used to talk about the "savagery" of terrorists who used bombs. These days, an explosion goes off and the lead story goes something like this; "A large explosion ripped through the World Trade Center today. Six are believed dead and approximately 60 are injured, some critically. No one *responsible* has called to take *credit* for the act."

If *responsible*, would these cretins murder innocent civilians? "Taking *credit* for the act?" Beg pardon? Since when is a terrorist act a credit to anyone?

Television, magazines, radio, and newspapers are supposed to be experts in the use of words. They're missing the mark here.

That we're willing to tolerate these distortions of fact, much less the acts themselves, is a reflection of our society. Our country spends much more on leisure than on crime. Yet crime costs us dearly. The cost in lives... loved ones lost to families, victims who will never again fully function because of the destruction to their lives... is the worst cost of all. It far outweighs the money spent.

Crime costs us *billions* of dollars a year. We all know it's getting worse each year. But we have the strength to deal with it. It will take discipline and commitment to do so. We all have to be willing to make tough decisions and get involved.

The next thing we need do is stop giving motive or cause to inanimate objects or an "excuse" to the criminal. The weapon is not the cause of the problem.

When California's drunk driving got out of hand, we didn't ban cars. We stopped offering "deals" to drunks. We made enforcement and capture more certain. When convicted, punishment was made mandatory. Unsurprisingly, the death rate has dropped on our highways. Now, let's do the same thing with murder. Make capture a sure thing, and if convicted, punishment, in the form of the death penalty, certain.

I hear the Amnesty International group and allied factions howling now. Despite their protestations, the death penalty *is* the answer. They point at statistics and scream, "There's no deterrent factor in the death penalty." Oh yes, there is. That *particular* murderer will never kill again. I question the statistics of these groups who say the death penalty is not a deterrent. It has not been used consistently enough in modern times to develop a database.

Let's buckle down and commit ourselves to a battle. One in which we all get involved. We can make it safe for a woman, unescorted, to walk down any street in the country at night.

We can make it safe for the elderly, teens, business people, and homeowners, if we buckle down to it. Refuse to be victims or fall to threats. Wherever and whenever possible, don't submit to home invading robberies, car-jacking, murder, and mayhem. Fight back and follow-up. Let's put the system back to work for society, not for the criminal predator.

One of our founding fathers said it best. But if he could see the "wishful thinking" the criminal justice system has employed, he would be disappointed in us for allowing the situation to deteriorate to this point.

This is his quote:

> *Government implies the power of making laws.*
> *It is essential to the idea of law,*
> *that it be attended with a sanction,*
> *or in other words,*
> *a penalty or punishment for disobedience.*

Alexander Hamilton

A GOOD PARTNER IS...

A good partner is a combination of many things. Someone who knows when silence is better than talking. Someone who knows your mind and your way of working without being too intrusive. Someone you know is going to be right there beside you, not back "guarding the car." Someone you communicate with, and rely on. Someone whose demeanor in and out of the car is a part of you. Someone whose actions and reactions often dictate how effectively you do your job.

Wow! Sounds complicated doesn't it. It is, and yet it isn't. Being one of a team can be very good. Being just the other person in the car, *not* being good working partners, can be very bad.

The actions of a partner influence the perceptions of the people you contact, as do your own actions. If you disagree with the actions of your partner, best do it in private if you want the partnership to remain viable. Both partners must be willing to compromise in their actions and behavior. If they don't, friction increases, and a patrol car is no place for animosity to be stewing.

Each partner brings a working knowledge into the car which differs from the other. The basis of the partnership is trust and a basic liking for the other person. I have had partners who were good friends, and partners who I never saw off the job. Some people weren't partners, and I got out of the car with them as soon as possible.

A lot depends on the person you are paired with. A partner is not someone who sets you on the opposite side of the car and says, "don't touch anything." If that happens, finish the shift if possible, and get reassigned to another person.

A good partner will not inflict basic bodily functions on the other partner. I can hear you laughing now, but this becomes more than a matter of politeness when you're cramped in a car in winter for 45-50 hours a week. If you have a partner who thinks these actions, or his accounts of conquests are "hilarious" or a matter of bragging rights, it can create a problem.

A good partner will communicate clearly when friction arises and before things get hairy. I have been part of partnerships with no overt sign of communication. In one instance, my partner and I were facing a very large, resistive suspect, crouching with fists clenched, who gave the famous line, "I'm not going to go to jail!" My partner and I never made any verbal reply, and I grabbed the suspect's right wrist. I hadn't announced my intention nor had my partner and I talked about it. Yet if he grabbed the left wrist any later than I grabbed the right, I couldn't tell it. The simultaneous grab was successful, the suspect was taken to the ground and handcuffed without injury to us or him. The concerted action between myself and my partner was the result of a long association and familiarity with each other.

Set the basis for trust and communicate with each other as partners. You love and rely on your spouse. But only under very rare circumstances will you take your spouse with you into danger and expect them to save your life, or into a situation where you have to save them. Partners frequently do this. You don't love your partner, but you should like and respect him as much as you do your spouse.

A partner is not a reason for complacency. More officers are seriously injured or killed in double cars than on single patrol. Possibly because there are more double cars in use than single patrol cars. Double cars are almost standard in larger cities, especially in high crime areas.

No cop can afford to forget that action is faster than reaction. We sometimes hear of both partners suffering because of a criminal attack. More often, we'll have examples of one partner suffering and the other reacting. This is a result of the action versus reaction dilemma. As tragic as it is, the surviving partner often takes onto themselves "survivor guilt."

The "If only I had..." aspect of the situation may inflict tragic results on the remaining partner. We need to come to terms with the nature of law enforcement. We're not an occupying force, suspects are frequently not readily identifiable as dangerous, and the three-quarters of a second reaction time is sometimes not on our side.

Good tactics, good working agreements between partners, tactical planning, trust, and familiarity can sometimes help win the day. A good partner is someone to protect by being on our toes, always.

I always considered statesmen to be more expendable than soldiers. (or police)
President Harry Truman (paraphrased)

HASTY RADIO
TRANSMISSIONS

I pulled into the parking lot of a local bar in my marked patrol car and saw three suspects standing in a fighting stance. All three saw me and dropped their fists, then began laughing and clapping each other on the back. It was clear no one wanted to go to jail for fighting. All three denied fighting, they were just "playing around."

No one wanted to prosecute for the cut lips and scrapes which were rather obvious. I made sure they all understood that the fight was not to continue. Since they had been drinking, I told them to call someone to catch a ride.

When I went into the bar with them to make the calls, I had a feeling it wasn't going to end there. I did my bar check - no problems - and left. At least that's what it looked like to them. I then pulled up to the top of a hill, switched off my headlights, and watched the parking lot.

Within 30 seconds, "Bud" came out and went to his car. The other two combatants came out of the bar and followed, kicking and cursing at the locked driver's car door. I began to drive towards them and picked up the radio mike. The two suspects broke off the attack and ran toward the front of the bar. What the hell? As I drove into the parking lot, I saw Bud get out of the car with a large revolver in his hand. I keyed the mike and transmitted, "245 (Section 245 California Penal Code: Assault With a Deadly Weapon) in progress." "Man with a gun, JohNicks Bar," and unloaded from the patrol car.

I took the guy at gunpoint and shouted, "Police, don't move!" The suspect looked back over his left shoulder and tucked the revolver into his waistband. He then brought his empty hands out to the side. Other units heard the transmission and came on the double. The suspects were taken into custody without further trouble.

The radio is not a shield, it is not bullet proof, and it does not help you fight off a suspect who is violent. We can't be sitting behind the wheel of our car fixated on making the radio transmission when the suspect walks up on us...or we could easily be found there later, somewhat the worse for wear.

If the air is clear, make the hasty radio transmission, if possible, and unload. Otherwise, use your portable at the first opportunity...after you take protective action. The hasty transmission is not suitable in all instances, but it can be a tool in extreme situations.

Later, I asked "Bud" what he thought he was doing. He told me he had been fighting with those two guys, who had called him "big, dumb, and slow." He was tired of them ganging up on him, so he decided to "equalize things." Not a smart move. "Bud" went to jail for brandishing a firearm. The other rocket scientists went to jail for drunk in public and vandalism. But... I learned something from this situation...

It is not my policy to start trouble...
but I invariably end it.

Forrest Macomber

PAUL BUNYAN: ANOTHER VERSION OF THE STORY

I stood looking at the man facing me and knew he was dangerous. He was also very drunk as usual. This guy wakes up with .20 blood alcohol content and gets worse as the day goes on. But I remembered a story about him, just before I was hired...

Jerry was drunk one night and went to his mother's house. This was not unusual - what was unusual was that Mama decided she'd had enough of Jerry coming home, raiding her icebox, raising hell, leaving his dirty clothes, and puking all over the house before passing out. Mama decided on the direct approach...she changed the door locks. Jerry went to the front door and found it locked. Mama yelled at him to go away. Jerry tried the key. It wouldn't work and Mama again told him to go away. Jerry was in his late thirties at the time, and since he was a full grown man, he wasn't going to take this kind of treatment from Mommy.

The call made to the Sheriff's Department was very hard to understand because of all the background noise. The snarling and straining of a small engine in the background tended to overpower Mama's cries for help. Dispatch sent four officers since the cries seemed to indicate a genuine disaster. The four arriving deputies were familiar with Jerry. They knew he cut and split firewood for beer money, and frequently carried a gun. He had resisted arrest in the past, was extremely strong, and had been in a gun fight with another local suspect not too long ago. But the cops never bargained for what they saw.

In Jerry's drunken state, reverse psychology must have made perfect sense to him. "Since I can't get in to Mama's house and she won't come out, I'll just move the house from over her." With that thought, he fired up his chainsaw and began cutting down the house. By the time the deputies arrived he had successfully cut through a third of the house at waist level, and had a big smile on his face.

The deputies stopped about 50 feet away and shined their spotlights on Jerry. He turned toward the light and revved the chainsaw in the air a few times. The deputies response was unanimous. They leveled their guns and shouted for him to put down the chainsaw. He again raised and revved it while advancing two paces.

One deputy shouted that if Jerry didn't put the chainsaw down, he would be shot. It finally penetrated Jerry's booze-sodden brain that the chainsaw might be a deadly weapon...and they really might shoot him. You got that right, Jerry! The chainsaw died a natural death as Jerry set it on the ground and meekly went along with the deputies.

Today, on this particular arrest, Jerry was again really drunk. From past arrests, I knew if I distracted him with conversation, he would be easier to handle. I remarked that I recognized his car as one of the Sheriff's Department's old unmarked Dodge Monaco's. "Gee Jerry, I remember that car. It has a 440 Dodge engine in it and it's got a fast top speed." Jerry went on to sing the praises of the car all the way to jail. That's all I wanted...if Jerry was talking, he wouldn't fight. His brain was so pickled it was hard for him to concentrate on more than one thing at a time.

All the booking paperwork was done, and the shift was over. I went home thinking about Jerry. He was a hard worker, and when not liquored up, a fairly interesting guy to talk to. Give him a chainsaw, a splitting mall, and a couple six packs, and he'd cut and split cords of firewood all day. He was not to be underestimated. But the booze had made a local character of him. Too bad.

I came in for the next shift and my partner came up to me with a mystified expression on his face. "Hey, did you hear about Jerry?" "No, what's he done now" I asked. Seems that Jerry sobered up and was released. But promptly decided he had too much blood in his alcohol stream and proceeded to get liquored up. Then, California Highway Patrol spotted him. A fifteen minute pursuit followed, ending with Jerry ramming into a Highway Patrol car and a Sheriff's unit. "Surely you don't think talking about how hot that car was convinced him he could outrun a radio," I questioned. My partner replied, "Who knows, but Jerry's looking at a couple years worth of time now." I met Jerry again after he was released from jail. When I asked him about the car as a matter of curiosity, he said no, he just got stupid and ran.

Experience is not what happens to you,
it's what you do with what happens to you.
Aldous Huxley

A CLEAR CASE OF OVERLOAD

Briefing was in progress and the sergeant was busy reading the crimes. There were a few bulletins worth writing down and a few jokes that got a laugh. Everyone was being cordial and trouble seemed very far away.

The door of the briefing room flew open and a rotund suited form came into the room at full speed. The hard look he gave everybody diminished the relaxed atmosphere of the room. This was a detective, and in a low voice he stated, "Stay the hell away from the hospital! If you have something to do there, a prisoner or something else, okay, but don't hang around, and if ******* ******* or his wife start talking to you, walk away. Just walk away! If anyone goes over there and says or does anything to screw up my case against this son of a bitch, I'll gut shoot them! Is that understood?"

We all nodded our understanding. This guy looked and sounded serious. The detective and his partner left as quickly as they entered. The briefing room stayed quiet after the crash of the closing door. I finally breathed out, "What the hell was that all about."

The sergeant looked around the room and said, "Listen, I realize you guys have to go to that hospital, but don't talk to this guy or his wife. There's a case over there involving a child with gonorrhea of the mouth, and old scars and stitches on his rectum. This victim is an18 month old boy."

The light dawned. The detective who spoke had a handicapped child himself, along with several other healthy children, and this case was eating him up inside. That diatribe was the only way he could ventilate safely.

This detective and his partner went on to interview witnesses, collect records, document the suspect's lies, break his story, obtain his confession, and send him away where he could no longer victimize the child.

Understand this. Some cases get very ugly. A policeman is not a machine and these things affect us. I've gone into the captain's office on one occasion and into the sheriff's office on another. The conversations went something like this, "Look, this has gotten to be too much. I can't continue to do this. If I do, it's going to end up hurting me or my family, or making hash out of the case. I won't do that. Take me off the case, and I'd like to take some vacation time."

Sometimes it's necessary. Things just get too ugly, too real, too personal, you get too close to it. Back off and take a breather. There's no provision for R&R for police. Create your own. Your bosses should realize there's got to be a very good reason for your walking into their offices. Know yourself, and know when you've reached your limits.

There is only one thing it requires real courage to say...
and that is a truism.

G.K. Chesterton

A HOLLOW CHALLENGE

It had been a quiet night in a single car patrol, but as usual, someone came along and loused it up.

I saw a darkened Trans Am sitting on the roadside and flipped up a spotlight lighting up the car's interior. I saw the driver get punched in the face three times very quickly. I made a radio transmission to let the office know what I had and where, all the while making a U-turn and getting behind the suspect's car.

I used the public address speaker and got the driver out of the car. He obeyed each direction, ending up in a kneeling position behind his car, facing away...very nice and cooperative. That's when things went sour.

"Passenger...slowly get out of the car with your hands on top of your head." The man screamed, "What?" out the open window. I repeated the demand and received a reply of "Fuck you!" I'd had enough of this. "Passenger...get your ass out of the car!"

The door exploded open and the suspect bounded out of the car with his fists clenched. "What you gonna do pig? C'mon man, shoot me, kill me motherfucker!" I looked at the man who was about 5' 8" and 160 pounds. There was no weapon visible in his hands and nothing visible in his belt. I replaced my sidearm in my holster and moved forward into the light of my spotlight.

I spun the baton out of the ring on my belt and dropped into a balanced stance with the baton displayed prominently in front of the light. I told the young man, "You don't want to screw around or you're going to get hurt." His reaction was immediate and sensible. "Hey, man, wait a minute...can't we talk about this?" I assured him that talking was not an option and he would either obey my directions or face the consequences. The suspect turned around on demand and I began the handcuffing procedure.

My suspect waited until I had one hand cuffed, and had begun to move the second hand for cuffing, before he began struggling. I powered the suspect's hands together and completed the handcuffing. I began trying to search the suspect and he started dancing and struggling. I told him to knock off the crap and continued. When I began to search the guy's legs, he raised up and tried to kick me in the face.

I reached up over his shoulder and grabbed a chin-cup, using it to take him to the ground. I then used a nerve hold momentarily and asked him why he wanted to try to hurt me? I again told him to relax and completed the search while he was in a prone position. This made him much easier to handle.

The suspect began this situation by issuing a "hollow challenge." He knew the situation was not sufficient to allow the use of lethal force, so his invitation for me to shoot him was bluster. He knew I couldn't and shouldn't shoot. When I de-escalated to impact force, his bluster was gone. The baton I held was not an empty threat and he knew it. Displaying the proper level of force allowed me to de-escalate the situation from impact force, which was not necessary to use, to bio-mechanical force when the suspect tried to kick me.

Use the right level of force and be assured there are criminals who know what the correct level is. The use of the proper level of force takes the wind out of their "hollow challenge."

Look at the hand.
Each finger is not of itself,
a very good weapon for either offense or defense.
But close it in a fist,
and it can become a very formidable weapon...

President Dwight Eisenhower
(paraphrased)

IMPACT WEAPONS: FICTION VS TRUTH

The radio call was strange anyway so how could I expect the situation to be anything less? "Suspicious person on Covey Road. We've had three calls from residents who have reported the suspect pounded on their doors and shouted that Reno has been bombed. Suspect then fled."

Ok, so what are we driving into? I went onto Covey Road within a minute, followed by another deputy who had just returned to patrol from a detective division assignment. We'd been talking nearby when the call went out. As we turned onto Covey Road, we were joined by a California Highway Patrol Officer who had obviously heard our call on the scanner.

I parked when I spotted a short, barrel-shaped man standing on the side of the road. The man was in his fifties, balding, wearing eye-glasses. He looked like he should be somebody's grandfather, as long as you didn't look at his eyes. When you did, it became apparent that "rational" was simply a word in the dictionary, and had no present connection to him.

His wide-eyed, darting stare was compounded by the hysterical monologue pouring from his mouth. "Reno's been bombed! Reno's in flames! The Japanese have attacked! I warned them about this. The government wouldn't listen. Now millions have died. I'm a major in the army! I'm in charge now!"

"Right!" I replied, "Now that we have that straight sir, let me take you to the command staff meeting" (meaning Mental Health). Our suspect refused, and trying to convince him I was a colonel and outranked him, didn't work. The man moved to his right and began pulling and pushing at a 1 1/2" diameter metal pipe buried in the ground as a fence post. If he got that pipe loose, this could get really ugly. I pulled my sidehandle baton and told our suspect to move away from the pipe. The suspect doubled his frantic efforts to pull the pipe from the ground, and my partner, Jeff, began to close in.

The suspect backed away from the pipe, turned toward Jeff with his fists raised and launched a punch. Jeff jumped backwards and the punch missed. I moved in with my sidehandle baton and struck the suspect's left knee twice. He turned around and I hit the right knee accurately and with power, shouting for him to get down. The suspect screamed, "What do you want me to do?" I shouted again for him to get on the ground. He flopped down on his face and the situation was over. We handcuffed the suspect and took him to the hospital for a physical exam, required any time we use impact force.

End result? No broken bones for the suspect, no injured officers, and one suspect residing in jail awaiting arrival of Mental Health.

How do we justify the use of force for police officers? Defense attorneys may not like the facts outlined above, but my use of force was well within federal, state, and case law guidelines. After the situation was over, Jeff came to me and said he thought he couldn't use impact force until he had tried to subdue the suspect with his hands. Knowing the laws regarding police use of force a little better, I was able to tell Jeff why I used the force level I did, and document my reasoning in the report.

First, our suspect did not respond to my verbal attempts to defuse the situation. Physical presence of uniformed police and attempts at verbal control didn't work. The suspect then upped the stakes (sorry) when he began pulling at the fence post.

A man armed with a 6' piece of pipe is not approachable, and deadly force may have to be used to stop him. I didn't want it to get to that point. When Jeff approached, the man backed off then swung a fist at him. That's when I struck with the baton. Jeff and I both had tried less intrusive means to control the suspect and they failed. Impact force was imminently justified here.

Dave Rose and I taught an Expandable/Collapsible Baton course through a Sacramento College where we are staff instructors. Police and sheriff's deputies from local agencies came to the class and we spent a day going through the drills and practice necessary to effectively use the baton. The Expandable/Collapsible police baton brands available include (in alphabetical order) the A.S.P., CASCO, and PPCT batons to name a few.

The class day included state and case law, departmental policy, and a use of force continuum we developed. This allowed us to tell students exactly when the use of impact force is permissible, what situations justify force, and what actions to take to ensure their use of force is justifiable. Instruction also included how to document the case and when and how to de-escalate from impact force to control holds. The rest of the day was spent in drills, techniques, and teaching.

The final examination called Confrontational Situation Training, or Realistic Situation Training was my honor. In many years of street police work, I have been hit a few times and taken some good hits from partners. I now had the privilege of wearing protective gear and letting my students hit me with full street batons. I learned more about the nature of impact force in that forty minute time period than I had learned in years.

The United States court says training must "approach realism." In short, the final exam for the baton class must be as realistic as safety allows, and student safety is of primary importance. Let's get one thing straight here, we can't let students get hurt during training. If a student is injured during training, it costs the agency for injuries that are job related. Also someone must be paid to work the injured officer's shift while he heals. Even injuries to the instructor may cause problems, so we conduct the training with safety uppermost in our minds.

I donned an athletic cup protector and FIST Protective Gear. The various straps and pads reminded me of when I played high school and college football. I had good mobility, but was very well padded on most surfaces. The students are then required to use the skills they had been taught in a realistic situation. They had to give verbal warning and directions and use the baton for an extended time period against my amply padded frame.

There is plenty of stress involved in this training and the stress is induced from many levels. The students perform the techniques in front of the class on an individual basis so there's some element of "stage fright." The instructor curses and acts like a highly resistive suspect. The other students also shout suggestions for techniques.

The instructor ties up the student by grabbing the student's head and pulling it in close and tapping the student in the face with a gloved hand simulating physical combat. Notice I said "tap." I used padded Kendo gloves to "tap" the student, and no bloody noses or even skin reddening was visible when the testing was over. This also antagonizes the officer and may reveal those who would "over-control" a suspect.

I felt each individual officer's strength. The most common problem was not too much power, but too little. I was able to verbally advise each officer to "step it up" when necessary or correct problems with targeting and accuracy. Dave Rose was standing by as safety officer should a student "over-control."

Inevitably, I made a mistake. I reached forward in an attempt to take a baton from a student. The student very properly used a fast, powerful extended shaft circle strike to hit me underneath the left arm on a completely unshielded portion of my anatomy. The result astounded me. The area under the arm felt like a large area burn, but it did not stop or slow me down!

This strike occurred about halfway through the class and I had the other half waiting to test. I continued with another 20 minutes of literally high-impact aerobics to finish the examinations. Near the end of the testing process, another student hit me with a glancing blow on the inside surface of the right elbow. I immediately knew I'd been hit, and that glancing blow cost me more in mobility and power than any other strike.

There is a popular theory being advanced by some police trainers that "nerve center and major muscle groups" are the areas which should be targeted for impact weapon strikes. I'm not convinced this theory is valid. The strike that hit me in the side hit the Latissimus Dorsai and Serratus Anterior, two major muscle groups. This strike was also near a major nerve center under the arm.

By the "nerve center and muscle group" targeting theory, I should have been unable to move or use the left arm fully. I assure you there are numerous students who would tell you in no uncertain terms I was not slowed nor hampered in any way. I did remain effective. Had it been a street situation, I would have remained dangerous through many strikes.

By contrast, the glancing blow to the right elbow which left almost no visible injury and no internal injury, cost me far more mobility than any other strike. In short, "major muscle group and nerve center" targeting will cause *more* impact weapon blows to be struck. I would not want to be the trainer teaching a method which needs more blows in order to control a suspect. Don Cameron and Dave Rose have been doing this training for over 12 years and have sustained minor injuries from nearly every impact weapon known to law enforcement. Their experience agrees with mine.

When the class was over, nearly every student came over to thank me and shake my hand. They had a new skill, one they had tested under "real world conditions." The students knew this skill could well save their hides.

It wasn't until I took off the gear and began to drive home that I located a large raised area on my left side under the arm and knew that strike had done some damage and was going to hurt. When I took off my clothes to shower, I found two full strikes; the one described under my arm, and another on the inside surface of the upper left arm. There were also three other strikes on my legs which had been partially absorbed by the padding, but had bruised the skin. In addition there was the glancing blow to the elbow.

Now folks, it's important to realize I was getting hit by full street batons wielded by police officers at full power. I'm not an overly large man, 5' 11" and 200 pounds. I absorbed two full strikes and three partial strikes, a glancing blow on a major joint area, *all without being in any danger of being incapacitated. Also the only thing I had in my system was adrenaline.* Anyone on drugs or alcohol would be harder to control.

The injury from the strike under the arm was quite substantial, a bruise about 3" wide by 6" long. I must stress again that it caused me no loss of mobility or power. I did not require a medical exam, nor did I miss one day of work.

Realistic Situation Training or Confrontational Situation Training, whichever you call it, law-abiding citizens should hope their local officers have been trained this way. Criminals should hope not.

Which army will win?
Which army is the stronger?
On which side are the officers and men more
highly trained? In which army is merit rewarded
and misdeeds punished?

Sun Tzu

CIVILIAN PERCEPTIONS: USE OF FORCE

Average civilians have not been in a fight for their life during their adult years. They have been in common childhood brawls and teenage scrapes, but infrequently will civilians face those who are determined, and really **trying**, to kill them.

Police service is partly to blame for the public's perceptions of use of force. During the 1960's the cry of "police brutality" was first heard. Watching television during an anti-war demonstration in San Francisco, I remember seeing a student being hit with a baton by a San Francisco Police Department officer. I would imagine very few people saw the officer's partner bend down and retrieve a switchblade knife in the grass near the suspect's outstretched hand. The public at large was too intent on the spectacle of the officer using the baton.

Citizens sometimes see the middle or end of a confrontation. They don't see the actions leading up to the situation. This gives them only a small portion of the picture which often can't be filled in right away. Whenever possible, without compromising an investigation, I try to explain the situation to any civilians who ask questions. If the questioner is belligerent or abusive, I won't argue with them. I provide my name and badge number and leave before the argument escalates. I also notify the department of the incoming complaint.

There are people who cannot conceive of any reason for the use of force. Some years ago, I had a brand new trainee in my patrol car. I hadn't even begun to question his experience before we got a call of "man with a gun." I pulled onto Highway 49, spotted the car, and pulled it over with High Risk/Felony Stop procedures. I ordered the suspect out of the car, into a prone position, approaching with a drawn gun. I secured the suspect's gun and took him into custody without incident. He was arrested as a convicted felon in possession of a firearm.

While doing paperwork after the arrest and booking, I received a telephone call. A woman driving by had been incensed by my "gestapo tactics." I explained to her that the suspect had been reported to have a gun and that I used procedures designed to ensure the suspect was safely arrested and I could go home that night. My handling of the arrest made the situation safe for surrounding civilians and even the suspect. I kept the suspect at a disadvantage so he could not fight effectively should he decide to start a fight. I kept my own and my partner's safety uppermost in my mind. I moved the suspect away from the line of traffic to somewhat alleviate any problem with compromising civilian safety.

The complainant couldn't understand how I could be "so offensive." "You actually approached that poor man with a drawn gun! It was barbaric! What if I'd had my grandchildren with me? They would have been scarred with mental anguish by the violent horror of a policeman with a drawn gun!"

I spent the better part of ten minutes telling this woman I had done what was right, proper, and what I was trained to do. I ended the conversation by telling her to call my office during regular business hours and file a complaint if she wished. Or if she wished, I could put a sergeant on the phone now who could help her file a complaint. She declined, saying she wanted to consider further my "violent behavior."

Apparently my wife and kids losing their husband and father didn't matter to this lady. She just didn't want any violence to encroach on her life. I hope she succeeds and she and her loved ones stay safe. I'll continue to do my job the right way.

There's a civilian perception, and a belief that's very pronounced with criminal defense attorneys, that police are violent. They may be. Violence may be part of a police officer's job and justified by the situation.

In those few cases where violence is justified, police should be *efficiently violent* to end the situation without inordinate danger to themselves, the public, or the suspect. More frequently I've seen cops go out of their way and endanger themselves **in order to keep from hurting a suspect**. Cops have been shot, stabbed, and lost their lives because they hesitated or warned a suspect, rather than use justifiable force.

Police trainers also reap some of this incorrect perception and ill will. The perception is that trainers are the ones who teach police, therefore, trainers must be even more violent. Untrue! In my experience, trainers get into far less physical contests with suspects than the average. The situation may be avoided before it occurs because we know what to look for and what to do. Those confrontations which do occur are generally over quickly without damage to the officer, with less danger to the public, and less injury to the suspect.

This lessening of danger through training is something every police officer and police trainer strives for. When police administrators and politicians bow to political pressure from liberals and those with an axe to grind, police and the public end up paying the price with increased injuries and deaths.

If the hands of the police become tied, the older officers will retire, the best people will quit, and police work will not attract highly qualified applicants. Police service will suffer as well as the general public. Police administrators, lawyers, courts, oversight committees, politicians, and media would do well to remember:

This is what extremely grieves us,
that a man who never fought,
should contrive our fees to pilfer.
One who for his native land,
never to this day had oar, or lance,
or blister in his hand.

Aeschylus

BUILT-IN RADAR

It was a warm spring night when I got a call of an armed invasion in Colfax. The man calling the Sheriff's Department complained there were armed men all around his trailer and he thought they might be either Colombians or the FBI. It didn't matter which, since both were trying to kill him. When I arrived, the man confided he was one of a very few secret agents who didn't have a "Double-O" number, and that I was safe since he didn't have his license to kill. Oh, and one more thing, please don't call him a spy - that's so melodramatic and amateurish.

After talking with the man and checking him for weapons, I had a second unit come out. I talked with the family, and the man's father was beside himself. "All I want is one good night's sleep. I can't take this, officer! He's never been violent. Never been suicidal. Mental Health won't help. He's just delusional. I'm at my wit's end. I'm ready to strangle him myself!"

I walked over to the Colfax police unit and asked the officer waiting there to hold onto the subject while I took a tour of the park. The delusional suspect said that masked, armed, camouflaged men were all over the trailer park and told me not to go in because I would never survive the battle. Taking my chances, I drove through the sedate, mainly senior citizen populated, trailer park where the most dangerous thing happening was an overdose of Geritol.

When I returned to the suspect's location in my marked patrol car, the young man was astonished I had survived my brush with death. He insisted the commando's were there. I told him they weren't. There was no convincing him, short of a demonstration. The radio was quiet that night, and I had an idea. I walked over to the Colfax officer and asked him to walk in front of my car when I waved to him, stay there for three seconds, and then walk back to his car.

I turned back to the suspect and asked him to look inside my patrol car. We had new radio frequency scanners in the cars and I had the LED read-out turned to the brightest setting. The blue lights chasing across the scanner made a ghostly light in the car's interior. I told our young friend, "Look, there's no one in the trailer park. I checked. Now, watch the blue light inside my car." I motioned to the Colfax patrolman to walk in front of my car. I keyed the microphone on my portable radio. When the scanner locked onto my radio channel, the blue lights quit chasing each other across the screen, a steady light shone brightly and static came out of the scanner's speaker. As the Colfax officer moved from in front of my car, I released the portable radio key. The blue figures began chasing themselves across the screen again.

I told the suspect, "See? All our units have new ground-effect radars installed in them. There's nobody in the park or I would have known." Our suspect was astonished. "I didn't know you guys had that." The suspect thanked me profusely, as did the family now that they were able to get a good night's sleep.

You can't say that civilizations don't advance,
for in every war they kill you in a new way.

Will Rogers

"VICTIMLESS CRIMES" (?)

The young man curled his lip in scorn and made an assertion for which his life experience didn't qualify him. "Hey, most everybody drinks, and there's no difference between pot and booze." The rest of the high school class leaned forward in their seats waiting to see how I would handle that comment. A flat George Bush style statement that marijuana was "Bad...Real Bad" would lose my credibility with the class, and I wasn't about to fall into that trap.

"Marijuana and booze. That's kinda like comparing apples and oranges, isn't it?" I replied. The young man got a puzzled look on his face. I continued, "Most people say that marijuana, drugs in general, prostitution, and bookmaking are 'victimless crimes'." The young man picked that up with, "Yeah, they are victimless crimes. Marijuana never killed anybody!"

I replied, "Wrong! Where's David _____? Anybody seen him lately?" He attended this high school, but it wasn't likely they had seen David in the last two months. He had been buried that long ago. A young life ended with a knockout punch combination of alcohol, drugs, and a car.

"Each year we have about 50 thousand lives ended on the highways. The majority of these deaths are due to drunk driving, or a combination of drunk driving with drugs. In addition, every year thousands of people in the U.S. and abroad die from the violence of the drug trade itself. That doesn't include the thousand who die from drug overdose."

"Tell the inspector from my office the pungi stakes he stepped on years ago were a victimless crime. The pungi stakes were surrounding a marijuana patch. Every year we get injury reports from people who are out enjoying national parks and public lands. A hiker goes down a forest path and finds fishhooks strung across the path at eye level. Many times each year some cretin with a gun steps out of the forest and threatens people with his firearm because they are getting too close to the marijuana plantation. Does this sound like victimless crime to you?"

I remember a case from many years ago. "Mindy" (not her real name) was a fresh-faced 17-year old. Her parents were going through a divorce, but it didn't seem to effect her much. Her parents were well off financially, and as a result, she had access to flashy cars and cash.

I knew she was hanging around with a crowd of drug users, and in conversations with her told her she was heading down the wrong path. She laughed and said she wasn't going to get caught up in the drug problems of her friends. Frequently when I talked with her, she would let something slip about someone and unknowingly give me enough information to pass on to the drug task force.

I quit working in that area a year after Mindy's parents broke up. The next time I saw her, I wasn't shocked. Mindy's apparent age was about mid-forties, even though she couldn't have been more than 22. When she was brought to jail, I asked her what happened.

In a capsule history Mindy told me she was using drugs even when I met her. (No surprise there). Commonly enough, she started with marijuana and alcohol, then graduated to speed (methamphetamine). In the intervening five years, she had become heavily involved in drug sales with some heavy duty people. She had two children by different fathers and both infants had been taken away from her because of her addiction.

Mindy's face was mottled and scarred by the "speed bumps" on her skin that itch intolerably. Her hair was dull and lifeless and her teeth were rotting. All this was an effect of the drug use. Physical deterioration that could never be reversed.

In addition, Mindy had been witness to two murders and had faced a range of violence which included being beaten, robbed, raped, kidnapped, and shot at. She told me of being kidnapped, taken to a cellar, and held for two days. Her captor was a drug dealer who hadn't decided if she was a "snitch." It was simple. If she was a snitch...she died. If not, she lived. She was chained to a wall of the cellar near a mattress while the dealer put a gun to her head and played "Russian roulette" with her life. He had also raped and beaten her in an effort to get her to "confess." Knowing she was dead if she broke down, she stayed defiant, survived, and broke loose after two days.

When she got out of jail from her own drug dealing charges, Mindy went back to her drug connections. I doubt if she's alive now, the odds are against it.

I looked at the faces of the high school kids in front of me. Should I tell them about Mindy? The addict and the marijuana user have one thing in common. They both say, "I can handle it." The dealers have a common refrain also, "Here, try this stuff. It's a better high." Marijuana to hashish, hash to white dope, it goes in small easy stages. In some settings, white dope itself is fashionable. It makes the dealer rich, and destroys the users, their children, and families.

No. No point in talking about Mindy. They wouldn't care, couldn't relate it to themselves, and would think I was just trying to scare them. Life can be scary enough all by itself.

If we seek merely the swollen,
slothful ease and ignoble peace,
if we shrink from the hard contests,
where men must win at the hazard of their lives,
and at the risk of all they hold dear,
then bolder and stronger peoples will pass us by,
and will win for themselves the domination of the world.

Theodore Roosevelt

OFFICER, LEAVE MY HOME NOW!

I went to the predominantly senior citizen populated mobile home park and met an obviously distraught woman standing outside her trailer. "It's my son. He came home and threatened me. He's been gone for three days and he's broken up the house before. He's scaring me." I took the information about the woman's 33 year old son and went into the trailer.

The tattoos on his arms spoke of prison work and when I checked, he had convictions for drug dealing. From his physical condition, pulse, respiration, and reactions, it appeared he was coming down from a central nervous system stimulant (probably crank). The suspect had been on a three day "run." There wasn't enough to make an arrest for being under the influence, since the drug had largely worn off. I found the suspect had no warrants and was not on a searchable probation or parole. The suspect was profane and uncooperative. I went back outside and talked to mama.

Sonny was working in a fast-food restaurant near home, making minimum wage. He would come home high, break up the trailer and shove mama around. Mama couldn't keep anything in the trailer because sonny would steal anything of value to sell. He rode a bicycle to work, but was trying to make mama buy him a car.

Mama was retired. I told her these should be the golden years of her life. The time when she had earned a rest and a break. I pointed out that by allowing sonny to live with her, she was saving him $400.00 a month in rent, which allowed him to buy more drugs and kill himself even faster. The solution, tough as it may be...throw him out. He was 33 and should be able to fend for himself.

I asked the lady what she wanted me to do. Did she want her son out of the trailer? "Well...no." Did she want to fill out a citizen's arrest form for battery when he pushed her around a week or so ago? "Well...no." "Then lady, I can't help you. Only you can do that. I can't help your son. Only he can do that. You can stop enabling him to spend more money on drugs, or you can keep suffering from your son's abuse and violence." The woman drew herself up to her full height and said, "Officer, leave my property now! The very idea. I call you for help and you accuse me of helping my son use drugs!"

I had the information for a Service Report. I took a copy along with my observations and forwarded them to the Special Investigations Unit (Narcotics). Sonny got busted dealing at the fast-food restaurant a couple months later.

Every time I hear about drugs being a "victimless crime" and liberals advocating legalization of drugs, I get angry. I wish they could see first-hand the squalor that children are forced to live in when parents abandon them for their drug habit. I wish they had to smell the hovels these kids live in, see the needles, razors, and garbage strewn throughout the apartment or house. I wish they could see the lives destroyed. Not only the user's - the family member or friend the user rips off - the children who are abused and sexually molested when "uncle" or "family friend" gets a nose or arm full of "go fast."

I would like to force a defense attorney to take the ambulance ride I took early in my career. A 13-year old runaway had been picked up by two heavily tattooed suspects. These paragons of society had proceeded to pack her nose full of crank and rape her in every possible way over a three day period. Her rantings and ravings about insects and spiders crawling on her continued during the 20 mile ride to the hospital. She ended up in a psychiatric hospital and the doctors didn't hold much hope she would recover. "Drug induced psychosis" was diagnosed. There was no chance she would recover enough to identify the attackers who made her last hours of sanity a living hell.

Legalize drugs is the liberal call. Not from where I stand!

I expect to fight that proposition until hell freezes.
Then I propose to start fighting on the ice.

Russell Long

THE HARBINGERS
OF DEATH

The average person will not see the end result of violent death. They may glimpse it as they pass on the freeway, or see it on the evening news and be properly "horrified." Most of the time, the average citizen will have the opportunity to say, "they looked like they were sleeping."

Not so for cops and emergency service workers. The hardest realization for an emergency service worker is that sooner or later they too will end their days in that same manner. No pulse, no respiration, no more lazy days in the sun, swimming and laughing. Never again the bite of a tart drink, the slow rasp of material against skin at night, nor the soothing warmth of a slow shower. The loss of all this is ahead of everyone, however, it is something we must not dwell on.

If you cannot stand the recurring reminder of death, find another field of endeavor. Each police officer knows he or she may become part of the two percent who are required to use their firearm during the course of their career. Some officers really don't come to terms with the use of lethal force unless it happens to them.

Much more pervasive are the scenes of death. Violent, accidental, quiet as a thief, or uproarious and malicious as next day's headlines. The aftermath of these repeated scenes of death will imprint you if you fail to realize they are a part of your work. If you come to terms with them, they may only haunt you for a short period of time. If they failed to bother me in the least, I would begin to worry for real.

The things that may imprint and bother you are varied. The smells of death can last a long time in your memory. Personally, the smell of ozone has bothered me for a long time because of the ozone generators used in the morgue to kill odors. But the smell of blood or decay may be what causes you trouble. Burning coffee to kill the smell, and dry cleaning uniforms after a horrid scene may help to ameliorate the immediate problem. But that's just a stopgap, not a solution. Dealing with the memories is our problem.

The sounds at a death scene are best left undescribed as are some of the sights. But know this input to your senses may well stick with you for hours, days, weeks, or longer. We deal with them for the short term so we can do our job. We won't know the cost until later when we come to terms with our perceptions of a particular scene.

When the family is waiting outside at the scene of the accident, suicide, or homicide, we know it's not going to be an easy case. To focus on the job which needs to be done will help us overcome some of the problems associated with the death scene.

The manner in which we come to terms with death will determine our effectiveness and our health. If we suppress these feelings and deal with them with alcohol, or engage in destructive behavior, we're not going to be very good for the people around us, not even to ourselves after a while. Come to terms with death. Realize as an EMS worker you're going to have it shoved in your face over and over. Don't be afraid to ask for help when you need it.

Also balance the death scenes with those of life. The look on your child's face when he asks a funny question. The tears in the corners of the eyes as mamma hugs the toddler you just found. The quiet time spent with your wife, family, and friends.

These successes can help brush the other perceptions aside.

Even his griefs are a joy long after
to one that remembers all that he wrought and endured.

Homer
The Odyssey

THE PRESENCE OF VULTURES

The highway was closed, with traffic backed up for seven miles on a Friday at 4 p.m. When the call came out of a coroner's case due to a traffic accident, I took the back roads to within a quarter mile of the scene, then flipped on the emergency lights to go the final distance on the wrong side of the road. As I arrived, a firefighter I knew walked past and said, "It's a bad one...a small child." I thanked him mentally, and would remember to thank him later for allowing me to prepare myself for the circumstances as much as possible.

I went through the processes necessary for the report; interviews with the Emergency Medical Technician who pronounced death, procedures done in an attempt to save the three year old, names of firefighters and California Highway Patrol officers who were first on the scene. The blanket covered figure on the road's shoulder spoke volumes about disaster. The crowd forming on the highway made things more difficult as crowd control became more of a problem.

A tall man burst through the lines of people and stepped across the small prone figure of my victim, demanding to know where the driver of the car was. I referred him to the hospital, controlling my frustration. He was a friend of the family.

The driver of the car had picked up his daughter for a court ordered visitation, and proceeded to get drunk and drive. Excessive speed and drunkenness caused him to cross the center line of the undivided highway and smash sidelong into a station wagon. The impact nearly sheared the car in half, ejecting the tiny 3 year old girl, killing her instantly. The smell of booze was heavy inside the car and an open liquor bottle and empty beer cans were taken by the Highway Patrol.

Focus on the job ... I took photographs of the victim and notes on the trauma for an on-scene coroner's viewing. I turned around and walked back to my patrol car. My eyes felt like they had ground glass pushed in back of them. My youngest daughter was the same age as the tiny victim.

I was met at the door of my patrol car by a sweating 60

year old man. He said he had walked over a mile through the line of cars, and demanded to know what was going on. I answered there had been a fatal accident and got into my car to check the arrival time of the morgue's transportation van. When I looked out of the car, I saw the man had moved so close to my door that I couldn't get out. I popped the car door latch and slowly opened the door to force him away from my car. The diatribe started, "I demand to know why one lane of this road hasn't been opened. What have you lazy bastards been doing?"

That did it! I snapped, "Mister, I don't know who you are, but this is a fatal accident scene and the road is closed for the investigation. I have a small child dead in the ditch over there. I don't know when the road will re-open, but I'll tell you one thing I'm absolutely positive about, if you don't get behind that patrol car, out of this scene and out of my face, you're going to end up in the back of this car in handcuffs for obstructing and delaying a police officer. That's not subject to debate, now back off!"

I continued with the information gathering, paperwork, and preparing the transportation of our victim. The man who protested the road closure was back outside the scene dominating the attention of two firefighters with his protests. The firemen probably didn't realize they saved him from being arrested. One more confrontation would have done it.

The road was opened after a wash down and the twisted wreckage pulled off to one side. I looked around the scene and saw people walking back to their cars in the immediate vicinity. The 60 year old whiner had disappeared. I could understand the folks from the cars in the vicinity being there. I know curiosity is contagious and a very human trait. What I couldn't understand was the two or three folks walking around the scene checking the ground. So I stayed just to double check the scene and ensure I left nothing of my victim's property for the souvenir hunters.

As two middle-aged couples crept through the scene in their Cadillac, I saw a blue haired matron hanging half out of the rear window of the car. She clutched a 35mm camera in her left hand, snapping pictures of the crushed car on the side of the road and the bloodstains on the road surface. As they cleared the south end of the accident scene, I saw her reach forward and strike the driver with her right hand shouting at him to slow down.

As I looked at the people searching the scene, I could easily imagine their necks stretching, thinning, and bending downward. Their heads balding and their noses elongating to form beaks.

Under normal circumstances, these people would very possibly say they detest and decry violence. Yet they will roll through an accident scene, one of violent death for a small child, snapping pictures for all they're worth!

Sorry, I still don't understand this. Can anyone enlighten me here?

*Hateful to me as the gates of hell,
is that man who hides one thing in his heart,
and speaks another.*

Homer
The Iliad

AN OUT OF PLACE CALL

Damn! I was just sitting down to a juicy steak dinner. A meal I try to treat myself to once a week while on duty. I was working the mid-watch and it was 5:00 a.m. when the telephone rang and the dispatcher told me, "We have a physical fight at...", and gave me the address. I went back to the restaurant booth, dropped money on the table, and told the waitress I had to leave.

Two other officers, Karl and Mike, were with me as we responded to the house, only a mile from the restaurant. The suspect's local history included charges of assault with a deadly weapon on his girlfriend. He had last attacked her with a hatchet. We pulled up and found a locked gate about 50 yards down from the house.

I looked up the terraced lawn to where a man was standing on the back porch of the home. He waved, smiled, and said, "Come on up. Everything's okay." I told Karl to watch out for this call. We all agreed it was out of place; wrong time of day for a family fight.

My partners and I went over the fence and walked up toward the back sliding glass door and the smiling, empty handed man on the porch. As we approached, Mike asked, "Are you Mark _____?" The suspect said yes, stepped back through the open sliding glass door and dropped a wooden prop in the door track, locking us out. He walked toward the kitchen as Mike tried the door.

Mike and Karl flanked around the side of the house and looked in through the huge plate glass kitchen window. I saw them draw their guns, and holler, "Put the gun down, put it down man."

Uh oh! I violated my own rule...where's my escape route? I moved toward the south side of the house and saw Karl and Mike jump backward behind a low retaining wall before my view was closed off by the corner of the building. The south wall of the house was mostly windows. Nothing for me here. I turned around and did my best to break the land speed record getting across about 20 yards of grass.

A low, flat dive took me beyond the next step down on the terraced lawn. I lay there hoping the lump in my stomach would dissolve in the rush of stomach acid. I felt like I could spit fishing weights. Karl hollered for me to cover him and then joined me a couple of seconds later.

The girlfriend had made it out the front door and was talking to Mike. She told him our suspect, Mark, had hit her and terrorized her throughout the night. She managed to call 911, but he caught her with the phone before she could give all the details. When we arrived, Mark told her if she screamed, he would get her later. When he dropped the wooden prop into the door, he walked into the kitchen, smiling at our victim saying, "I'm going to get us on T.V." She ran out the front door at that point.

Up side...no hostage situation. Down side...barricaded suspect. I notified the office.

Doesn't look like I'm going to get home on time this morning. I went back to the car and got the Mini-14 rifle issued to me as a Special Enforcement Team member. After some negotiation and a couple of hours, the suspect surrendered. He wouldn't surrender to Sheriff's Department people because we were too violent (?) He invoked his Miranda rights and shut up.

There were several things of note upon my review of the situation later. I had broken my own rule of not having my escape route planned. That caused me to have to run 20 yards with a breezy feeling over my rump waiting for the shot to catch me. Not a comfortable feeling, and one I'll go a long way to avoid in the future.

Mike and Karl ended up standing a couple feet away from the huge picture window on the kitchen side. Both had their sidearms within a foot or two of the glass. What would have been the result if they had decided to fire? Glass has a nasty tendency to "spall" or shatter and throw glass back toward the shooter. It wasn't something I considered until after this situation, but a hand or arm thrown up below the level of their eyes might have afforded a little protection.

Other than that, once our suspect decided he "wouldn't be on T.V." he gave up. A positive ending to the situation.

In order to provide for your safety,
I must first see to my own.

Author Unknown

A MORNING STROLL
IN THE WOODS

This was our third SWAT call-out on this guy and we were getting decidedly tired of him. He changed names like other people change shirts, and had about $200,000.00 in drug warrants following him. We'll call him Hessinger.

The team went to a rally point a mile or so away from the site of the raid. We took the main house down..locked, unoccupied, deserted...Damn! The second half of the team was busy sneaking down a dry-wash below the small cabin, when the suspect came out on the porch to answer the morning call of nature. The team was so close when he began to pee, he nearly got them wet, and Hessinger tucked in without ever knowing they were there. The radio earpiece crackled and one of the team members said, "He's in the clapboard cabin about 200 yards behind the main house!"

The major problem now was how to surprise the four suspects sleeping on the carpet outside, take them into custody, and not tip off Hessinger. One team member, Chris, crawled forward and got within 10 feet of a man sleeping at the north end of the carpet. He picked up a pine cone and bounced if off the sleeping figure's head. A little stir, resettle, and the guy went back to sleep!

A second pine cone bounced and the man's eyes snapped open at this informal wake-up call. His eyes opened wide at the sight of the camouflaged man holding a carbine with the flash suppressor leveled at him. Chris brought his off hand forefinger up to his mouth and said quietly, "Shhh!" The man, sensibly, decided he didn't want to challenge the reality of this nightmare. He whispered back quietly, "What do you want me to do?" Chris replied quietly, "Shut up!"

Chris had the man crawl to him and handcuffed him. The other three suspects had similar rude awakenings and the perimeter was secured. The prisoners said there was no one other than Hessinger inside the cabin. At that point, the call went out identifying us as Sheriff's Department and demanding Hessinger's surrender. He tried unsuccessfully to convince us he had a hostage inside. That was a silly ploy on his part since it would have increased the threat level of this confrontation and increased the jeopardy to himself. He came out meekly some minutes later, after we told him we were going to use gas if he didn't give up.

Turns out Mr. Hessinger had been living under an assumed name for quite some time and had been collecting welfare and food stamps while running from his drug warrants. It isn't a novel approach on his part, it's actually done all the time. Wanted by the state on one hand, and at the same time paid by the state to live on the run.

*When more of the people's sustenance
is exacted in the form of taxation than is necessary
to meet the just obligations of government,
and expenses of its economical administration;
such exaction becomes ruthless extortion
and a violation of the fundamental principles
of a free government.*

President Grover Cleveland
1886

GETTING EVEN? WHO ME?

Randy was my training officer and my partner. I was supposed to trust him with my life, right? When he asked me if I could write while the car rolled, I said yes and didn't think anything of it. The patrol car rolled slowly through the rural back roads as I slaved over the vandalism report he would later mercilessly tear apart. But I was learning.

It was a hot July day, naturally the air conditioning didn't work, and my passenger window was rolled down so I could catch any breeze to cool off under the ballistic vest I was wearing. I didn't pay much attention to the road since Randy had suspended the unnerving practice of asking me exactly what road we were on and what the next cross street was.

I didn't mind when he stopped the car at the top of a hill and only half heard the power steering pump whine. The car lurched backward and I heard a heavy thump on my side door. I looked up and saw my "partner and training officer" had hit a beehive, and the entire hive was boiling up toward my open window...oh shit!

I rolled up the window at mach speed and Randy lay back in the driver's seat howling with laughter. I turned toward him and shouted, "You son-of-a-bitch!" All the while clenching my right fist. Randy turned his face my way and was laughing so hard he had trouble saying, "I just wanted to see how you would react under stress, boot!" I sat stunned, knowing I didn't dare argue, because it had put me under enormous stress. Especially since I'm allergic to bee stings. I vowed to myself that if I got the chance...

The graveyard shift came and rolled on by. Randy was very fond of asking me if I wanted to find a beehive and laughing uproariously with other training officers. Another shift began and we drew the Lincoln beat, a valley agricultural area with flat straight roads. My heart began pounding when we received a report of a kidnapping. We had just stopped at a local convenience store to get 20 ounce containers of scalding hot coffee to help us stay awake. The car we were driving had a very flat dash and Randy had me stop the car so we could put the coffee cups on the dash, write down details and ask for clarification of a few points.

I put my foot on the brake and my right hand on the gear shift lever. Randy told me not to go anywhere. I assured him I wouldn't move while he was writing. I put the car into gear with my foot pressed firmly on the brake. Our Dodge patrol cars have a fast idle and there was plenty of slack in the drive line so the car jerked when I put it into gear...about one foot, **real fast**.

The 20 ounce cup of coffee jumped like it had come alive and homed like a laser guided missile for Randy's lap. The resulting explosion of coffee and flurry of activity was gratifying to see. It was my turn to lay behind the wheel helpless with laughter while Randy stood outside the car holding his smoking pants away from sensitive, steaming, and somewhat scorched vitals.

Randy screamed, "You son-of-a-bitch! I told you not to go anywhere." I started to say I hadn't...I just put the car in gear...then I thought to myself, aw what the hell. I told Randy, "I just wanted to see how you would react under stress!" Randy's face blanked out and I could see the light begin to dawn as he began to grin...malevolently. He had the last laugh. "Just wait till you see this next evaluation, boot!" I knew we still had the kidnapping call to handle and I was sure he wouldn't chew me out much with the call waiting. With all fairness to Randy, my next evaluation was alright, with a minor deficit for "ability to follow direction."

I always considered it a miracle that I passed probation.

P.S. The kidnapping call was unfounded...a jilted boyfriend trying to get back at his former girlfriend.

Strategy is the craft of the warrior.

Miyamoto Musashi

THE SLEEPER

I wasn't having much trouble staying awake. I'm a night person by nature so graveyard shifts weren't too bad for me. The other training car wasn't so lucky. The training officer, Kent, had a perpetual problem with his trainee, Scott, nodding off in the passenger seat. Finding something that would work to keep this guy awake was becoming a problem. Kent decided to solve the problem with a little practical demonstration.

The night started routinely enough and the normal small calls were easily handled. No reports were left to write, and Kent was driving the "Three S Method," slow, straight, and smooth. Guaranteed to put anyone to sleep. The trainee, Scott, was nodding in the right passenger seat as Kent threaded his devious way across the flatlands to a dirt road, miles from the nearest street sign. Kent reached down and pulled the microphone plug from the back of the radio, put up the spotlight, and turned it on. He was ready for the demonstration.

Kent threw on the red lights, hit the siren, slammed on the emergency brake, bounced out of the car and screamed, "Stop you son-of-a-bitch!" Kent bounded into the darkness, over the levee, and out of sight before the startled Scott could react or get fully awake. He turned off the siren so he could hear, and looked around...panic time!

The roadway was no help, a plain dirt road about 15 feet wide with a gravel surface. No car in front to get any idea of what was going on, and no street signs or buildings for miles. Another panicked look around and a shout for his training officer produced nothing. Scott's tone of voice suggested nothing less than the cry of a puppy who has misplaced its mother. The panicked Scott ran back up the road about fifty yards looking for a street sign. He then figured he'd better not leave the car idling with the keys in the ignition. He returned to the car, picked up the microphone and began to transmit, deciding correctly it was time to take his medicine.

Kent was close enough to hear the strained voice of the trainee as he said he was on a dirt road, with his training officer in foot pursuit of unknown subjects at an unknown location. Scott never noticed the radio's red transmit light was not on, and Kent heard not one word over the portable radio on his side.

When Kent stepped back into the light some five minutes later, he had just one question, "Think you can stay awake now?" It worked.

■ ■ ■ ■ ■ ■ ■ ■ ■ ■ ■ ■ ■ ■ ■ ■ ■ ■ ■

Jerry M. was riding patrol with his female partner, Tina, who was known to have a love of practical jokes for co-workers. Tina was driving in circles in quiet, rural areas, and the radio dispatch traffic cooperated by staying quiet. Even then, it was hard to put Jerry to sleep, but she finally succeeded and Jerry was out. Tina drove to a place she had already "reconned" knowing it would suit her purposes. This hill belonged in San Francisco. At the bottom of a long straight stretch was a dip...no...it was a **huge** dip in the roadway. The road went on straight afterward, so loss of control was not a problem. Tina got to the top of the hill and accelerated the car smoothly and rapidly. Just before she hit the bottom of the dip, she screamed, "Oh shit, we're both gonna die!"

Jerry awoke to see the roadway like a wall in front of the car hood. The patrol car hit the dip and slammed upward under Jerry's drowsy rear end. This rocketed Jerry into the headliner. After his third rebound between headliner and seat springs, Jerry succeeded in getting his hands up, and stopped imitating a super ball thrown under a table.

The incident highlighted two things. One, Jerry had great bladder control. Two, Jerry would drive from now on in this partnership. Myself, I thought that last point was petty of him.

It is necessary to relax your muscles when you can,
Relaxing your brain is fatal.

Stirling Moss

SUCCESS IS A RELATIVE TERM...ISN'T IT?

This was a very bad boy. Nineteen years old and he had taken a crowbar to a friend of his who was now being treated at the hospital. It would take quite a few stitches to close up the victim's head. The up-side of the situation was the suspect resided in handcuffs in the back of my patrol car. I had all the necessary information and was looking at booking my suspect into jail, then taking the three-plus hours necessary for the report.

As we went into the jail, I felt pretty good about the arrest. It had taken a little bit of investigation to find the guy and arrest him, but with the large number of witnesses, he should get some decent time in jail before he got another chance to crowbar someone. After Miranda warning and a waiver, I questioned the suspect. He admitted he was on parole from California Youth Authority, the "prison" level of California Youth Corrections. It would take a **very** bad boy to make it to that level.

Okay. That changes things some. Knowing California law somewhat, I knew that Youth Authority could retain jurisdiction over their juveniles until age 25. That would be a longer stretch than he would get as an adult and it would be reasonable they would want their boy back pronto, right? I called the parole officer.

The P.O. was not happy to hear from me at 2 o'clock in the morning. I briefed the Parole Officer on the situation, witness statements, and evidence I had on the arrest. The officer said California Youth Authority did **not** want the parolee back and he was going to **end** the suspect's parole. I beg your pardon?

The parole officer confirmed he was going to conclude the parolee's term now, immediately. I was stunned. The P.O. then said, "Yeah, we turn him over to adult corrections and it's just a statistical thing." I asked if that meant the juvenile's parole was being ended as a success. The P.O. told me, "Well, yeah. I mean, success is a relative term, right? He's going into the adult system for a felony, so it's a wash."

No wonder the "rehabilitation rate" is so high with juvenile justice systems. They can point proudly to their statistic of "saves" and not reveal that the books are, to some extent at least, "cooked."

I booked the suspect and as I feared, since this was his first "adult" crime, his sentence was light. How could I possibly change a system into which I had no input? Winner, suspect. Loser, society at large.

No man is justified in doing evil
on the grounds of expediency.

Theodore Roosevelt

THE SUCCESSFUL INTERVIEW

The cell door shut behind me at the Sacramento County Jail. When I looked at Mike I wondered how he had aged so much in so few years. He looked up at me with despair and helplessness on his face. He knew his ship had sunk out from under him and there wasn't anything he could do about it now.

"Hello Mike, how ya doing?" Mike replied he'd be a lot better if he weren't in here. I agreed with him. I sat down and told him "You know I've got a job to do..." then I read him his Miranda rights and got a signed waiver form. I took his personal information, and remembered a couple of ride-along tours he had taken in my patrol car 10 years before. I asked him "Mike, tell me what happened?" He said he had been living in Boise, Idaho and left because it was getting rough for him there. This was the time to haul him up short, I couldn't let him think he could snow me and get away with it. I had spent three days with Boise detectives who had flown in looking for Mike and his son, Kevin, for an armed robbery and kidnapping in Boise.

"Whoa Mike. You and Kevin had to leave because things were getting too hot for you over an armed robbery and kidnapping you did in Boise, isn't that right?" Mike hung his head and said, "Yeah." He went on to tell me about a golf course burglary he and his son committed prior to the armed robbery and kidnapping then stealing a car and running to Reno, Nevada. In Reno, Mike and his son gambled, drank, partied, and bought dope until the $7,800.00 from the Boise robbery was gone.

Mike and his son traveled into my California county and committed three commercial and one residential burglary. When I asked if he would be willing to show me what he had done and where he had dumped the stolen car, he quickly agreed. The Sacramento County Lieutenant was glad to turn Mike over to me since all he had was a fugitive warrant and I would be able to get fresh charges from this. I spent the next

133

day with Mike going from location to location, recovering the stolen car, and getting particulars on methods of entry, what was done inside this business or that house, and where stolen property had been pawned.

When I was done, I had Mike's confessions to one commercial burglary in Boise, one kidnapping and armed robbery in Boise, and three commercial burglaries and one residential burglary in my jurisdiction. I also recovered a stolen car, and knew where the stolen property from my burglaries had been pawned. I also found out that Mike and his son, while pulling two of the commercial burglaries, had ripped the safes apart, and taken two-way portable radios in preparation for a burglary and safe job at a local bank.

I listened to Mike for about 20 minutes, while he brought me up to date on what had happened to him since the last time I saw him. I heard about his "fall from grace" so to speak. It was a common enough story, with drugs and alcohol leading the way. But the remainder of the confession poured out of him like a landslide. After letting him talk, until that first lie, letting him know I knew it was a lie, and setting the ground rules, he went off like an unplugged fire hydrant.

It was worth doing, and cost me nothing more than a lot of listening and some commiseration over how bad things were for him. I've had other interviews go the other way and nothing would get them to say a word. If the suspect shows even one flicker of an inclination to talk, let him. Don't interrupt. Listen. Don't take notes. Remember the information as well as possible. Record the information on a tape recorder if you can, but **let them talk**. After the initial purge of information, ask if it's okay if you clear up a few points. Then go back to the front of their story and ask a question about something. At this point, pick up a pencil and take notes. They will usually be so engrossed in the details, they won't even notice when you start taking notes.

Mike is currently serving 4 years in a California state prison and when that term is finished, he will be going to Boise, Idaho where it's expected he will be sentenced to 10 to 12 more years. The hardest part of this method of interviewing is it seems to work best on those who have some semblance of a conscience.

No man is above the law and no man is below it. Nor do
we ask any man's permission when we require him to obey it.
Obedience to the law is demanded as a right; not asked
as a favor.
Theodore Roosevelt

FELONY STOP FOLLIES

It was raining like Noah should be around somewhere, and the night was decidedly *not* quiet. I don't know what had gotten into people, but they had decided tonight was the night to get nuts. I was about a mile away when I heard my partner go out on a felony traffic stop on a possibly armed domestic violence suspect. I pushed the limit getting there to back him up since he was a single unit.

As I approached, I saw that Scott had the suspect out of the car at gunpoint, and face down in the road per felony stop procedures. Scott knew I was on the SWAT team and called me to do the hands-on with the suspect. I went through the prone-control handcuffing techniques and put the first handcuff on the suspect's left wrist. As I looked down over my left shoulder at the suspect, the thought occurred to me, "Oops, I'd better get this guy up pretty quickly." The rain had flooded the streets and as I looked down I saw the suspect was blowing bubbles from his mouth into the floodwater. Not a good situation.

I placed the second cuff in a speed-cuff technique then spun and pushed the suspect to a kneeling position so I could search without drowning him. This wasn't the first time I had been caught by the "Felony Stop Follies."

It happens nearly every time, some small mistake, procedural error, or glaring "brain fart" occurs, and what began as a police procedure ends up looking like a bad silent movie. I remember some of them; some went right; some went wrong...

The suspects, a man and a woman in a brown van, were wanted for kidnapping, rape, and torture. They kidnapped a 12-year old girl and the woman held the girl down while the man raped her, then burned her breasts with a lit cigarette. This had happened in Truckee, California.

The suspects in their van, were now headed down westbound Interstate 80 with a lone California Highway Patrol unit unseen behind them. The suspects were white, a male and a female.

My partner and I were on the off ramp and when the van and CHP unit passed, we fell in behind them. I was astonished by the number of police units pulling onto the highway at the next ramp. The freeway looked like a Christmas display with all the flashing colored lights.

The van stopped and one CHP unit pulled past them and blocked them in. The CHP officer got out of his car and pointed a handgun at the people in the front of the van, "Let's make a point right here folks, **don't do this**."

When the officer pulled in front of the suspect van blocking them in, he kept them from running, and turning this into a pursuit. However, he also placed himself directly in the path of the suspect, making himself subject to a ramming attack. He also placed himself in the direct crossfire of the officers directly behind and to one side of the suspect vehicle. Those officers might as well have holstered their guns because they stood a good chance of hitting the officer if they needed to fire on the suspect.

The male suspect was removed from the vehicle, searched and secured. The female was called out and put face down on the ground immediately thereafter. She lay prone on the ground for a few seconds and there was no officer taking the lead to handcuff her. I secured my firearm and approached, telling her not to move.

I went through the prone control techniques and handcuffed the woman. I checked the back of her belt and rear pockets to ensure she couldn't get her handcuffed hands to a hidden weapon in those areas. I then spun the woman to her feet and went through the search procedures I had been taught in defensive tactics. The woman was a violent felony suspect and I had every right to search her according to police procedures and case law. I think no one was willing to approach her because they were unsure how to proceed with the search.

I grasped and checked all loose clothing on her body. Visually and physically checked the waistband, and used the back of my hand to check the lower chest under the breasts, and groin area. I performed the search quickly and was looking for the telltale bulk of the firearm they were supposed to have, or any other weapon. I also checked the arms, legs and feet.

The last procedure I performed was to grasp the woman's bra at the center of the cleavage and pull it away from her body and shake it. This procedure is designed to allow anything stashed under the lower wires of the bra cup to fall free. This woman was fairly well endowed physically, and I couldn't help wondering at the fact that she had been in the van, and we were arresting them both for rape.

When I finished the bra under-wire shake, a spontaneous cheer broke out from the assembled officers at the felony stop. The only standing ovation I know of in felony stop history...they were obviously glad to get these two into custody.

That woman has the dubious distinction of being the only woman I know who was convicted of forcible rape, kidnapping, and mayhem, and you can bet she served a nice long stretch in prison.

If you are a cop, don't hesitate to perform a cross-gender search in justifiable circumstances. You have a right to protect yourself and your community. When the circumstances dictate, search. Be aware that any abuse of the search procedure will be cause for discipline. Interestingly, women officers searching male suspects rarely have complaints filed against them. Male officers searching female suspects cause the majority of complaints filed.

Another "felony stop folly" I remember was a combination of "an awful lot of things going wrong" and a "stupid crook."

The pursuit started in Roseville, and the four suspects were wanted for armed robbery. They had taken $400.00 at gunpoint from a victim, and fired a shot in the air near enough to the victim to make him run. I pushed the unit to catch up, and was the lead unit on the stop.

The deputy who first spotted them was in an unmarked unit without emergency lights and couldn't do the stop. I had a marked Sacramento Sheriff's unit on my left, blocking that lane. When the suspect stopped, I stomped the emergency brake on my car bringing it to a sliding stop. The deputy next to me put his car in park...at 15 miles an hour. I heard the transmission clunk, and out of the corner of my eye, saw his head whip back and forth until he put his foot on the brake stopping the rear wheels from turning. Somewhat distracting for him, but no major gig.

My spotlight and several others were directed into the rear of the suspect's car which had stopped just past a filling station and near a hotel. A family station wagon picked that moment to pull partially between me and the suspect's car. I could see the kids noses pressed against the left side window of their car as the driver looked horrified at the cops pointing guns in his direction.

I shouted and waved the driver backward and his squealing tires showed he definitely understood and wanted to be anywhere but where he was...fast. The suspect vehicle hadn't been more than partially blocked by the family car. Again, these things happen.

I gave the verbal commands and brought the suspects out one by one. Myself and another officer completed the hand-cuffing, while Sacramento Sheriff's personnel covered the remaining suspects then cleared the car for us.

As I spun and pushed the last suspect to his feet (we would later learn he was the trigger man), a Sacramento deputy clapped me on the shoulder saying, "Good felony stop." I thanked him. To my astonishment, the suspect said, "Yeah, that was a great stop, man." Well I thought to myself, that's one for the scrapbook.

I walked back to the car with the suspect and told him, "You realize you're under arrest, don't you?" The suspect said, "I didn't do no 2-11, man." When I smiled a mile wide, the suspect got suspicious and asked why I was grinning. I told him I hadn't advised him why he was under arrest, and that he had made a useful admission to me just now. He was under arrest for armed robbery, Section 211 of the California Penal Code. Only cops and cons call an armed robbery "a 2-11." The suspect was not a happy camper from that point on. Especially since he was out on bail for a prior "2-11."

Seems like for everything that goes wrong, if you're persistent and thorough, something has to go right at least once in a while. The main point is, we do our best to do the job right and hope to go home at the end of the shift.

Murphy was an optimist!

O'Toole's commentary on Murphy's Law
as cited by A. Bloch

FISHING THE BACK ROADS
OF CALIFORNIA

The briefing was interrupted by a call from dispatch. The sergeant picked up the phone, said "yeah" a couple of times, then cradled the phone. He looked over at me and said, "Get to Weimar. Walt's out there with three men held at gunpoint and one woman who ran into the brush. They're suspects in two residential burglaries."

With all burners on, it still took me about 12 minutes to make the 15 miles. I arrived to find Walt with two California Highway Patrol officers just cuffing the last of the three male suspects. Walt was still a little out of breath while telling me his side of the story...

Early that morning, the woman and three men were seen at a small road off East Weimar Crossroads. Several people passing to work had witnessed the suspects acting suspiciously.

The woman had walked into a house where the male homeowner had just finished his morning shower and was getting into his underwear. The homeowner looked up in surprise as the unknown woman walked across his kitchen as if she owned the place. He confronted her, she smiled, rambled on that she knew him, and tried to solicit him to bed. When our victim's wife entered the room, the suspect fled, under threat of attack from the irate homeowners. I think the victim's wife was the more dangerous of the two at the time.

Not one to be deterred, the suspect went to the next door neighbor's house and walked in. The homeowner was expecting a contractor to work on his house that day. When the woman said she would wait for her friends, the homeowner assumed she was waiting for the contractor.

The female suspect wandered around his house, and the homeowner asked her to stay in the front room. He later found her wandering in an upstairs bedroom and told her to leave the house. She left, threatening to sue him, with one of his gold necklaces in her pocket.

Meantime, Walt had arrived and taken the three male suspects' identification. When the calls began coming in about the woman committing burglaries, he knew he had her get-away vehicle and accomplices. He held the suspects in the car while waiting for back up.

The female suspect approached Walt from behind, babbling about her friends. Walt grabbed her and she immediately went down on the blacktop on her back, kicking mightily at him with her heels. The driver of the car, a 6', 200 pound, tattooed male with a nice long rap sheet, picked this moment to get out of the car. Walt abandoned his attempt to take the female into custody because of the bigger threat...three men.

The woman ran into the woods next to the road, and later search efforts didn't work. I participated in the search and asked for an evidence team to process the homes. Karen, a good friend of mine, an evidence technician and the wife of one of my former training officers, arrived to process the scene. The search personnel began to gather statements from the victims and witnesses, of which there were many. I went to the house of the first victim to see if Karen needed any help, just as the radio came alive...

The female suspect had been sighted by a neighbor walking down East Weimar Crossroads. Karen's face lit up with a wide smile and she said, "I'm going with you. There's no close backup." I knew Karen had worked as a dispatcher and processed female prisoners in Tahoe. Besides, stopping Karen from doing something she's set her mind on is like trying to stop an avalanche barehanded. Not a fun thing to do.

We went slowly down East Weimar Crossroads and over a small rise where we saw the woman trying to hitch a ride from passing traffic. I pulled within15 feet and got out of the car. I shouted at the woman, "Police, get down on the ground." The woman put both hands out in front of her body, and began backing away screaming about another officer who had tried to kill her.

As the woman continued to back away, I snapped out an ASP tactical baton in my right hand and repeated the command to get on the ground. The woman fled into the woods along the road. I could hear Karen calling in the foot pursuit on my portable radio as I ran about 10 feet behind the female suspect, all the time shouting for her to stop.

The woman fell on the frost on the ground and I caught up. She went into a half-sitting position on her back and started kicking at me with her heels. I couldn't get a clear swing at her with the baton. I reached for an arm as she scurried out from under a dead fallen tree. She fell again and as I was deciding which ankle to hit, I saw a blur of motion from the corner of my eye. Karen was running down the hill to join in the fray. The suspect went for Karen like a bass after a fishing plug, "Help, save me. They're trying to kill me." The woman extended her right hand to Karen and I recognized the glint in Karen's eyes. Karen bent the woman's wrist and applied a very professional arm-bar to roll the woman over. When the woman realized she had "been hooked," she started to fight. I got my baton out of the way and completed the handcuffing Karen had started. I "boated" the fish Karen hooked. I later told Karen that one of the basic points of police work is "You catch 'em, you clean 'em!" She was going to have to live up to that the next time. Karen looked up at me and calmly said, "We're going to have to do this again some time."

If it hadn't been for Karen, I would have been forced to hit the suspect with my stick, and I'm glad it didn't happen that way. The woman had committed one burglary the night before in addition to the two for which we arrested her. When Karen searched the woman, she found three pocket knives in her pants pockets. Turns out the suspect was trying to support her drug habit. She was basically psychotic on speed, crank, CR, methamphetamine or dope. As a general rule, burglars are dopers, and dopers are burglars. If it weren't for Karen, that woman's ankles or knees might not have felt too comfortable. If knives had entered the fight, one or more of us might not have had a tomorrow.

There are periods when to dare is the highest wisdom.

William Ellery Channing

Karen dared.

THE DEFENSE SENTENCES YOU ...TO DEATH

My day was going to be just fine. Although I did plan on ruining someone else's. I knew that Greg had $200,000 in warrants and was a "chemist," a cooker for a methamphetamine lab. I called my sergeant and we went to Greg's house to pay a call. As we pulled up, I saw Julie coming out to the yard. I walked up near the door and met Julie. She said there was nobody else at home. From prior experience with Julie, I knew she didn't have even a working acquaintance with the truth. My sergeant, Larry, went to the garage and found a man working under the hood of a pickup. Strike one, Julie. I heard Larry ask the man, "What's your name?" The man replied his name was Gary. I told Julie she had lied to me once, and I'd be more than happy to arrest her for obstruction if she lied again. I asked her for the name of the man who was under the hood. She couldn't have heard Larry or the man's reply. She told me, "Greg." Alright! We had our man.

I walked to the pickup and saw Greg with engine grease up to his elbows, and wearing no shirt. I said, "Hello Greg. You need to get out of the truck slowly, and we need to get these warrants taken care of." Greg seemed resigned as he complied, and asked me, "Do you mind if I get my shirt." I almost let him, but as his feet hit the ground, I put a twist-lock on his right wrist and speed-cuffed him in less than five seconds.

I searched him and found a jar in his right front pants pocket. The jar was about one inch in diameter filled with nearly a half-ounce of crank. Okay, another drug charge Greg will answer to. We called detectives and did a protective sweep of the house to make sure that suspects weren't inside destroying evidence or getting ready to come after us.

I took Greg and booked him, then put together an affidavit and search warrant. We went back to the house where the detectives were waiting. A short while into the search, a detective came to me with a question. "Greg asked you if he could put on his shirt?" I told him, "Yeah...so what?" The detective gave me a big smile and said, "You're one lucky son-of-a-bitch, you know that?" The detective took me over to a pool table inside the garage and lifted up Greg's shirt. Under it was a loaded stainless-steel .357 magnum. I felt like I'd just been kicked in the stomach when I saw the gun. I picked it up, unloaded it, and examined it. I knew I wouldn't have any trouble going to the bathroom for the next couple of days. Matter of fact, where's the john now?

We went to court on Greg. It was an interesting experience. Despite his lengthy history, and two drug arrests in a four month period, his defense attorney pled the case convincingly (at least from a judge's point of view). The general theme was, "Judge don't send my young client to prison...prison is an Evil College for Criminals, where he'll be victimized and only schooled and hardened to a life of crime."

The judge wanted to believe. Despite Greg's lengthy criminal history that began at 16 years old, he sentenced him to a two year prison term, then commuted it to "No State Prison" by telling Greg he could do one year of county jail time, get credit for time served and "time off for good behavior." Greg was out in less than a year.

Greg wasn't a quitter though. He also wasn't real impressed by the efforts of his attorney or the judge. Six weeks after he was out, he was in a drug lab in Yreka, California. Julie, "standing by her man," went with him.

Greg made a mistake. He took some crank "right off the glass" fresh from the cook. Either he thought he still had tolerance, or he wasn't as good a chemist as he thought. In minutes, Greg was having grand mal seizures. Julie and her friends thought, "We can't call for an ambulance. We're in a drug lab and they'll find the drugs in Greg's system." By the time they decided to call, it was too late. Greg died a few days later.

If he'd been in prison...who knows? The most unlikely people have decided prison is not something they want to repeat. I thought it was a novel situation that a successful defense sentenced the criminal to death. More frequently the rest of society suffers before the criminal gets put away and poetic justice is served.

Do you want to be free from fear of the one in authority?
Then do what is right and he will commend you.
For he is God's servant to do you good.
But if you do that which is wrong be afraid,
for he does not bear the sword for nothing.

Romans 13:3-4 N.I.V.

DESPERATE PEOPLE USE DESPERATE MEASURES

This "raid" was not going well. A relatively inexperienced SWAT Team had been called for the bust. The deal was to buy a couple ounces of speed, and order several pounds of methamphetamine. The suspects would have no trouble filling the order since they had a drug lab and had made major sales before.

I was working patrol and had been briefed on the operation. Myself and my trainee would be providing transportation for the suspects, and the raid would be in our area. All day I monitored the state channels. I found out what happened later...

The commander of the lead SWAT Team had been briefed on the situation including suspect identities, layout of the house, and resources. Tim, the main suspect in the case, was the chemist, very violent, and known to carry a gun. There were also several rifles in the house. When the back-up SWAT Team leader asked his counterpart how they intended to do the entry, the SWAT Leader said they were "not comfortable" with fast, dynamic entry techniques, and planned an announcement by public address system, then introducing CS gas if the suspects failed to come out.

Department administration would not rotate the more experienced back-up team to primary, and decided to allow the inexperienced team to go ahead with the "call out method."

After the usual starts and stumbles due to both the Confidential Informant's, and suspect's unwillingness to cooperate, the raid got off the ground. The SWAT Team moved into a perimeter around the house and made an announcement over the PA that the house was surrounded and the suspects were to come out the front door with their hands in the air.

The suspects; Tim, two women, and two other men, began running around the house like crazy, obviously destroying drugs. The back-up SWAT and narcotics teams wailed and gnashed their teeth as the Primary Team used their ultimate threat, "Come out or we'll introduce gas into the house!"

145

The two women retreated from the front room, came back a minute later refusing to come out, and held two screaming infants up to a picture window in the front of the house. A desperate tactic, but very effective. Scratch the teargas idea. Tim wanted to shoot his way out of the house, but was talked out of it by the women.

By the time the suspects came out, they had time to destroy between four and seven pounds of drugs. The lab was seized. I took the male suspects to jail, and all the way to the cell Tim threatened to kill everybody involved. The women went to jail as well, and the kids went to a receiving home. DEA was understandably very unhappy with the way the raid had been planned and *not* executed.

About six months later a friend of mine who works as a cop near the California/Oregon border called to say they had made a major drug bust on an underground lab. I asked if the suspect was named Tim _____? There was silence on the phone before my friend said, "How the hell did you know?" Tim was bailed out of jail by a money man within hours of his arrest. He never came back to answer the charges. The warrant from our County case was never entered in the computer due to a clerical error, and Tim was free to cook and be violent again.

Eight months later, a drug task force missed Tim by mere minutes. He drove up to a drug lab they had just raided and was involved in a short pursuit with Sacramento police before they lost him.

About two years later, I was called to the Gold Run California Highway Patrol Station to process a car for latent fingerprints. Two suspects had run from California Highway Patrol and there were guns, ammunition, holsters, and drug paraphernalia all over the car's interior. When I looked under the front seat, surprise, surprise...what was Tim's driver's license doing there?

It had been raining hard for a week and Brian, one of my former trainees, tried to make a traffic stop on an erratic driver. There was no way this guy was going to stop. He went berserk, driving like a maniac into a remote area, where he ditched the car and ran with Brian not far behind.

Brian was lucky. As he passed two people who were walking in the woods, he was told the man he was chasing was carrying a large revolver. Brian notified the office, and despite the help of deputies, lots of back-up, and a thorough search, the suspect disappeared.

About five days later, a couple of young girls were walking along a now dry watercourse, that only a week ago had been a rushing torrent. They saw the body of a man draped over a log at the bottom of the canal. The frantic girls found a water district employee who went over to take a look. Near the body, he saw a revolver. When he picked up the gun, it went off. It had apparently been cocked while Tim was running. A very desperate and dangerous gamble.

Being the coroner's office, we got the call. When I heard what was going on, I went over. We brought a booking photo with us and it was pretty obvious this was Tim. Apparently he had been running from Brian, decided to try to jump the canal, and didn't quite make it.

Tim had manufactured drugs for years. I don't know that he directly murdered anyone during that time, but I'm convinced it was just a matter of time. His desperate measures caught up with him before we did.

All creatures kill.
There seems to be no exception.
But of the whole list, man is the only one
that kills for fun,
The only one that kills in malice,
The only one that kills for revenge.

Mark Twain

THE BUTT OF JOKES

A friend of mine moved to Nevada to work for a sheriff's department. Karl was a good cop and we did some physical skills training together on handcuffing, and arrest and control techniques, which his new department would not recognize. We kept in touch by telephone and one night I got a call.

"Hey Rocky, how's it going? I just called to ask you why the hell you California cops can't keep your bad guys in jail?" My reply was nowhere near printable. Karl went on to explain that he had been injured on duty. The case went like this...

Karl got a call of suspicious circumstances at a house out in the valley area of Washoe County. When Karl arrived he learned that a female resident was convinced her boarder was trying to steal her child. This woman had met the boarder only casually, but said she was down on her luck. In exchange for baby sitting and other small chores around the house, the woman invited the boarder in to help out and to better herself in the process. A good samaritan gesture.

The lady of the house arrived home from shopping one afternoon to find the boarder and her toddler daughter had disappeared from the house. Panic ensued since there had been no permission given for the boarder to take the child anywhere, and it was getting dark.

Karl was taking the details of identification and descriptions, just as the suspect came home with the toddler safe and sound. Karl asked for the boarder's identification and she suggested a physically impossible act. Karl took her verbal I.D., and gave it to dispatch for entry in the computer. It came back as a registered alias for the woman, so Karl tried the real name on the woman. The suspect acknowledged the name, but said she didn't use it anymore. It is understandable that she didn't use her real name since there was an arrest warrant for her in California for child stealing. The warrant was a felony of such severity that the California authorities would extradite.

149

Karl told the suspect that she was under arrest and took control of an arm. The woman began struggling and Karl moved in close quickly, performing a hair-pull take down and struggling with the woman on a porch swing and the floor. Karl succeeded in handcuffing the cursing, fighting, screaming, kicking woman and took her to the patrol car. When Karl sat down in the car he thought he felt something wet on his hip. He brushed the back of his pants and his hand came away with blood on it...his own.

Responding back-up units took control of the suspect and found an open four-inch buck knife on the cushions of the porch swing. The suspect must have hidden the opened knife horizontally behind her belt buckle, because that's the only area she could have reached so quickly. Karl did not hear the knife open and the woman would not have been able to open the folding knife with one hand.

The suspect had inflicted several stab wounds where Karl sits. He was the "butt" of many good natured jokes from his peers, but Karl is convinced had he not closed with the woman as fast as he had, she would have gutted him like a fish.

Instead of acknowledging that cops are going to get hurt by armed suspects occasionally, his department administrators wanted to discipline Karl. I don't understand that attitude except to say they probably have not tried to subdue an armed adversary lately. The portion of the anatomy attacked may not be subject to display as "honorable war wounds," but the attack was no less dangerous. If your officers go into a fight, knifing, or gunfight...expect them to get hurt occasionally. The best training can't always make up the "action v. reaction" gap.

Of men who have a sense of honor,
more come through alive than are slain.
But from those who flee comes neither glory,nor any help.

Homer
(*The Iliad*)

THE UNBELIEVABLE
IS VERY POSSIBLE

The type of work done by police officers is often subject to second guessing. The level of scrutiny currently focused on police is unrivaled in any period of our history. Yet the worst type of second guessing is not leveled at us by the press, administrators, courts, public, or our peers. The worst type of second guessing often occurs late at night when you are alone, often when you are trying to get to sleep. It is the second guessing leveled at us...by ourselves.

Learning to live with the problems brought on by working as a cop, or any other type of emergency service work, will not be easy. Compartmentalizing work and never bringing it home may be an answer. It can also lead to "burn out" because you have no safety valve, or an inappropriate safety valve. Promiscuity, alcoholism and other safety valves are destructive to any type of settled life style and an unsettled life just leads to more stress. A cycle which can be impossible to break without help.

The worst type of situation is one that we "Monday morning quarterback" to ourselves. For example, one night, about ten o'clock, I was sitting in my patrol car writing a report. I was behind on quite a few reports and it was a foul night. There was a high wind and rain showers. Despite the wind, I had my driver's window down a couple of inches, and could hear the storm noises outside.

As I wrote, I heard something different. A high pitched squeal which was very faint. I rolled the window down and listened more closely. I smiled and thought that some of the area cats from the apartment 200 yards behind me sure picked a terrible night to be fighting and prowling. I continued with my report writing until I got a call and left the area.

Three weeks later, the body of an infant was found at the base of an oak tree 75 yards from where I had been parked. The body was in advanced stages of decomposition. It must have been a fluke of wind that brought the baby's cry to my window. Not recognizing it as a cry, but thinking I heard neighborhood cats, is just something that happened. Hind-sight is 20/20 and thinking back on it, I'm positive it was that infant I heard.

It doesn't help to let these things eat at you. Life is a series of experiences, learning, and compromises necessary to living. Some nights, collective experiences can be, in street terms, "a stone bitch." We have to learn to live with it. It won't always be easy. Sometimes it won't even be pleasant.

Death is always and under all circumstances a tragedy.
For if it is not,
then it means that life itself has become one.

Theodore Roosevelt

A LITTLE INFORMATION
IS VERY POWERFUL

The informants were very nervous about giving any information. The information was given because I was known to the informants and trusted not to reveal my sources.

They had seen a house with a room lined with rifles and shotguns, and handguns strewn throughout the entire house. Our Special Investigations (Narcotics) unit heard a rumor of a motor home traveling through the county cooking crank on the move.

The case developed rapidly for a little while. Agents began identifying and following drug dealers to Bakersfield, the San Francisco Bay area, and points in between. The people involved in this case were large scale dealers with plenty of drug related convictions between them, and a fairly far flung network they were supplying with meth.

Our agency didn't have the resources to follow it out, so Investigations referred the case to the California Department of Justice. They began categorizing the people involved and making charts of the network. I knew that would take a lot of time, which we didn't have, and would result in a huge bust.

When I came on swing shift, I heard a patrol car go out to the Lincoln address of the surveillance on a coroner's case. I immediately got on the radio, flipped it over to the scrambler to prevent anyone listening to the radio transmission, and briefed dispatch and the responding deputy. It was not general knowledge that the surveillance was going on. At the sergeant's direction, I went to the house to help out.

When we took the coroner's case, we found the deceased on the toilet which is common. People who suffer heart attacks frequently feel they have to go to the bathroom and end up dying there. But when we checked the victim's inside left elbow, there was a needle mark. It turned out that family members who came to visit had removed the needle from the arm of the body and cleaned up the scene.

When detectives came back with the search warrant, we went through the house beyond the scope of the coroner's case.

We went through the guns and found only a few which we could prove were stolen. The R.V. used as a crank lab was behind the house with all the glassware. There was also jewelry and unset diamonds worth $110,000.00 in a display case in a bedroom. The diamonds and jewelry were from an armed robbery in San Francisco. Also found was one and one-quarter pounds of 80 percent pure heroin.

The heroin was the cause of our coroner's case. The deceased had been watching the house while the suspects were away on a delivery. He found the heroin and thought he'd take a taste. Not knowing the heroin was nearly pure, he fixed...and never even got the needle out of his arm.

The case widened and the focus moved out of our jurisdiction. But I couldn't get over it. All this from a little bit of information.

Man is the only animal that contemplates death;
and also the only animal that shows
any sign of doubt of it's finality.

William Ernest Hocking

AN INITIATION TO BODY WEAPONS

We had been having trouble with our local mental health facility for many years. I had often taken people there who had tried to kill themselves. After hours of waiting, getting the person medically cleared, and many pages of frequently redundant paperwork, the mental health worker takes over the case. They ask, "Did you try to kill yourself? Do you feel like killing yourself now?" If the subject lies in any convincing way to the first question, and says no to the second, they may often be set free immediately.

I had this point brought home to me one cold Thanksgiving Day when I brought in a young man who was attempting suicide. He had run away from relatives and we found him outside the railing of the Foresthill Bridge looking at 700 plus feet to the American River. It had taken a hostage negotiator to talk him down. When I brought him to the mental health lock-up, he lied convincingly. The mental health workers went into a huddle and when one came out I asked what was going on. The worker said he was going to call a relative and see if they could take care of the suspect.

I hit the roof! I asked them how they could even consider turning the suspect loose. Not too long before, one of the people they had turned loose killed two people and then himself. It seemed like they just wouldn't learn until one of *them* was injured by a mental case.

Sometimes the local mental health facility received an extremely violent suspect for lock-up, yet, the staff would object to us bringing in a police baton. "It looks too offensive and upsets the other patients." A few incidents would change this attitude. Among them:

Henry was well known to most of the deputies on our department. He had a local history of assault with a deadly weapon, burglary, and drugs, in addition to the mental health problems. I got a call to go to the Mental Health facility for an uncontrollable patient. Gerry and Ken decided to go with me.

Joe, the mental health worker, told us that since Henry was being aggressive, he had obtained a doctor's order to restrain and sedate him. Okay. When we stood in front of the door, Henry went off with threats to kill all of us. He said he was a CIA operative and if we messed with him he would "piss on all of you in front of President Reagan's desk." I told Joe to open the door, back out of the way and let us handle it. Joe agreed, put the key in the door, opened the lock and followed the door inward. SHIT!

Henry backed up into the room, then charged. He launched a picture-perfect right fist to Joe's jaw. Joe's glasses jumped, he slammed backwards into the door and slumped against it. Henry backed up with both fists clenched, then squared off in the center of the room. He couldn't decide whether to pursue the quick victory with Joe or swing at me. He turned his head for a second to look at Joe. MISTAKE!

I charged forward and hit Henry under the chin with my right forearm carrying him toward the far wall. I took hold of Henry's right arm on the way across the room and we landed on the bed. Ken and Gerry moved into the room and took hold of Henry's left arm. It was over for now. Joe followed with a hypodermic syringe of Thorazine, making Henry do what cops and medical people call "the Thorazine shuffle." He was hospitalized in a state institution for a while following that incident. With the body weapon strike and my forward motion, I had managed to move Henry about ten feet across the room. That's an indicator of how powerful body weapon strikes can be.

Immediately after this incident, the department came up with a policy that allows the officer to decide what equipment he or she needs to resolve the problem, and to hell with any other agencies' restrictions or policy. About time.

There is nothing wrong with winning.
There is a great deal wrong with losing.
Those who bear arms should keep that in mind.

Colonel Jeff Cooper

THE SAGA OF
THE LAND SHARKS

It was a normal evening with a lot of partying in Squaw Valley. Normally not something to worry about, but tonight would be an exception to the rule. Dave got a call to go to a parking lot in Squaw Valley because of a man who was drunk and fighting. Dave got there and confronted a man who refused to go along with any verbal directions. The man backed to the door of his van and opened the door, calling out, "Get him!"

A pit bull dog burst out of the front of the van immediately becoming a red-eyed ball of fur and fury. The dog grabbed Dave high on his left thigh and pulled him to the ground. The pit bull let go of the thigh and sunk his teeth into Dave's face biting through his left cheek about an inch below his eye.

Another deputy, Chal, arrived to see this modern day land shark standing with a forepaw on either side of Dave's chest and hind-paws on either side of his waist. Chal knew he didn't have any room to miss if he shot, but he squatted down in place, took aim, and carefully shot the dog off Dave.

The brindle hide of the dog showed the hit of the bullet as the dog yelped, quit chewing on Dave's face, and tried to run. Chal shot the dog again, killing it. The suspect was arrested for assault with a deadly weapon, in addition to the original charge of drunk in public. A misdemeanor. Figure that one.

Dave was taken to a South Shore Lake Tahoe Hospital where a specialist took more than 140 stitches in Dave's face. I first met Dave a few years later, and when he told me the story he was smoking a cigar in his living room. At the end of the story Dave reached over to his left, raised the upper jaw of a large skull, flipped cigar ashes into the lower jaw, then absently patted the skull's head, smiling all the while. Nice puppy.

About seven years later, Mike C., a deputy with our office was going to a house in the Auburn area to serve the home owner with civil papers. Mike ran into yet another dog who decided his impression of "Cujo" was called for, and tried to make good on his intentions to eat our deputy. Mike, being a

157

fairly big man, pulled his side handle baton and hit the dog as hard as he could behind the head.

The owner was immediately outside and boy was he pissed! Despite the attack, the dog owner threatened lawsuit, giving the dog's value at several thousand dollars, and demanded the sheriff's department pay the vet bills for this dog that had suddenly been gifted with a pedigree. He also made it clear he was personally going to obscenely sue the deputy and the sheriff's department silly.

Mike tried to explain that the dog had attacked him and that he had only defended himself. The dog owner went off into another profane tirade. Mike innocently asked the irate dog owner if his name was Charles _____. The dog's owner belligerently said that it was, and so what? Mike tore the staple out of the civil paper, handed it to him and said, "you're served." This did not calm the dog owner.

Mike left before the complainant could do something really violent or stupid, and went directly back to the sheriff's department. He met with the Undersheriff and explained what happened. Shortly after Mike arrived, a pickup screamed to a stop in the parking lot of the office and a disturbance began out front.

Mike confirmed the man screaming in front of the office was the dog owner. The price of the dog had skyrocketed amazingly during the drive from home to the sheriff's department. The Undersheriff took a look at the dog which lay twitching and whining in the rear of the pick up and told the owner he should take the dog to the vet and get it looked after. The owner could then file a county claim form for the vet bills.

The owner went off on another tirade about how he was going to sue everything and everyone even remotely connected with the dog's injuries and the county was going to pay for all vet bills. The dog picked this moment to give one last move, yelp, and die.

The chief looked sadly down into the bed of the truck and told the dog owner, "Well, I guess that takes care of that. No vet bills now," as he walked back into the office.

We don't allow our deputies to get mangled or eaten by land sharks.

> *When you want to be quick, you don't succeed;*
> *Act carefully and you cannot miss.*

> Ying Shaowu

A PLACE TO
WRITE REPORTS

After recovering from his dog bites and still working the Tahoe area, Dave was at an accident scene in the busy resort area near Tahoe City. Dave asked another deputy, Russ, to toss him a road flare. Russ threw the road flare. Either he threw it like a major league pitcher or Dave turned away, then back, just in time to get the road flare in the mouth. Teeth hit the pavement from the impact. Dave lost several front teeth...seems like he just couldn't win.

After Dave transferred to Auburn, his troubles weren't over. Near his house, Dave found the perfect place to write reports. He pulled around the back of an old ice house near the railroad tracks and onto the loading dock. From there he could do his reports, watch an intersection, and Highway 65. A good spot to be.

Dave was totally engrossed in a report when a young local man came through the intersection and across the state highway doing his best imitation of a jet dragster. Dave fired up the patrol car's engine, threw his notebook onto the right seat, put the car in gear, and floored the pedal. In his haste and distraction, Dave forgot all about the four foot loading dock at the end of the concrete strip. Dukes of Hazard time!

When the car came to a stop, Dave knew the situation was going to get real ugly. Prepared to take his medicine, he called his sergeant who came to the scene of the accident. The sergeant looked at the car. In the night light the metal on the car didn't look bad. The gauges were all working within range. The sergeant made his command decision and told Dave to drive the car back to the substation.

The next morning when another deputy checked the car, he found that all the "crumple zones" on the car...*had*. And most of the car's "running gear"...*wouldn't*. The sergeant caught some grief over that one, as well as Dave spending "time on the beach."

Sometimes, it's nice to work a shift with someone like Dave. He draws all the administrative "heat" away from the rest of us.

> *In life, as in a football game,*
> *the principle to follow is:*
> *Hit the line...Hard!*

Theodore Roosevelt

Dave just "hits the line" a little harder and more often than the rest of us.

A WISECRACK
AND RADIO TRAFFIC

When I was in the Police Academy, our Physical Training Instructor, Mr. Clark, was an obnoxious, indestructible shit who was a track man. I've always hated running, and three to five miles a day was not my idea of fun. Mr. Clark was not well liked, and obviously had delusions of Police Academy being like the Army because his favorite running songs began, "C-130 going down the strip. Airborne daddy gonna take a little trip...", the song went downhill from there. When Mr. Clark got tired, one of the students would pick up the chant. I had been in the military and this was getting old and tired.

This morning Mr. Clark stopped the chant and there was a hesitation before anyone picked it up. I decided today was as good as any. I chanted, "If I had a low I.Q., I could be an instructor too!" The well-ordered ranks of cadets immediately dissolved as people fell out onto the grass holding their sides with laughter.

Mr. Clark spun around, demanding to know "who said that." No one gave me up, but we had to run an extra mile. I made sure the squad leader knew that "I had to do it one time," but had no intention of repeating the chant. I didn't think anyone would top that one very easily. I was mistaken.

It had not been an average New Year's Eve. The radio was extremely quiet at 3:00 a.m. which was unusual for the early 1980's. I was working on reports in my patrol car when the police scanner stopped on a Sacramento agency radio channel. A deep slurred voice came over the radio. "Boy am I fucked up!"

There was a short, stunned pause then the dispatcher came on the air saying, "Unit calling, identify." Another long pause. After about 20 seconds, the unknown caller struck again. "Oh man, am I fucked up!" The dispatcher's voice was edged with fury as he immediately keyed up the radio, "Unit calling, identify! Unit calling, identify immediately!"

The whole Sacramento area was listening and locked to the channel when a calm voice came on the air and said, "This is Captain Green. Unit calling, identify."

The radio crackled again and the anonymous voice said, "I'm not *that* fucked up!"

The air went dead for a few minutes. The Captain's calm voice came back on the air calling the nearest unit to the station, and ordering his sergeants to rotate *all* units into the Sacramento office.

It took me quite a few years to lean that the Captain met with each one of the officers and took them individually to the intoxilyzer machine. Each officer on shift that night had to take a breath test. I don't know who the prankster was, and I hope his co-workers never find out.

> *Cynic: noun - A blackguard whose faulty vision*
> *sees things as they are.*
> *Not as they ought to be.*

Ambrose Bierce

"THE MULES"

The night was extremely cold and very slow as far as radio traffic was concerned. I got a call to go to the intersection of Gold Hill Road and Highway 193. This should prove interesting because there's nothing at that intersection. The dispatcher told me and Dennis Healy, the other patrol officer, to use the radio coder. She said we would be meeting Special Investigation Unit narcotics people at the intersection regarding one of their cases. More interesting yet.

I met with Gerry Thompson, Rick Armstrong and several other SIU agents. I parked my car facing west and Dennis parked facing east. There were unmarked agents cars parked haphazardly around ours. Gerry said we didn't have a search warrant and they were discussing going to the residence for a "knock and talk" prior to going for the warrant.

The house, Gerry told us, was known as a drug lab, and "lo and behold" when he had been at the house earlier in the day, he had looked in the front window and saw the back of a television set with its serial number scratched off. Hallelujah! This was such an unlikely and unbelievable set of circumstances that they risked a second approach to have the Special Agent in Charge verify it personally.

Suddenly, a red MG Midget came to the stop sign about 50 yards away from us with a blue pickup with a camper shell following it. Gerry hollered, "Oh shit. They're both mules. They're carrying dope for the lab. Get 'em!"

I jumped into my car and revved it toward the intersection. The MG turned toward me and I decided to let it go to the agents behind me. I accelerated toward the pickup which had taken one look at us and decided distance was desirable. I caught up easily and flipped on the overhead lights while calling in the stop location to dispatch. The pickup came to a stop in the middle of the road and Healy breezed by me in the other marked unit and stopped even with the front seat of the pickup. Dennis jumped out and leveled his gun across the top of his car directly at the front seat passengers. I called the driver out using normal felony stop procedures, searched, handcuffed, and put the driver, Mr. Cox, in the back of my car. I called out the middle passenger and she stepped out of the front seat. This is where things went to hell. The woman opened her hands and let about a dozen bindles of drugs fall to the street all around her. Gerry dashed into the middle of the stop, picked up the crank and pushed the female up against the patrol car.

This was the most unsafe thing I had seen done on a felony stop at the time. My shouts to Gerry wouldn't make him back out of there. Gerry was too focused on saving the dope to realize he had placed himself in a position where neither Dennis nor I could have helped if the remaining passenger had decided to fight.

Gerry handcuffed the woman and pulled her out from between the cars. I used normal procedures to get the third passenger out and handcuff him. I booked both the men, and another officer transported the female for possession of drugs for sale, and transportation of drugs. When I finished my shift, I went home.

When I came back on shift the next afternoon, I heard the Agent in Charge of the Special Investigation Unit ask if there was anyone who knew about exotic weaponry. I answered and went to the drug lab location where the suspects had been. What I saw made my heart rise up in my throat.

Next to the pickup Dennis and I had stopped last night I saw an Ingram MAC 11 with a silencer. This boxy little gun and several others had been in the truck we stopped. From experience with this gun, I knew it was a little firehose with a real penchant for throwing lots of bullets in a real short time.

I picked up the weapon and field checked it. The gun tested out to be capable of full-auto fire. Damn! These guys had a sub-machine gun with a silencer when we stopped them last night! I told the agent what I found. He told me he had found $12,000.00 in cash in an envelope lodged in the wires under the dashboard. The suspects also had enough cash on them to make bail, immediately after they were booked on the drug charges, to the tune of $15,000.00. All this happened prior to asset forfeiture laws going into effect, so all we could do was look at the money going out, know it was from "ill gotten gains," and be pissed.

But, lo and behold! There is a God! What should pull up next to the house but a Chevy with Mr. Cox and company aboard. I looked at the Special Agent in Charge and reminded him that Mr. Cox had not been arrested on any weapons charges and that I would be more than happy to take him back to our local accommodations. The SAC agreed. I walked up to Mr. Cox and placed him under arrest for the weapons charges. I don't think the news thrilled him.

Since the Ingram was fitted with a silencer, I booked Cox on charges of possession of a machine gun and silencer. The search of the house brought a quantity of drugs, more guns, and an investigative link to a storage area in Twenty Nine Palms, California.

The agents followed that lead and traced it to a warehouse which was a clandestine drug lab outside Twenty Nine Palms. The seizure of that lab was a real accomplishment. The lab had the capability of making about 60 pounds of methamphetamine a month and producing some of the precursor chemicals needed to make crank.

My part in this whole thing was minuscule. My hat is off to Gerry Thompson and Rick Armstrong for their hard work and the danger they faced to make the case, get the information, and follow the investigation out. That lab was, at that time, the largest methamphetamine manufacturing operation in California history. Thompson and Armstrong broke it.

Wars may be fought with weapons,
but they are won by men.
It is the spirit of the men who follow,
and of the man who leads that gains the victory.

General George S. Patton

THE CARE AND FEEDING OF INFORMANTS

The call was fairly routine, "See the R/P at the Rock Creek Plaza regarding a fight." I went into Rock Creek Plaza knowing there was a small carnival there, the one held every spring. Let's get one thing straight here and now, "Carnies" are not my favorite people. I've arrested too many for narcotic sales, sexual battery to minor girls, and various other crimes. However the call was still there.

When I got there, the victim began telling me about these three people he had gotten into a fight with. I knew two of them, and knew they weren't nice people. I finished taking the report, and began talking with the guy. Where was the carnival going next? Was there some way we could get in touch with him? Did he want prosecution? Pretty standard stuff.

I asked the victim if he wanted to see a doctor. Right there I hit a nerve. He refused the doctor (I knew his injuries were minor) and the fact he had been hurt made him mad. At that point, in his eyes, I became a friend. I left him standing there feeling righteously vengeful, and from his information, wrote out an intelligence report which resulted in the narcotics arrest of two of his attackers and put the third one in jail for several burglaries he had committed.

Did I really feel sympathy for the victim? It was important that *in his eyes, I did.* The result far outweighed the effort I put forth. *Showing a little humanity* netted the arrest of two dope dealers and a burglar.

Informants can work from a variety of motives. Revenge, fear of prosecution or retaliation, excitement, jealously, and just plain hate. You always have to be aware that what they're telling you may be a lie. Get corroborative evidence; a detail nobody but the criminal (or someone he's told) would know; personal observation of stolen property or contraband; locations of physical evidence (hiding place of stolen property); or some other unique detail that's not common knowledge.

Now we're cooking! Remember, informants always need to justify themselves, most importantly in their eyes, but also to you. Listen to their justifications and play it with a sympathetic ear. Be very cautious in trying to lead them. It can be seen as being patronizing. Mostly, just listen and be non-judgmental.

When they have justified themselves enough, they will start to tell you the things you love to hear. *Don't interrupt them with questions!* Let them talk, then ask questions. Remember any particular points that interested you or could lead to another crime, and come back to those later.

This is no time for taking notes! Remember, or have a tape recorder on. Once they've gone through their story, ask if they mind if you make a few notes. If they say no, exercise your memory. *You need to look them in the eyes and be sympathetic.*

Be careful not to let sensitive information slip when talking to an informant. Don't try to "prime them" with information or identities. A smart crook will give you history, take your sensitive information, and apply it to his own benefit. An even smarter crook will remember all the identities and situations you gave and will spread the word through his network as counter-intelligence. It can also tell the crook too much about how you work or what you need to be able to get a search warrant.

The most common type of informant operates on fear. I once arrested a man and woman for possession of a sawed-off shotgun. The man was an ex-con. I talked to the woman and got nothing. The ex-con wasn't saying anything either. I looked over at the reserve officer in the interview room and shouted, "He's going to hide behind a woman's skirts. Get this _____ out of my sight."

I had judged him correctly. The criminal stood up and said, "Wait, wait, I'll talk to you...I just didn't want to talk in front of him." The crook indicated the reserve officer standing behind him. The reserve officer left at my request and before I left, I had information that lead to three drug labs and 13 pushers. The informant also worked for the Special Investigations Unit for six months before he burned himself.

This brings up another point. *Don't ever burn an informant on the street.* Word will get around that this cop or this agency said that "X" is an informant. The small amount of satisfaction you get from the burn will be far outweighed by the amount of trust you will lose. When a crook finds himself facing you at the moment of truth, he will remember the "burn" and you won't get anything.

I have an informant now who gives me a piece of information then says, "I don't know why I'm talking to you." It's not important for him or her to know why. *It's crucial for me to know!*

Try it. With a little practice, a "routine" call may be very profitable for you and make suspects very nervous. Take care.

How over that same door was likewise writ,
be bold, be bold and everywhere be bold.

Edmund Spenser

"SHARE AND SHARE ALIKE..."

My formative years as a cop were in the Military Police where I was lucky enough to have good partners to keep me straight until I got my feet on the ground. I made plenty of mistakes at the start of my career. I don't think anything imprinted on me the way a certain thief did, and for the best and worst of reasons.

Sgt. Dumbjohn did *not* want to be a Military Policeman. *No way* did he want to stay a cop! He was a screw-up of the first water, but he made the mistake of telling the platoon sergeant he wanted to be shipped out to *any* other company than one with a bunch of cops. With perfect military precision, the powers that be decided they would leave him as a cop, "to make him toe the line and teach him a lesson." This had the added benefit of making those under this lazy bastard's supervision miserable.

The military rules from within by discipline and fear, backed by punishment. When I came into the police station (called the Provost Marshal's Office) that day in June of 1975, I could taste and feel the fear and anger around the office. Not something I had felt before and definitely not a comfortable feeling. A buddy of mine quickly told me that Sgt. Dumbjohn and another patrolman had been arrested by Criminal Investigation Division agents that morning. "Huh" and other bright comments followed on my part.

Dumbjohn had taken the most stupid route back to an infantry company, and one I would never have thought of. He began to steal toys from the front yards of homes on base late at night. When that didn't get him caught, he waited until he found cars on the highway with military field gear locked in them, broke into them and stole the gear. *All of this was done on duty!*

The patrolman arrested with Sgt. Dumbjohn had not participated in the thefts, neither had he reported them. Therefore, he was also guilty. *Private* Dumbjohn went back to the infantry company after a lengthy stay in the brig. The patrolman who failed to report the crime also did time in the brig and was busted. The effect this had on me and other MP's could be felt around the post for the next six months or more.

The word of Dumbjohn's arrest made it to the local papers. For the next six months whenever we issued a traffic ticket or arrested someone for anything, some wise ass would smirk and say, "How much did you steal this week, Mr. Policeman?" There were plenty of smirks cleaned off plenty of faces during that six months. We felt soiled as an organization. We worked ourselves to the bone to remove that stain. Plenty of folks went to the brig on justifiable charges scratching their heads and wondering what happened.

When I came back to California, I thought I would be somewhat immune. The headlines often give me flashbacks..."Cops arrested in drug seizure skim." "Corrupt cops caught." It brings back the same sting. What to do about it? Work a little harder, and ensure you and the people you work with are on the straight. Sometimes things happen to let you know you're in the right place...

Healy made a traffic stop on a brisk fall night. Approaching the car carefully, he asked for and received driver's license and registration from the driver. Carefully tucked between the driver's license and the extension card was a folded one-hundred dollar bill. Healy looked at the bill and said, "What's this?" The driver was all slimy smiles when he told Healy, "It's for you, officer, if we can just forget this unpleasantness." Healy told the man, "You're not joking are you?" The motorist assured him he was completely serious.

"Okay," thought Healy, "It's my word against his about the offering of a bribe." How do I improve the odds? Healy told the motorist that he had to call his "Sergeant" since good old Sarge was in for a cut of the money. "You know, share and share alike?"

The motorist agreed to wait. Meanwhile Deputy Bunch arrived and was briefed. Bunch strolled up to the motorist's car with Healy in tow and asked the citizen, with his most disarming smile, if it was true he had offered a hundred dollars to Healy to forget the ticket. The motorist assured Bunch it was true and even offered to kick in an extra twenty for "Sarge."

Our rocket scientist motorist kept shaking his head and wondering what happened on his way to jail. The real irony was he had been stopped for a traffic infraction which would have cost him less than the bribe offered. Now the violator was booked for a felony - Attempting to Bribe a Peace Officer.

I hope this citizen's little one-hundred dollar bill had plenty of brothers, because his defense attorney was surely going to demand them for his client's felony trial, and the speeding ticket he received after all was said and done.

His resolve is not to seem, but to be the best.

Aeschylus
456 B.C.

YOU'VE GOT ONE SHOT!

Roger Burnett, Tony DeCarlo and Sgt. Keven Besana were friends. They had worked together for years and knew each other socially as well as on the job.

In December 1982, Keven saw a stolen pickup with Florida plates at a house in Lincoln. He knew there was a warrant for the driver of that pickup, a man named Baker, who had committed rape and car theft in Florida. California law lets police serve an arrest warrant if they know of the existence of a warrant. They don't have to have the warrant in hand. Keven called for Tony and Roger as backup to help him serve the warrant.

Keven and company went to a small cabin on the property, and were denied entry by Baker's family. They said Baker wasn't there, he was in Texas, and the cops could not check the cabin. Lovely people that family; Marlene, a school teacher and mother of Julie, our suspect's wife; and Matt, brother-in-law of the suspect. This miracle family demanded to see a copy of Baker's arrest warrant. Keven went back over the hill to his patrol car where he radioed Lincoln Police to bring a copy of the warrant.

Tony DeCarlo and Roger Burnett were being their usual genial, persuasive selves and finally succeeded in talking their way into the cabin for a look around. Tony went to the back of the cabin, down a short hallway, checking a bedroom on the way. When he came to a closet at the back of the house, things went to hell in a hurry. There were books stacked against the door of the closet. Books stacked there by one of Baker's family members, sealing him in with a shotgun. As Tony opened the closet door, the barrel of a shotgun began descending through the opened crack of the door toward Tony's face.

Baker slammed against the inside of the door and knocked Tony backwards down the hall where he lost his footing and fell to his knees. Roger Burnett had been checking the living room when he saw the gun barrel descending. Roger pulled his own gun as Tony began his pin-ball trip through the hall.

Roger thought, "I've got one shot." With Tony ricocheting around the hall, it wasn't going to happen. Tony went down on his knees and Baker came to rest behind Tony with the 12 gauge shotgun muzzle jammed at the back of Tony's skull. Baker screamed for Roger to put his gun down. Roger was still looking for that "one shot" but he knew if he didn't kill Baker outright...Tony would die.

Baker became more and more agitated and Roger was afraid he would pull the trigger without meaning to. Roger made a decision then and there. He went against all his training and everything he had ever been told. He put his gun down.

Baker began calming down almost immediately and relieved Tony of his gun. Baker then demanded that Roger and Tony call Sgt. Besana into the house. Roger and Tony refused, telling Baker that Keven was outside and couldn't hurt him. Baker dropped it.

At Baker's orders, the rest of Baker's family, Marlene, Julie and Matthew went scurrying through the house making up a travel pack for Baker, (the rapist, and now kidnapper) to take with him on his long journey to "prove his innocence." (Obviously, he was going to stop by Vacaville Prison and pick up Charlie Manson so they could both "prove their innocence.")

Roger had noticed that Baker often gestured with the shotgun and then raised it nearly to a "port arms" or across the chest position. Baker said he was going to take them into a nearby barn. He began to herd Roger and Tony toward what they knew would be their execution-style deaths.

Baker again gestured with the shotgun and raised it across his body. Roger lost no time in dotting Baker's eye with his right fist. The shotgun went off into the ceiling of the small cabin and Tony was knocked part way out the front door. His first instinct was, "that son-of-a-bitch shot Roger." He looked back at Roger on the couch and didn't see any movement.

Roger had knocked Baker back onto a sofa and the shotgun had fallen to the living room floor. Roger fought with Baker on the sofa and was successful in getting two revolvers out of Baker's belt. Baker however, had other ideas. From somewhere in the couch, or on himself, Baker produced a .22 pistol and all Roger could see was the red dot on the side of the gun that says, "I'm not on safe!" Baker began moving the gun toward Roger's head and Roger fought him for possession of the gun.

Tony was about to go out the door when he looked back and hesitated. He saw Roger with Baker under him and realized they were fighting. Tony ran back into the room and grabbed the pump shotgun. Tony worked the slide and racked a fresh round into the pump action. The warm muzzle of the shotgun inserted firmly in Baker's right ear halted all action. One look at the face of Tony Decarlo ended all thought of resistance and Baker was taken into custody.

I don't know what great stories Baker is telling in the Florida State Prison, but I do know he is currently serving a 113 year sentence. The bottom line is Roger and Keven are still working and Tony recently retired. It could easily have been otherwise. Baker tried hard enough to make it so.

A man who has had a bull by the tail
knows five or six things more than the man who hasn't.

Mark Twain

POSITIVE AND NEGATIVE ANCHORS

In a police officer's working life there are points which I prefer to call "anchors." These anchors, foundations, and points of stability, help to keep an officer healthy in mind and body. With professional and personal stress comes mental and physical effects. The officer who is so stressed or rushed "he doesn't have time to work out, or keep in shape" is playing a dangerous gamble. Those who are "too busy doing the job to train for the job" are also playing fast and loose with their own welfare, as well as that of their co-workers and the public. Both should hope they are not going to meet a determined, aggressive assailant any time soon.

One anchor to help keep the officer healthy is the officer's family. Others; his friends, community, church, and positive personal outlets. Positive personal outlets can include relaxation activities such as fishing, hunting, hiking, bicycling or any myriad hobbies or physical activities.

On the reverse side of the coin are the negative outlets which can include alcohol abuse, sexual exploits, or other negative behaviors. The officer must understand that negative outlets only add to stress. Gender is not a factor in negative or positive stressors. The officer who is worried about a negative outlet "catching up with him" often cannot fully focus his attention on the job. When personal life stress intrudes on job performance it can become a vicious cycle with negative stress off the job adding to negative job performance and each stressor reinforcing the other. Breaking this cyclic behavior requires outside help and frequently cannot be broken without intervention.

On the other hand, positive outlets reduce the stress level and help the officer de-compress in his off time. The officer comes back from a vacation or set of days off feeling re-charged and able to concentrate and focus on the job at hand. Positive outlets, "positive anchors" help to keep a cop's perspective above the crime and violence he must deal with every day.

179

In a world where "peace" officers face trials of all kinds as a result of their job, the officer may become cynical, hardened and remote. I say the officer *may* become these things...but not necessarily. If you take satisfaction in a job well-done, satisfaction in a harmonious home life, pleasure in physical activities and enjoy your "down time," everything comes into focus.

Over and above the positive anchors mentioned, there are people. One of the benefits of a "public service job" is the various people you meet and the wisdom they can impart to you. The people you see on the job are frequently under huge stress, however, in the course of law enforcement, you are going to meet many good people as well. Allowing yourself to enjoy and benefit from the contact with average good citizens will help minimize the cynical side of policework.

Whenever my civilian friends look at me in a sideways manner, I check and see if my sense of humor isn't skewed too much toward the "dark humor" that cops are known and famous (or infamous) for. I usually find I've become too cynical or crossed a line. My task then is to re-align my mindset to uproot the cynicism that finds its way in, like weeds growing through a crack in a sidewalk.

In caring about the citizens and demonstrating that care, without compromising your safety, position, or integrity, you will find yourself in a positive, reinforcing feed-back situation. One of the hardest things in a cop's negative world is to realize that there is basic honesty and kindness among the majority of the populace. Really...two percent of the populace cause 80 percent of societies' and cops' problems.

Positive outlets help you to do your job in a focused, efficient, positive light. The officer who can use positive outlets and remains in a balanced frame of mind is a precious commodity.

A true warrior, and law enforcement officers should be warriors, knows that *he* controls how he feels. Over time, anger, resentment, hatred, and cynicism only serve to eat up the officer from the inside out. Get rid of those negatives and you can become a solid stone in the middle of a stream. The negatives flow around you and leave you present...unchanged and seemingly unchangeable. Young enough at heart to see the good. Careful enough about your safety to survive. Unworried enough to recognize problems and stop them before they get out of control. Centered enough within yourself to react correctly and instantly when it's necessary.

For other officers who habitually engage in negative stressors, you will find your anchor is not holding you to positive values. Negative stressors become the anchor around your neck, and the water can be real deep in front of you. Get help now. For those who habitually choose to engage in negative compensations, remember this quote:

Don't look back...something might be gaining on you!

Satchel Paige

THEY'LL DRIVE YOU OFF THE JOB

I worked construction before I became a cop. The same conditions applied when I started construction as when I became a cop. There were always established people who saw it as their mission in life to "run you off" if possible. They would make things as tough as possible for any "new kid on the block." Any lousy duty they could throw your way, any dirty situation that could be given away would land on the rookie.

The only thing to do with most of these folks was to smile as much as possible, know they would ease up on you eventually, and continue to do the work. Most would become friends later. There was always a piss-ant in the group with an overbearing attitude for any new co-worker or one whom they didn't like. In construction it could get dangerous to be in a confrontation with the piss-ant. It can also be dangerous to confront your department piss-ant.

Steve was the department piss-ant when I joined. A loud, obnoxious, vulgar man whose best mood was like a bobcat with a toothache. His obscene manner of speech and crude jokes alienated many of the people he came in contact with, both on and off the job. His favorite polite address for me was, "Hey do this, you fuckin' boot!"

For a long time my only reaction was a smile, a reply of, "Sure Steve" and doing whatever dirty job he pawned off on me. This was not my normal manner and I wondered if I could keep it together long enough to get past probation, or Steve's juvenile antics. I tried to keep my mouth shut and just do my work. The remainder of the people I worked with realized that I could do the job and left me alone or better yet, offered help. But piss-ant Steve just kept loading it on. I knew I had reached my limit with this guy, and the next confrontation with him would set the tone from there on.

The next graveyard shift came and Steve was intolerable. My field training officer thought this little set-to was funny and that it was a good way to evaluate my "ability to work well with others." He found every possible instance to throw me into contact with Steve. "Do this boot! Do that rookie! Fucking ree-cruit!" Building searches, back-up requests, even during dinner, I was subjected to Steve's lack of social graces.

After the shift ended, my training officer, Randy, invited me to a local park to have a beer. I asked calmly if Steve was going to be there. Randy got a funny look on his face and told me Steve was part of the shift and would be there. I bowed out of the invitation. Randy asked why I wasn't going and I told him I considered Steve a fucking Neanderthal I had to tolerate during shift, but didn't have to on *my* time. Randy left commenting, "Well, if you change your mind, come on down."

After he left, I asked myself why I should let Steve drive me away from a beer with friends and co-workers? I've always been one to grasp the nettle firmly once I've decided it's necessary. I went to the park. Upon arrival, Steve shouted, "Go get some fuckin' beer, boot!" I smiled at him, knowing it was the last time, and said, "Sure Steve." I went across the street and bought my brand of beer, which I knew Steve hated. I went back across the street psyched-up and ready for whatever came. I popped the cap off a beer and handed it to Steve and said, "Steve, you know, I owe you an apology." He got a puzzled expression on his face. "No, no, I'm serious," I went on. "I owe you an apology!"

Steve had a half-grin on his face now but wasn't certain what I was leading up to. He asked "What are you apologizing for?" I looked up at him. He was a full head taller than me and probably outweighed me by 40 pounds. I moved closer and said, "Steve, I owe you an apology because I told Randy I wouldn't drink with you." Then I shouted in his face, "BE-CAUSE YOU'RE A FUCKING NEANDERTHAL! YOU'RE NOT A FUCKING NEANDERTHAL ARE YOU? SO I OWE YOU AN APOLOGY...RIGHT?"

Randy was laughing until I thought his sides would split. The rest of the shift was in shock thinking they were going to see spilled blood any second and counting on the majority of it being mine. Randy looked at Steve and told him, "I think you've found out how much he's willing to take." Steve finally laughed and pounded me on the back.

From that day on, Steve and I never had any trouble. He just wanted to know how hard I could be pushed. He was actually a fairly adept cop, until booze, and later disease, ruined him.

Success lies in achieving the top of the food chain.
Dr. Robert Heinlein

YOUR WORST ENEMY...
THE FIVE SENSES

The job has its definite drawbacks. The assault on your senses sometimes seems to be the most definite hazard. The sights and, even worse, the smells associated with it are lasting. The first time you walk into an unfit home with cat, dog, and human feces odors mixed together will stay with you a long time. This isn't something you'd do unless the job requires it. All too frequently it's necessary to take a rat or flea bitten child or infant from the home.

I took a coroner's call at 4:00 p.m. on a fall afternoon and went to a house in Roseville. The elderly, senile woman I encountered there smelled bad in the open air and her story was strange to say the least. Her brother was older than she and had died that day. I asked what time the brother had died. She said he had died just after 8:00 that morning and she had busied herself clearing a path inside the house for us to use to get her brother out. *Eight hours to clear a path?*

I went toward the door of the house and ten feet away the smell hit me. INCREDIBLE! I continued on inside. The entire interior of the house was stacked better than six feet high with cans, bottles, jars, papers, food scraps, feces, clothing and other things I didn't want to examine too closely. The smell defied description.

I examined the body and confirmed death, cold to the touch, pupils fixed and dilated, no respiration, post-mortem lividity and rigor mortis all present. Photos were taken and I went outside and called for the coroner's removal van as well as Adult Protective Services. The way I saw it, this elderly lady couldn't continue to live in this fire trap, unsanitary, roach infested hovel. I shouldn't have bothered.

The woman from Adult Protective Services, Sharon, and her co-worker arrived and I briefed them on what we had. I suggested they wait to go in until the coroner's removal van arrived and we could remove the body while they took a quick look around. Sharon, was known to be a complete feminist, very vocal in her disdain for men and very vicious to any real or imagined slight by co-workers. Sharon's favorite motto was, "The best man for the job is a woman!" Her co-worker was very competent and did her job well. Unfortunately, but not surprisingly, Sharon was senior of the two. She seemed to receive promotions frequently through (in my opinion) the unlikely method of being obnoxious to all around her. I guessed they promoted her to get her out of their hair.

The coroner's van arrived and I put on a pair of rubber gloves. Sharon was ahead of me as I began walking toward the front of the house. When we reached "the line of stink" near the front door, Sharon began to slow. Nearer the front door, I heard the heavy bass sound of her retching in front of me. Sharon peeled off to my left and fled in one huge hurry. The other female APS worker continued into the house with us.

I went in with the morgue worker and we removed the body through the twisting, rat-maze of garbage. This was no easy matter since the deceased had to weight in excess of 300 pounds. Meanwhile, Sharon's co-worker had seen enough and left the house.

The morgue worker and I came out of the house and found Sharon parading around in her expensive pants-suit, holding forth at length how she shouldn't have to be subjected to these types of calls. I couldn't resist. "Sharon, next time I see you, you can tell me again how the best man for a job is a woman!" "WELL IT IS," she replied. I thought her screaming lacked conviction.

Sharon's female co-worker, an acquaintance of mine, who had shown real fortitude by touring the house, looked at me with a small smile. She told me, "She's vindictive. She'll find some way to take it out on you." I wondered how Sharon could make life hard for me. File a complaint? I hadn't done anything wrong. Complain to my boss? About what?

I then found out how she could get back at me. Sharon held forth again. This elderly woman needed no help from Adult Protective Services. This was her lifestyle. If I felt the need, I could do something, but they were not needed here. Her co-worker and the local police argued against her for a while, but Sharon was adamant. This was the elderly woman's lifestyle and who were we to interfere with it?

The senile, elderly woman came up to me, as she had to Sharon, and said she was afraid. Her brother had been her protector, and now he was gone. How was she going to live? I watched Sharon collect her co-worker, get into the county car, and coolly drive away. She hadn't even had the guts to confront the problem. She just avoided it, the same way she'd avoided the house.

Sharon had taken her pitiful measure of revenge. I had no answer for the old woman. The agency that was designed and funded to help her had just gotten petty and vindictive, then driven away. I made do with a call to the Fire Marshal's office and worked through another agency that I knew would do the job without having "their sensibilities offended."

People who win their spurs in battle,
almost always show more compassion
than those who never fire a shot in anger.

William Stevenson

OFFICER'S OBSERVATIONS

I was part of an officer-involved shooting in 1982. There were six other officers on the scene with me. There were seven accounts of the events that night, and seven statements which could have been titled, "What I did was..."

One of the officer's on scene said the round the suspect fired at us ricocheted off the ground. I didn't hear the sound of a ricochet. The officer may have heard the Doppler Effect and not understood it. I don't know.

Another officer said he saw the round glint in the light after being fired and believed it passed about three feet to his partner's left. I've had bullets register on the eye while on the range when weather, lighting, and angle are correct. But, as the defense said, I'm not going to get out in front of the muzzle and let someone shoot near me to find out if it's possible from the front.

The point is that I wasn't standing where these officers were, so I can't say. Each officer's observation was uniquely his own. Observations are defined by a number of factors, namely vantage point, training level, experience level, environmental, and physical factors. Complicated isn't it?

How many times have we heard the famous line, "You look...but you don't see." In law enforcement, seeing can save your life or the life of your partner. An unseen weapon in a car, or a bulge in clothing can be disastrous. So, how do we go about seeing? Here are some suggestions:

#1 Of paramount importance is having enough light. ALWAYS have a flashlight. You're working dayshift and don't need one? WRONG! Carry a small mag-light if nothing else. You may find yourself searching a darkened building, looking for a lost child under a freeway drainage tunnel or under a house, or most commonly, searching under car seats.

#2 DON'T have preconceived notions about what you are going to see. During a training scenario, I put a dark colored toy gun (with light colored grips) on the rear seat of a dark colored car. Very difficult to see unless you spot the grip panels and recognize them for what they are. Expect to see ANYTHING AT ALL, not just a rear seat, floorboard, etc. If you expect to see the car seat, THAT'S ALL YOU'LL SEE!

#3   Change your point of view and look again if you're not certain. Take a different angle of view on the object and see if more of the object is visible. Also be curious. If it looks suspicious, check it out!

#4   Carry a mirror in your pocket. Pocket size camping mirrors are available from $2.00 - $4.00 each. Metal mirrors don't distort much and don't scratch easily. Acetate mirrors scratch easily, but have crystal clarity. *Hint* - a small amount of acrylic floor wax, like Future, applied to the plastic and buffed vigorously will take the scratches out of acetate mirrors.
   A mirror has a second advantage - talk about changing your angle of view! Hold it under something like a couch or car and take a look. What's that? Too dark under there? Take the flashlight you bought after reading #1 above and shine it upward or downward into the angled mirror. You should be able to see just fine now, above or below any search object. This can also be a life saver in this age of needles, AIDS, and Hepatitis B. In order to spot razors, needles, knives, and such, you need to look real sharp (pardon the pun) because these items don't have much visible width.

#5   Training and experience. This is a tough one. Where one person only sees a chain, another may see the weights attached to the ends. But, so what...unless you know that Section 12020 of the Penal Code makes possession of a "Slungshot" a felony. One person may only see a square piece of folded, slick paper. Another person would recognize this as a "Sno-Seal" or pharmaceutical fold used to contain cocaine or crank.

So how do you get the training? You train by doing. By getting out and looking, by being redundant. Have someone else take a look at anything of which you are not certain. There can also be a certain amount of luck to observing.
   During my term in the Detective Division, I served a search warrant on a property in Meadow Vista. The stolen property in question was over $18,000.00 in checks, cash, and food stamps from a supermarket burglary. My partner searched a small

camper the suspect lived in, while I searched the house and tried to get information from the family and girlfriend. My partner concluded his search and told the patrol deputy he hadn't found anything. The patrol officer must have been as frustrated as I was at that point.

Then a uniformed deputy stepped inside and kicked at a pile of dirty clothes lying on the floor. A stack of bound cash rolled out of the clothing. Over $4,500.00 in cash and food stamps were recovered because of that kick. The suspect was convicted of the burglary.

When you learn by doing, you are going to make mistakes. Do it! I would rather have someone make an honest mistake and learn from it then have to push a "shrinking violet" who makes no mistakes, but also doesn't make any observations. We all try not to make mistakes and I'm not advocating making mistakes on purpose. Our goal is if we make mistakes, we should make sure we learn from them and *don't* repeat them. There are mistakes that are *final*. We shouldn't make mistakes with weaponry, vehicles, or safety. These should be considered, anticipated, and avoided wherever possible.

Oh Yes! #6? LOOK UP! Cops DON'T look up enough. A co-worker of mine recently told me the story of a Pennsylvania Black Powder rifle found on an American Revolution battleground. It's pretty certain that rifle's been there for 170 years or so. How do they figure that? Because the rifle has grown into and become PART OF A TREE! So, look up!

> *Far better it is to dare mighty things, to win glorious triumphs, even though checkered by failure, than to rank with those poor spirits who neither enjoy much nor suffer much, because they live in that grey twilight that knows neither victory nor defeat.*

Theodore Roosevelt

THE PATROL RIFLE: POINTS TO PONDER

The face of law enforcement is changing, and with it, the methods and equipment we utilize. Some people mistake technology as a replacement for the training and materials necessary to do the job. As the requirements of our profession change and evolve, so must the training and tactics. Sometimes new technology itself requires an invention or evolution of training and tactics. Keeping this in mind, let's consider the peace officer's offensive weaponry.

In the U.S. the police shotgun has historically been an approved police offensive weapon. This is exactly the opposite in European communities where the shotgun is seen as "inhumane" for use against people and is strictly a "fowling piece." However, a policeman on the street corner in Europe with a carbine or sub-machine gun is not even noteworthy.

Increasingly in the United States, a patrol rifle in various configurations has either replaced or supplemented the shotgun. The shotgun's beneficial factors include:

1) It's sheer power and devastating effect when properly utilized.

2) It's versatility. The fact that it can be used with everything from ferret rounds which introduce CS gas, lock-buster ammunition for forcible door entries, buckshot in various sizes, slugs, or plastic shot for less-than-lethal use.

The disadvantages of the shotgun are as follows:

1) It is a dispersion-type weapon. The further away the target, the more chance for an extended range miss and projectiles flying toward disaster.

2) The often held, but mistaken belief that the shotgun is addressed to anyone in front of the muzzle, and that the "scattergun" can make up for poor marksmanship. In close quarters, the shotgun must be aimed nearly as precisely as a rifle.

3) At any range, because of the misconception or simply from dispersion, there is an increased likelihood of misses simply because of the shot spread.

4) If there is a miss because of #1, 2, or 3 above, there are somewhere between 1 to 12 projectiles headed for potential disaster.

5) With certain qualifications at any extended range, the shotgun is not "specific" enough to let an officer select and direct force against a certain assailant, and *only* that assailant.

6) With some exceptions, patrol officers don't carry slugs, lock-buster or ferret rounds with the patrol shotgun, so the argument for diversity of use is a moot point.

7) In most configurations, a shotgun has only four or five rounds of spare ammunition, therefore, is limited in its capacity and utility.

8) Recoil, recoil, and more recoil. Officer's generally do not prefer the shotgun because of it's recoil. If they don't like that fact, they will not retain training, and are less likely to use it.

Please don't get me wrong. We teach Tactical Shotgun and if you look at the listed considerations, you will see the advantages argue more for the shotgun's use with tactical teams.

For patrol work and with officers generally trained, not specially trained, the advantages of the patrol rifle are as follows:

1) Specific force can be brought to bear on a specific assailant. One assailant can be singled out.

2) Misses, when they do occur, are ONE projectile, NOT 9 to 12.

3) The patrol rifle gives the officer an extended range capability which far surpasses the capability of the short sight-planed service sidearm and prevents the dispersion miss of the shotgun.

4) Patrol carbines can be made compatible with service sidearm ammunition. Not a large consideration, but an advantage.

5) Weight factors. Some rifles, depending on configuration, are lighter than shotguns. With the number of small stature officers we have, this can be a consideration.

6) Recoil. In all carbine configurations and some rifle calibers, the recoil felt is much less than with the shotgun. This factor combined with weight means the patrol rifle will be

used more frequently and possibly more effectively, since the officer is not shy of it's weight and recoil.

7) Ammunition capacity. After four to eight rounds, a shotgun is a large paperweight and almost as handy. A patrol rifle is still live in most configurations.

The disadvantages of a patrol rifle are as follows:

1) Depending on caliber and ammunition selection, rifles may over-penetrate.

2) If you use a specialty ammunition to try to "cure" the tendency to over-penetrate, you give away the ability to penetrate intermediate barriers.

3) Ammunition capacity. Larger capacity may bring up the tendency to "spray and pray." A subject for training.

4) Patrol rifles are not something frequently seen except in the hands of tactical teams and may evoke a reaction from the public. Shotguns are "politically acceptable" in large part.

Of particular note are the jurisdictions who have begun to remove shotguns from the patrol car without any replacement of offensive capability. Those jurisdictions are walking a tightrope of liability. If an officer or citizen's injury or death was preventable by the use of an offensive weapon and it has been removed from the patrol car, the governmental organization and chief executive officer who took away that capability may very well stand to lose.

The patrol rifle requires long gun training the same as the shotgun. If either gun goes sour, officers must be taught to go through a clearing drill or go to the defensive sidearm. The marksmanship training for each is necessary. Firearm retention instruction for each is necessary. We should, therefore, give the officer the weapon which best suits the need. If the need is to apply specific force to a specific target *and only that target* without unacceptable losses, then the more accurate and less dispersion prone weapon is something worth considering.

There is one condition to the patrol rifle that we all agree on. In any configuration, PATROL RIFLES SHOULD NOT BE SCOPED. NO TELESCOPIC SIGHTS!

This is going to cause some firearms instructors to disagree, and all owners of Steyr Aug's mad, but here's the reason. Whenever a scope sight is used, an observer is needed. The scope does several beneficial things; it magnifies, makes target identification easier, and focuses attention. But it also makes it impossible to see what's happening just outside the rifle user's field of view. This is critically important in the use of an offensive weapon and crucial in traversing with a moving target.

If an officer is traversing, following a moving target, with the rifle scope and as the trigger is pressed, the suspect runs in front of a non-combatant, the officer's field of view is restricted until the shot is fired. It's not the officer's fault, the officer just bumped his nose into an equipment shortcoming - one he may not even have known existed.

One of the other equipment "shortcomings" of telescopic sights is that they should be trained with, installed for, and retained by one person. The eye relief for a scope depends on the installation and can be "opened" immediately for the intended user. However, trade the rifle to another user and the length of pull, cheek weld and eye relief combine to close the view for a second or two. Critical time!

Add to these factors, the narrowing of field of view when the weapon is shouldered and it may force the shooter to "search" for the threat when they can't afford the time. All of these factors can be remedied by diligent training. But that's not always possible because of time or fiscal restraints. Especially in larger agencies, this may be a reality of our profession as trainers.

We need to have high quality training in the area of patrol rifle. It's new enough in some jurisdictions that it's possible to lose the use of this valuable tool.

The gun is the individual arm,
But the emphasis is on the man.

H. W. McBride
(paraphrased)

HONEST OFFICER...
THAT'S HOW IT HAPPENED!

It was late at night and George and I were in our patrol area making the rounds looking for a couple of suspects who had arrest warrants. The radio came alive with our "call of the night." An Iowa Hill local, Moe, was in the emergency room suffering from a gunshot wound to the upper left thigh. The sergeant wanted us to go to Iowa Hill, check out the scene, and talk with witnesses.

Iowa Hill is an historical "49'er Gold Rush" town with nothing much there anymore. It's atop a steep mountain divide in a beautiful forest setting. In the early 80's our standard statement whenever we crossed the American River toward Iowa Hill was, "we just hit a time warp and dropped about 50 years. We'd better be able to take care of ourselves here!" Everyone carries guns, it's forested, and there are both four and two legged varmints to worry about.

We went to the Iowa Hill Store and found a jeep parked about 50 feet beyond. My partner started toward the store and a man came out to meet us. "Larry" identified himself and gave the following account of the "gun accident."

Moe, Larry and a third person he refused to name had been driving around in the jeep. They came to the campfire outside the store and had a couple of beers together. A .22 rifle had been leaned against the jeep and it slid off it's rest and fell on a log. The gun went off and Moe got hit in the leg.

I looked into the jeep and spotted a 50,000 candlepower spotlight plugged into the cigarette lighter. The back and right seats of the jeep had water on them from being freshly washed down. I reached over and retrieved a scope-sighted .22 semi-auto rifle out of the back of the jeep. I asked Larry if there was anything he wanted to change about his story. Larry looked confused and said he had told me how it happened...honest! I looked at Larry directly at close range and told him he was lying. I interrupted Larry's shocked look and stammering with, "Let me tell you what happened!"

"To start with, the story about the gun falling is bull and

197

you know it. The wound to Moe's leg is straight across not an upward angle like it would have to be if the gun had fallen against something. So that part's a lie." (No, I hadn't seen Moe's leg. This was a shot in the dark on my part, pardon the pun). Larry was now getting a little green around the gills.

"From the looks of the jeep, it's pretty obvious Moe was wounded while in the jeep and brought back to the store. The jeep was washed down to get the blood out of the back and right seats. The jeep has a roll bar on it. Moe was standing up in the back of the jeep hanging onto the roll bar using the spotlight to light up deer. The driver was going too fast when a doe or buck was spotted on the passenger side of the jeep. The driver drove past it and stopped."

"The right hand passenger had the rifle. Whether it was you, Larry, or your unknown buddy "Curly," I don't know, and could care less. The poacher got out of the right hand seat and began to follow the deer with the scoped rifle. The deer, in self preservation, started to run and with perfect instinct, ran behind the jeep."

"The gunman, swinging the scoped rifle to follow the deer, pulled the trigger just as Moe's leg came into his field of view. BINGO! I'll bet Moe was pissed! He's not known for his low-key temperament." (Moe and the anonymous gunman had just found out having a scope on a rifle can be a disadvantage. You can't see what's moving into the field of view until it's there).

From the sick look on Larry's face, I knew I had hit pay dirt with the account. "Well Larry, you have the right to remain silent." Larry stood on his Miranda rights and refused to say anything more. I had what I needed.

I took my observations and Larry's reactions and wrote them up for the district attorney. Nothing happened with the district attorney's office which was what I expected. It's one of those, "circumstantial evidence cases." We all know what happened, but proving it is another matter.

Strange though, Moe, Larry and Curly were arrested a couple of months later...for poaching. Seems the game warden was interested in my report and observations. I must have let slip what I saw and heard. Another case of my big mouth getting deserving folks in trouble!

In battle, the only bullets that count are those that hit.

Theodore Roosevelt

Winner ... the Deer!

A VACATION DAY

It was one of those rare days off. Rich Taylor and I were cleaning up our diving gear. Rich is a former Sacramento Sheriff's Department SWAT member and we had gone to high school together. It had been a great day of diving, we each had our limit of abalone. There would be abalone, fish fillets, scallops, and crab for dinner tonight. We were standing under the fresh water showers at a state campground near Mendocino, California on a beautiful sunny, calm day, cutting the salt water taste out of our mouths with a beer. What a vacation!

A marine biologist checked our abalone when we got to the beach. All were well above the legal seven inch minimum limit across the shell. A couple of low class citizens had dragged up on shore just after us and the biologist was checking their abalone and found they were all under sized. Now this is not a small matter. It takes about 13-14 years to grow a seven inch shelled abalone. When people take the youngsters, it destroys the abalone harvest for future years.

The marine biologist asked these citizens to take the abalone back to the rocks since they were below limit. These slobs basically told her obscenely they had no such intention and were obscenely going to keep the abalone.

Rich and I watched the exchange and the biologist walked away. She went to the gate of Van Dam State Park across the road and Rich and I looked at each other knowingly. Within a couple of minutes, a game warden came hauling down Highway 1, and pulled into the parking lot directly behind the pickup where our two slobs were loading dive gear and illegal abalone.

The two slobs began to get a little heated under the collar about the game warden checking their shellfish. The game warden was polite, but firm. Very professional. He took the under-sized abalone, searched the truck, photographed the shellfish with a ruler in the picture, and issued a citation to the slobs. A wrecker showed up and towed the slob's four-wheel drive truck. All slob-owned dive gear went into the back of the game warden's truck.

Rich and I were still in our wet suits and watching the fun. The game warden came over and asked us if we would mind taking the abalone back to the rocks. We both said we would be happy to. The warden measured our abalone by eye and commented they were good sized. We told him we were cops and with which agency. Rich said, "Just out of curiosity, how much of a fine are those two looking at?"

The warden was a pleasant kind of guy and he smiled and said, "Well to tell you the truth, each abalone is worth about $500.00 a piece. Each person had four undersized, so figure a $2,000.00 fine a piece. $4,000.00 total fine between the two. Their truck and dive gear are liable to be forfeited. Add to that, the fact that their hunting and fishing licenses can be revoked for up to five years and it gets stiff." Rich and I both grunted. We knew burglars who received less punishment and fine.

In conversation with the game warden after we re-planted the abalone, we found things are different for game wardens. Apparently, the "exclusionary rule" does not bind Fish and Game cops as it does other branches of law enforcement. Their aim is "preservation of a species." If they do a search with that aim in mind, anything they find is producible in court. I would guess this situation would give defense attorney's diarrhea of the first order.

But it makes sense. People downgrade Fish and Game and Forestry police. Calling them "fish cops" and "tree cops." Make fun if you want, but the vast majority of them I've run into are smart, dedicated people, and they know what they're doing and how to go about it. They work in very remote areas, where people are almost always armed. Back-up can be many hours away. They're frequently attacked by some cretin who doesn't get the idea a dead doe or some over limit fish isn't worth killing someone over. Tough job.

If you want to take game illegally, I'd like to hear how you make out when you get caught. I'll keep my hunting and fishing licenses intact, my car at my disposal, and my wallet contents for myself and my family's betterment, thank you very much!

We must especially beware of
that small group of selfish men
who clip the wings of the American Eagle,
in order to feather their own nests.

Franklin D. Roosevelt

UNMITIGATED SAVAGERY

On a late morning in March 1988, my trainee and I were called to a local school where we were told to contact the vice-principal. Dispatch went over the "coder" and scrambled the radio traffic so the whole county wouldn't know what had happened. A 12-year old girl had just been dropped off at the railroad tracks near her elementary school. She had come to her class, promptly began crying, and told a friend she had just been raped.

I got to the school and found the vice-principal in a side office with a female teacher's aide and the victim. I motioned to the vice-principal to come outside which he did. He briefed me on the student's time of arrival at school and the fact "Sissy" had apparently been raped and sodomized by a stranger.

I took my trainee and began to go into the office to interview the victim. The vice-principal walked in with me. Whoa! Time out! I asked the girl to excuse me for a second and backed the school official out the door, closing it behind me. This diligent school official said he needed to be present at the interview with Sissy. I told him his presence was flatly impossible. The man didn't get the point because he replied, "I have notes to complete on this, and she's my student." The vice-principal's attitude was a little belligerent.

I said, "That little girl sees you every day and every time she sees you she's going to remember this day and that you were there. I'm a uniform and someone that she's going to seldom see. Don't push this." I flatly told him, "She stopped being your student when she became my victim. You're not going in."

Mr. vice-principal began to puff up like a self-important toad and insisted he had a right as a school official. I replied I wouldn't even go in that room if I didn't absolutely have to. Conducting a rape interview is one of the hardest things imaginable. If he insisted on getting in my way, my trainee was going to escort him to my patrol car where he could remain during the interview. When I completed the interview, I would gladly cite him for resisting and obstructing a peace officer. He backed down. The entire exchange had taken no more than two minutes.

I went back in the room and asked the girl if she felt she needed a doctor. She replied no. I introduced myself to her, then to the teacher's aide. The victim gave her full name and I told her I'd like to talk with her about what happened if it was okay with her. Due to the initial questions about her welfare and asking for her permission to talk with her, she was willing to be interviewed.

The story came out that she had been forced into the car by the suspect. A 12-year old girl really has no defense against a 43-year old man. The suspect's car was a late model Chrysler LaBaron. Sissy went on to describe in heartbreaking detail the suspect's description, the acts committed, the description of the car's contents, the color of the blankets in the car, the location of the rape, and everything she could remember. A very courageous little girl. I let our patrol people know the descriptions of the suspect and his car and had dispatch re-broadcast it for other local agencies.

Two days later, a sharp-eyed Sacramento County patrol deputy spotted a stolen beige Chrysler LaBaron. Through investigation the identity of our suspect was learned. It was another of those obvious "success" stories of the criminal justice system.

In 1972, "Joey" committed a series of violent rapes and went to prison. In 1975, Joey was allowed to re-join society on parole. Within two months his parole officer and police were looking for him for another violent series of rapes. Joey had stayed in prison for 12 years that time and been paroled for his third chance in 1988. Joey was known to have a real affinity for Chrysler LaBarons and his modus operandi matched the crimes to Sissy.

Within two weeks of his release, Joey raped a real estate saleswoman in a San Francisco Bay area town and stole her Chrysler LaBaron. He went to Modesto, California, forced a woman into the back of the store where she worked and raped her. Joey went to Sacramento and ended up on a college campus. A co-ed walking through campus was attacked from behind, slammed to the ground, her clothing cut off with a knife, and raped. During the rape, the suspect had made the mistake of letting his hand stray near the victim's mouth. She clamped down like an enraged alligator and chewed the suspect's left little finger with diligence and authority. The suspect stabbed the victim four times in the buttocks in an attempt to make her let go. A mutual agreement was reached where she would let go of the suspect's finger if he would let her go. Both suspect and victim made a retreat without the victim ever seeing the attacker. A couple days later, Joey raped Sissy.

When Sacramento Sheriff's Officers found out Joey was in their area, they went into an all out effort, found and arrested him in the stolen Chrysler LaBaron. Joey had a very badly chewed little finger on his left hand. The bite marks could be matched with dental casts from the college campus victim. Tie him to one rape. The victims in the San Francisco Bay area and Modesto made positive identification from a photo line-up. Tie Joey to three rapes.

Our detectives went to the Sacramento towing agency that had taken the stolen Chrysler and recovered the blankets and the shaving kit Sissy had described down to such fine detail. Tie Joey to four rapes. The victims ranged in age from 12 to 45 years of age.

There was little chance of fingerprint identification from most surfaces of the car. But the attempt was made and results shipped to the Department of Justice. When my department found out Joey was in the Sacramento jail, they sent a copy of the interview with Sissy and the crime scene investigation report. Sacramento County Sheriff's Detectives did the interview with him.

My interview with Sissy had been very exhaustive, figuratively as well as literally. A detective from my agency picked up Sissy at the end of the interview and took her for a medical examination and preservation of fluid and particle evidence. During the ride to the hospital, Sissy turned to the detective and told him, "I don't know if it's important, but this guy asked my name before he raped me. I didn't want to give him my real name so I told him my name was Jean." The detective noted this and included it in his report.

In Sacramento, the detective interviewing Joey told him how badly he'd hurt all the women, and bore down on the fact one of them was a child whose innocence had irreparably been stolen. The detective said sometimes it helped the victims if the suspect wrote a letter of apology.

Joey started one letter, "Dearest Jean."

The court sentence was 76 years.

■ ■

The most dangerous person I've ever met is six-foot two inches tall and 210 pounds of the most violent rapist imaginable. He has spent all but about two years of his adult life in prison, and was well acquainted with California Youth Authority as a pre-teen and teenager.

His name is Eddie and his idea of "picking up women" includes running their car off the roadway and doing whatever his twisted mind comes up with.

One of the times Eddie was arrested, he was trying to buy drugs. The deal went sour and Eddie went after the dealer with a sawed-off shotgun, firing three rounds at the running drug dealer. When arrested, Eddie's statement to the arresting officer was, "Fuck you! You're a cop, I'm a con. I'm going to tell you exactly what I want you to know. What can you do to me? I've got a boyfriend at Folsom Prison that I'm dying to get back to!"

■■■■■■■■■■■■■■■■■■■

Between these two men, there are probably 40 or more victims who will never forget their faces. Women who will have nightmares, crying jags, and problems of a greater or lesser degree for the rest of their lives. Simply put, these two criminals are not worth the shedding of one tear from any of these victims. They should never have been allowed to come back out repeatedly just to victimize more.

But, society will continue to let them out. People who are known to be violent and continue to make victims out of innocent people are let out every day. In a grand perversion, the courts frequently order them out because of "overcrowding" in their facilities.

Makes perfect sense, right?

Degrees do not matter.
One does not bargain with inches of evil.

Ayn Rand

THE POLICE GAMES ANNOUNCER

The Porsche slammed through the gears and fled eastbound on Interstate 80 at speeds well in excess of 120 miles per hour. The driver was not the owner of the car, and this thief didn't care what happened to the car, as long as he got away.

The pursuing patrol units from my Sheriff's Department and the California Highway Patrol had other ideas. Several units converged onto the area. The stolen car went onto frontage roads, back down the freeway, and off onto another frontage road. The driver of the stolen car made a mistake, went onto the railroad right-of-way, then tried to jump the railroad tracks leaving the car high-centered.

Our suspect jumped from the car and decided to absent himself from the vicinity. Running through brush, he approached the back of a house, broke a rear window and went in. He packed some clothing, canned goods, a disassembled rifle, and ammunition into a backpack. Leaving the house, he walked parallel to the tracks for about half a mile before going back onto the tracks and walking north.

Our patrol deputy, Jerry, and his partner drove onto the railroad right-of-way bumping along in the patrol car. Lucky for us and bad news for the bad-guy, CHP Helicopter 20 was overhead and the scene was set. The helicopter observer was a cool sort as his radio frequency opened and he calmly told Jerry the suspect was on foot directly ahead about one-quarter mile. Jerry made the quarter-mile in good time, radioed in that the suspect was running down the hill, and unloaded from the patrol car. The left-hand rear window of the patrol unit rolled down, and Jerry's partner came out of the patrol unit...MEET GRIZZLEY! One hundred five pounds of trained, experienced German Shepherd.

CHP H-20's radio traffic went on, rising in pitch and excitement as the scene unfolded. It went something like this.

"The deputy's out of the car...The dog is out...The suspect's running downhill...The dog is going down the hill...THE DOG

IS DOWN...THE DEPUTY AND SUSPECT ARE DOWN...THE DEPUTY, THE DOG, AND THE SUSPECT ARE DOWN...!"

Right feet slammed down on area patrol car accelerators as the radio went quiet. There's a calm before the storm in any incident. The worst sound is the emergency tone on the radio. Knowing that your friend is out there in a fight, and no radio traffic telling you "it's okay now." There are many silent prayers and more than a few silent pleas of "pick up my coordinates and beam me aboard Scotty!"

The police announcer overhead in H-20 finally came on and said, "It looks like he's got him in custody." Breath whistled out through numerous clenched-tight police jaws. Two units arrived on scene and no more were needed. The arriving units also radioed that Jerry was okay. We waited until end of shift to find out what happened...

Jerry got out of the car and sent Grizzley toward the suspect who was running down the embankment. The suspect saw black, tan and teeth gaining on him from behind. He stopped and picked up a manzanita stump. He set his feet, waited for the dog and delivered a smashing blow to the dog's rib cage knocking him into the brush. Jerry was following the dog and saw Grizz get knocked into the brush. He charged down the hill and the suspect swung at him. Jerry knocked the suspect to the ground fighting with him. Grizzley returned to the fight in short order and his disposition had *not* been improved by being thumped in the side.

Jerry was off for a time because of a separated shoulder and Grizzley had some broken ribs. Both returned to duty after a short healing break. The suspect had trouble sitting down for awhile and got some prison time to reflect on the efficiency of police dogs and his own stupidity.

*If a grasshopper tries to fight a lawnmower,
one may admire his bravery...but not his intelligence.*

Dr. Robert Heinlein

BAITING THE TRAP

The local restaurant was having trouble. Located alongside Interstate 80, it was a local landmark and did a very good business. A quiet place with good food and cordial owners. Leave it to some enterprising criminal to rip off the place. By the time the owner caught the error on the books, the loss was about $2,500.00. The grief of the situation was the owner suspected an employee. I was working detectives and had to do something about the situation. There was no way a suspect interview was going to help, the stolen property was all cash. The suspect could lie, deny, and demand proof. I had no proof to give. Another solution would have to be found.

I had used surveillance equipment from the California Dept of Justice. With a "see in the dark video camera" and special VCR, I had the cash drawer under constant surveillance. Patrol was briefed about the surveillance and knew to notify me if the suspect was caught in the act by the owner.

A couple of days later, I was absolutely stunned. The suspect had found the surveillance system, *turned if off, then committed the burglary anyway*! Boy, was my face red, and I was pissed! I went back to the Department of Justice, took the ribbing from the technicians, and backed up the surveillance system with an alarm and other equipment.

That night, the restaurant owner called and told me he had found a restaurant door prepared so it could be opened from the outside. I called a reserve officer and we did a stake out waiting for the suspect. Understand this, I had worked the entire day, was ready for bed, got the call about the door preparation at 11:00 p.m., and went on stake out until 4:00 a.m. the next day. I was really whipped by the time I called off the stake out. All I wanted was to go home and crawl into bed.

I arrived home, shucked clothing and went to bed. Forty-five minutes later the phone rang and my tolerant wife hit me in the head with the phone receiver. The dispatcher was breathless as she told me, "You better get to the restaurant, it's been burglarized and shots fired!" Aw Shit!

I broke land speed records getting into my clothing and my unmarked car. Dispatch told me the suspect was last seen riding a bicycle north from the business. I went to the area Code 3 then cut my red light and cruised a little slower. I met the first responding patrol unit about five miles from my house and we swapped areas. I was to look where they had been, they would double back on my track.

One quarter-mile later I passed the suspect on his bicycle, did a turn around and went back to confront the suspect. It was 5:00 a.m. and we were the only people in the area. As I got out of the car, I shouted, "Police, don't move! The suspect made the most common statement in police history, "who...me?"

I approached and took a twist-lock control hold then hand-cuffed him. The suspect's immediate comment was, "He shot me," indicating the outside of his left leg. I looked down at the leg and found a 1/2 inch wide abrasion mark along the outside surface of the calf, halfway between ankle and knee.

Sergeant Jeff, a former homicide detective, arrived. I've seen my share of bullet wounds and Jeff's seen more then I have. Both of us looked at the scrape on the kid's leg, looked him in the eye and chorused, "Bullshit. That's no bullet wound." I continued, "You scraped that running through the brush kid. There's weeds and blackberry brambles all over you." The kid looked sheepish and admitted that he "might" be wrong about the "wound." The patrol unit transported and booked the suspect into juvenile hall.

I went back to the restaurant and the owner met me at the door. "That little shit! I was sound asleep when that alarm went off. I went pounding down the stairs and chased him through the hall, into the kitchen and out the side door screaming his name and telling him to stop. When I cleared the side door, I fired two rounds into the air. It just put high octane in him. Made him run faster." I agreed that gunfire was a great motivator. The suspect generally either freezes in place or does a gazelle imitation over the horizon.

The kid decided to talk to me and told me "Jimmy," the restaurant owner, could afford it. After all, he had that restaurant and cars and all. He just took the money for CD's and pizza parties with his friends. Our suspect felt kinda like it was "owed" to him. Why should he have to work so hard? It just wasn't fair!

Knowing your enemies capabilities are one thing.
But what are his intentions?
Military Intelligence Quote

A FORMAL INTRODUCTION

I had worked a full day in Investigations - Burglary Division, and was on my way home. It was 5:30 p.m. and I had worked a little late at the office. The radio piped up and gave a report of a burglary which had just occurred on Swanson Lane.

I knew there was a standing order from the captain *not* to go on patrol's calls unless requested. I also knew there was no close back-up for the upper beat car and this was one directive that was going by the wayside. I wanted to drop by and assist since I knew I would get the case for investigation in a day or so. I couldn't get into trouble with the captain if I just stopped by and gave an assist. Right? C'mon, somebody twist my arm a little here. Aw hell with it! The captain goes home at 4:00 p.m. anyway.

I swung off the highway and arrived before the dust settled on the narrow dirt road where the burglary occurred. We had four witnesses who had seen the suspect. They all described his Levi jacket with burn holes on it, Walkman with headphones, and small yellow pick-up. The physical description of the suspect was consistent among the witnesses with only minor variations.

The patrol officer, Jeff, and I went to the house, found a smashed sliding glass door and made a quick building search. The house was small, but very expensively furnished. We began walking back toward the cars on the 10 foot wide dirt road. We heard the witnesses screaming, "There he is! The yellow truck! It's him! He just came over the top of the hill, saw us and backed away fast."

I ran the 20 yards to my unmarked car, slid behind the wheel and fired up the engine. My unmarked was a Mercury Sable with a siren under the wheel well and a flip down red light. I had insisted on the emergency equipment when I got the car. I backed up at about 30 miles per hour, a skill I'd practiced, and whipped the front of the car around in a slew turn while backing into a driveway.

As I started forward, I saw the yellow truck just disappearing around the corner, 50 yards south of me. This guy couldn't back as fast as I could...a point for me. I picked up the radio mike from between the seats of the car and let dispatch know I was in pursuit. The road turned into blacktop just a little way ahead and widened to 15 feet. This guy wasn't going to stop...he was running about 55 miles per hour despite the lights and siren.

We went out onto Ponderosa Road and turned right. I hadn't been able to get close enough to get a license number, but I didn't think the guy had enough engine to get away. The truck met another pickup on a curve and passed him. The obliging motorist saw my red light and pulled over letting me by. (Thank you very much sir, should you ever read this!) We went down the rural county road at 60 to 70 miles per hour.

The local store was coming up and I left the siren on as the suspect whipped past another truck in front of the store. I could see local people running out to see what the hell was going on. I kept on the suspect's tail, yet far enough back to give me stopping room and reaction distance if he pulled something stupid.

We accelerated to over 100 miles per hour on a straight stretch of road. I had kept up a running radio commentary during the pursuit; constantly updating speed, location, and direction of travel. The guy couldn't drive as fast in "go-behind" but he could sure haul in "go-ahead." We passed another car and he went up on two wheels on a hard left hand turn.

I dropped back a little to give him room to crash should it happen. When I began to come out of the turn, I floored it and caught up with him a little. My suspect turned onto Yankee Jim's Road and unless he knew the road, he was in for a nasty surprise. That road gets really narrow and rough while heading through mountains and past cliffs toward the American River Canyon.

I closed up enough to get a license plate just after we went onto Yankee Jim's and before it changed to a dirt surface. I let dispatch know the license number over the radio. The dust was flying and the suspect swerved from side to side trying to throw rocks up onto my windshield. I knew this road too well. We went into the narrow portion of the dirt road. Now it gets tricky. One false tap on the brake, or a corner a little too fast, and you end up in the mountain, over the cliff, or both.

A mile and one half later, I saw the suspect's brake lights come on solid prior to the curve ahead. I knew he'd made the mistake. I fully expected to see the tail lights disappear over the 100 foot cliff which waited on the right side of the roadway. Somehow the truck stopped with 18 inches to spare.

I slammed on the emergency brake and slid my car to a stop since the road was straight where I was. I came to a stop about 30 yards away from the truck and bounced out of the car with gun in hand, "Police, Don't Move!"

The dim figure in the dust put up both hands and walked several paces away from the truck. I shouted for him to stop and turn around facing away from me. He complied. I radioed the final location of the stop and said I had one held at gunpoint.

Nearly a minute later, Jeff pulled up, accompanied by Colfax Police, another patrol unit from my agency, and the California Highway patrol. I had the suspect back up toward me and put his knees on the ground. Jeff walked forward to do the hands-on arrest and the suspect began to bring his off-hand down toward his body. I flanked out around the suspect so I could continue to cover him with my sidearm in case he was going for a weapon. Not to worry. This guy had been through this before a time or two and was just trying to get his hand down and in back of him where he knew it was going to end up anyway. Cooperative soul.

I looked at the suspect's face and got a shock..."Brad, is that you?" I had gone to high school with this guy. He looked up, "Hi Rocky." I said to the cops around me, "Gentlemen, meet Brad."

Jeff leaned forward and said hello, then each of the cops on the scene, five others in all, came up and said hello to Brad. Since the formal introductions had been made, Brad was spirited off to sit in the back seat position of honor in the patrol car.

I went up to the pickup carefully and cleared it in case there were other guests for our local lock-up. Empty. Jeff was pissed. He had tracked behind me during the pursuit, but where people had gotten out of the way for me, he had every soul on the road take their sweet time getting over and out of the way. He knew when this ended, I would need back-up fast, and was near blind with frustration by the time he made it to my stop.

When all was said and done, I recovered a Levi jacket with burn holes, a Sony Walkman with headphones, and plenty of stolen property from the pick-up.

I called Department of Justice and was able to collect blood samples for analysis from inside the house. I got identification from neighbors and later from the victims about the stolen property. I took another day and more on the investigation and evidence. I also prepared a Search Warrant for a forcible blood draw from the suspect if it became necessary. When I went into court for the preliminary hearing, the District Attorney and I laid all our cards face up on defense counsel's table. It was an impressive case with all the ducks in a row.

I have to give Brad a little credit here. As he was lead out of the courtroom to the holding cell, he cordially said hello, and I answered in the same way. He knew he was caught, but there was none of the common garbage. He didn't hold a grudge, or threaten me or my family. That shows me a little bit. In my opinion, it's only the cheap crooks or animals who will threaten to hurt someone's family.

Brad knew he was caught, and when he gets out, if he decides to try again, we'll meet on even footing. I hope it doesn't happen. I'm a cop, he is who he is, but he does have one touch of ethics. Brad pled guilty before trial, sentence - six years.

There may come a time when the lion and the lamb will lie down together, but I am still betting on the lion.

Henry Wheeler Shaw
1818-1885

COME GET YOUR DAMN DOG!

A police dog is a bundle of instinct and training. There are two ways a trainer can get a dog and have him certified for patrol work. Dogs can be purchased as puppies and painstakingly trained for basic obedience, advanced obedience, then trained for "protection." This is a long, expensive, and time consuming project. If a handler does not have the time, or money, he can get a dog which has already been trained.

Dogs have frequently given their lives for their handlers and they make police work much safer both for police and the public. Believe it or not, it's often safer for the suspect too. Were it not for the presence of a dog, lethal force might have to be used more often.

Patrol dogs are frequently trained for tracking as well as "protection." Yet the dog's ultimate goal is the protection of the human handler. The handler must be the acknowledged master or superior of the dog. It is a partnership, but the handler must rule. Sometimes it doesn't always go that way...

It was time for Jerry's old dog, Grizzley, to retire. He was having trouble getting through the obstacle course the dogs are required to run for certification on the street. Grizz needed his "time in the sun" on the family porch, not to be banging around in the back of a patrol car. Much as Grizz loved to work, and hated being left home when Jerry put on his uniform, it was time to start looking for a replacement.

Schutzen "trials dogs" are trained nearly identically to police dogs, but are not used for police work. They go through their years competing against other dogs for prizes, and protecting their masters and families, not nailing criminals. This is a worthwhile living for a dog and "trials dogs" are working dogs.

Jerry saw an ad for a trials dog in Washington state and made a call. The price was right, and Jerry saw a very impressive video of the dog at work. Turns out the dog was a little too strong and willful for the owner. This happens occasionally. The dog just needed a stronger hand, and since Jerry had been training dogs for many years he figured this would be tough, but do-able.

Jerry sent a check for the dog. "Yago" was scheduled to fly into Sacramento Airport on a specific day. Jerry had some business to attend to which could not be ignored on Yago's arrival date. He called the airport and told them he would be a little late. Jerry went blissfully about his business. After all, how much trouble could a dog be? Yago was going to arrive in a crate and no one would take him out. He'd be taken to the freight terminal and left there for pickup...so no problem.

Jerry finished his business and headed for Sacramento. His cellular phone rang and his wife asked him where he was. Jerry said he was enroute to the airport and should be there in 30 minutes. With some merriment, his wife said the airline had called three times in the last 30 minutes asking when Jerry would be arriving *to get this damn dog!*

Jerry hung up the phone and called the terminal. A harried shipping clerk answered. Jerry heard the unmistakable growling and barking of an enraged German Shepherd in the background and told the clerk he would be there in 30 minutes. The clerk replied, obviously relieved, "Please hurry!"

Jerry pulled into the terminal area and over to the shipping building. The barks, growls, and snarls were audible from outside the front door. When he went inside, Jerry saw the commotion emanated from a ring of shipping crates placed around the angry dog. Yago couldn't see, and that had not made him any happier.

It sounded like Yago was doing his best to claw and chew his way out of the fiberglass shipping crate. Jerry walked up to the worried counter clerk. In his meekest, most mild-mannered tone of voice, Jerry asked the clerk, "Is my dog Fluffy here?" The clerk's mouth dropped open and the verbal explosion came next, "Is that what you call that dog? Get him out of here, mister!"

In due time, and with unnecessary caution on the shipping people's part, Yago came to rest in Jerry's Blazer and they started the drive toward Yago's new digs. Jerry talked in a calm, low voice to the dog while Yago kept up his litany of anger for the b.s. he'd gone through that day. It was clear that flying was not his favorite pastime and being in the car with this strange man was also not his idea of fun. He let it be known in no uncertain terms that he blamed Jerry.

Ah, home at last. Jerry looked at the snarling, snapping dog in the cage and knew he was going to need help with this one. He called Dave, another very experienced dog handler, to come over. It was necessary to let the dog out inside a room of the house which was specially prepared for him so he could have the feeling of getting used to the house and new people smells. The leash was snaked through and the dog was put on the lead without bloodshed, then released into the room. Jerry barely got out in time.

Later, when the dog had calmed down in the home setting, Jerry and Dave made a cautious approach into the room. Yago was cautious, but had dropped the annoying tendency to want to imitate "Cujo" for the minute. Jerry identified himself to the dog, let the animal get used to him and picked up the lead. Dave and Jerry made their slow, cautious way toward the kennel outside the house.

On the way to the kennel, the setting sun lured both men and Yago down to a small pond on the property. The men stood with the dog watching the sun set for a minute or two, talking amicably. Yago was interested in his new setting, and wasn't being overtly aggressive. The dog wandered for a moment and pulled at the lead. From instinct, Jerry commanded him in German then gave a correction with a sharp tug on the lead. MISTAKE! Yago did *not* acknowledge this stranger had any right to correct him, and was immediately red-line pissed! He reared up on his hind legs and placed both front feet on Jerry's chest, baring leering fangs into Jerry's face. Yago jumped down and repeated the performance for Dave. Both men knew these dogs would not bite unless the target moved. They stood frozen like stone. Yago's frustration was still not vented. He bounced down off Dave's chest and thrust his bared muzzle up under Jerry's legs, directly into his groin! Growling and snarling for all he was worth, it was as if Yago was telling Jerry, "I own you pal! If you mess with me you *will* regret it!" Jerry could only look upward, not move, and plead, "Please God, don't let him bite me there!" Dave spoke softly out of the corner of his mouth..."I'm going to run and leave you here! That dog's going to eat you!" Jerry replied, "This dog's on a 50 foot lead and I'll let him go!" They tried to keep from laughing which would have caused them both to be bitten. Eventually, eternity passed, and Yago simmered down. The two shaken men took the dog to the kennel and succeeded in enclosing him safely in the compound.

After all was said and done, Yago stayed true to his training and did not bite Jerry. If you don't want to be bitten by a police dog, the solution is simple, *don't move.* Oh...they hate guns, gunfire, clubs, and knives. If you have anything in your hands, drop it before the dog gets there. If you try to shoot one, remember, dogs never quit and are very tough. The dog is going to be a tough target, moving fast, and even if you hit him, he's going to chew on you for awhile anyway.

It was a long row to hoe, with lots of work for both handler and dog, but Yago and Jerry are a team now. They are in fact one of the premier handler/dog teams in the area.

For all the talk about knowledge
being such a wonderful thing,
instinct is worth forty of it for real unerringness.

Mark Twain

HOT AND COLD

This is not a book about dogs, but canines are integral to police work. They protect their masters, tackle felons, search and find lost children, conduct area searches, sniff out flammable substances at arson scenes, and find articles of evidence spread across far-flung crime scenes. Dogs also locate drugs and bombs which are most definitely not lost, thereby again serving their masters and the public.

Police dogs are frequently taken into schools and preschools. They are actually safer to be around than other dogs. Police dogs are tested and trained. They will bite only when the handler is attacked, or on command from the handler. They do not bite out of fear or anger. When taken into a school, these dogs pant and wag their tails like any other dog. The kids love them and pet them just the same as any other dog. The dogs in my jurisdiction at least, live in a home setting with the family of the handler. They need the opportunity to be homebodies, socialize, play, rest, and wind down at least as much as the handler.

Quite a few years ago I was involved in a training course where my partner and I made a felony stop on a suspect vehicle. The suspect got out with his dog, a beautiful German Shepherd. The suspect began pacing back and forth and the Shepherd was obviously keyed in, ready to attack should the owner let him loose. I stood behind my car door with a drawn firearm and told the dog owner to put the dog back in the car. The owner refused saying he needed him for protection.

I tried to negotiate with the dog owner. I wasn't successful. The owner began walking the dog closer and I warned him I would shoot the dog if necessary. The owner protested and walked the dog closer yet. I fired. The training blanks went off like firecrackers, and the dog exploded in fury.

The Shepherd bounded into the air and landed barking and snarling. The suspect/role player called the dog off and put him down on the ground. I was then told to put down my blank gun. The gun was absolutely useless against the dog, and I threw it onto the front seat of my car. The handler released the dog which made a charge right at me, jumped up onto my chest and knocked me back into the car. I found my face thoroughly licked by this dog who had acted like he thought I would make good dog kibble15 seconds earlier.

That was an interesting experience with dogs, and illustrates how highly trained and discretionary they are. I also had a similar experience in the field...

I had gone to this house on one prior occasion. I was trying to find and arrest a 19 year old car thief who had arrest warrants. I was sure he was there, but his family was hiding him at the house. I asked Danny and his Rotweiler partner, Luther, to come along with me on this visit. I went around the house to the right side and Danny and Luther went around to the left toward a garage.

From the detached garage, the suspect looked out the door and saw Danny's patrol unit. Having a touch of rabbit blood in him, our suspect did his best to get out of the garage and into the brush post-haste. Danny, knowing this was a felony suspect, verbally warned the suspect to stop and then sent his canine buddy, Luther. Danny continued to warn the suspect to stop and not move and he would not be bitten.

A little description of Luther is in order here. He is a prime Rotweiler, tipping the scales over 140 pounds, and very quick and agile for his size. The suspect looked back and saw black, tan, and TEETH gaining ground. A look toward the brush convinced the man he couldn't make it to cover before Luther made it to him. The suspect stopped and Danny called off Luther. Luther slowed but did not return immediately. He walked around the suspect in a complete circle, glaring, and growling before returning to sit at Danny's feet. Danny termed it "counting coup." Luther just let the suspect know, "You're lucky you stopped buddy. I would've caught ya!"

I approached and handcuffed the suspect. When I searched the suspect's legs during the search for weapons, I found he was wearing fairly tight jeans. I also saw his pants cuff was trembling...looked like about 450 oscillations per minute. All the suspect's nerves were obviously firing. I think we could have hooked him up to a copper line and powered a good-sized city.

No force used, suspect enroute to jail, another canine-use success story.

Be not afraid of sudden fear.
Proverbs 3:25

A WALK THROUGH HELL

These guys were gold miners, and arrived at the Forestry Station in Colfax with a unique story to tell. At about 5:00 that afternoon they had returned to camp to find Eddie B. in their tent stealing their food and what gold they had been able to extract from the canyon. This was July 1985, but claim-jumping and thieves were as big a problem now as they were in 1849. The two miners shouted across the gully confronting Eddie, and he came out shooting, unloading six rounds from a revolver. Showing discretion, as they were both unarmed, the miners fled.

Eddie then burned out their camp, starting a forest fire on the west wall of the American River Canyon. As the two miners fled, they frequently stopped and hid, at one time for several hours, fearing Eddie was hunting them. It was now after 11:00 p.m. on a warm summer night.

My partner, George, was a long time cop, and the boss in our partnership. He had recently moved from the Los Angeles area and had only been working the Sierra Nevada Foothills for a couple of years. He listened to the miners' story, and with eyes glittering, he announced," We're going into the canyon after Eddie. We've got enough to arrest him for Assault with a Deadly Weapon."

I questioned the miners a little more closely and when I found out their camp was located down Stevens Trail at the bottom of the American River Canyon, I wanted to stop the idea of going into the canyon. "George, we can't do this. That canyon kills people every year. Forestry is fighting the fire on the Lover's Leap side, and in some places that trail is only three feet wide or less. You're perched over 1,200 feet of drop. Don't do this!"

George insisted, "I'm going. This is adventure!" I let myself be persuaded, but said, "Alright, you won't go alone, but this isn't adventure, it's freaking stupid." We geared up with some water and a shotgun and started into the canyon just after midnight. The walk down was worse than I remembered from years ago walking it in daylight. My Streamlight flash-light shined off yawning side canyons, some of which were overhangs, and I waited for the irresistible force of gravity to take hold.

We made it past the top and began a more easy descent down the canyon side toward Green Valley. The forest fire was raging and lit our way without need for flashlights. Then we reached what I thought was the end of our night trek. The line of fire was advancing toward us down the canyon wall. To me it looked like we should be beating feet back up the path.

The two California Division of Forestry Investigators with us went into a huddle and decided we should take a look at this side of the fire, and if it was impassable, take a branching trail down to the river level and walk along the river to get around the fire. If not impassable, we'd walk through the fire!

I admit, I was silly enough to let myself be talked into this in the first place, so now I'm committed. Cute! The lead Forestry man said, "Listen, I know this part of the trail and it's straight. I think we can walk through this. Here's what you do. Cover your head, hyper-ventilate, hold your breath and close your eyes. Concentrate on walking straight ahead. If I shout 'No' turn 180 degrees and walk back out. If I shout 'Yes' I'm out of it, just keep walking."

RIGHT!!! I looked at the forest fire burning briskly through the dry grass and brush alongside the trail. The flames met 40 feet overhead and formed an arch over the trail. The noise was deafening and the bang and rush of timber exploding into flame up the canyon made me wonder if Dante hadn't been near here in his dope dreams.

We all started hyper-ventilating and looked at each other grimly. One Forestry ranger, then George disappeared into the fire. The other Forestry man would be behind me. Okay let's take a walk. I placed one foot in front of the other, leaving the prescribed five yards between me and George, then plunged into a slice of hell.

I found that I was completely disoriented immediately, which I had expected. I held my breath and plodded ahead for a couple of hours before I heard the shouted, "YES" ahead of me. As if I could have turned around and made it back now! The rush of air on the far side of the fire was blessedly cool and the smell of charcoal rather than hot swirling smoke, was a great relief.

After checking the miner's camp, we checked several other camp sites hoping Eddie was around. We had already walked three miles getting in here and we walked another mile or two along the broken river bed looking over the camps. During a rest break, I entertained myself by watching the Ponderosa and Digger pines rooted on the canyon walls explode into flames.

Up and at 'em. One more camp site to check. We made a silent approach to the site and found nothing. About 4:00 a.m., I made a mistake. I was stepping over a knife edge rock and the heel of my left boot caught on the top. I leaned on the foot trying to maintain my balance and unlucky for me, the heel let go just as I put my weight on it. My left foot rocketed down into the football sized quartz rocks on the far side of the boulder. Shit fire and damnation! I took the boot off and looked at the foot. Probably something broken from the way it felt, but nothing to do about it now. I put the boot back on and tested some weight. It hurt, but it held.

The night was about 500 years too long, but finally the eastern sky began to lighten. It would take until sometime mid-morning for the sun to show itself above the canyon walls. Long before that, I wanted to be out of there.

The small shambling man walking along the canyon trail looked out of place, but matched the description of our suspect. Hey, Eddie! The man looked around for the source of the voice and spotted my partner. Eddie admitted who he was, but denied being involved in anything. When we told him about his rights he changed his story around to where he was the victim.

A conference decided that Eddie should be handcuffed in front since, if a helicopter was unavailable, we would have to hoof it back out of the canyon. Not my favorite thought with this gimp foot.

Eddie talked about himself as we waited for the helicopter. He'd begun his criminal career in New York at the age of thirteen where he'd been jailed for a long time for murder. Not that he'd done it, mind you, but that was what the cops and courts thought.

Suddenly, Eddie stripped off his shorts and stood naked atop a boulder. "As God is my witness, I stand naked before him and proclaim my innocence." I told Eddie to put his clothes back on, there was nobody here shocked by that cheap shit. Eddie looked at me reclining on a rock, cradling a shotgun, then at George sitting atop a boulder. He pointed at George and said, "You...you're bad in your own way...but that guy there is a blue-eyed killer," while swinging his finger to point at me. I couldn't help it, I started to laugh. This comical, naked, wrinkled 56 year old man, an incarcerated murderer at 13 years old, now under arrest for Arson and Assault with a

Deadly Weapon, was calling me a killer? The unreality of the accusation was funny as hell.

The helicopter arrived and the co-pilot unloaded to allow room for the prisoner and myself. George was worried about my ability to get out of the canyon on my bum foot. I made it clear to Eddie that if he goofed around in the chopper during the flight, I would hold him down and use nerve holds. I promised he wouldn't enjoy the experience.

The foot was broken and I spent six weeks hobbling around in a cast. Eddie was free long before that. The "victims" never showed up for court.

If a thief is found breaking in,
and he is struck so that he dies,
there shall be no guilt for his bloodshed.

Exodus 22:2

MODERN DAY
FOSSIL FINGERPRINTS

I knew it was a SWAT call-out, but the powers that be hadn't figured it out yet. The suspect was armed with a .44 magnum and was drunk. He was arguing with a neighboring camper, and the camper called our Sheriff's Department. Deputy Mike arrived and talked with a daughter of the suspect and the complainant. The daughter returned to the campsite and shortly thereafter Mike heard the shot. People fleeing the camp said the daughter and father had been at the campsite and she had been shot in the face and killed.

Mike called for help and plenty of units responded. At about 12:30 in the morning, the powers that be decided they had better call the SWAT Team. We geared up and moved. I drove the unmarked Plymouth Sebring containing half the SWAT Team. We wound along the twisting mountain roads and arrived with no brakes. I used the emergency brake and what mushy pedal I had left to stop us just above the campground.

There was a patrol deputy on the north canyon wall where it was agreed I should set up as counter-sniper. The deputy's position provided a good overview of the campground as well as a height advantage. The range was about 110 yards, should it be necessary, but there was no better position available. I went across the bridge and dropped off onto the trail to climb to the patrol officer.

The trail climbed then suddenly dropped back to river level. I could hear the deputy 50 feet above me. I decided to go up the canyon wall rather than make a lot of noise backtracking and trying to locate another path. The wall of the canyon fell away steeply, and after I got off the path I tried to go over a boulder about as big as a three bedroom house. The surface of the rock didn't look too bad in the night light, but it got worse as I scaled the surface.

I found myself perched about 40 feet above the river with somewhat precarious hand and footholds. I looked down between my feet at black water flowing by in the headlights of cars lighting up the campsite on the other side. I would have been okay if I hadn't had a load bearing vest with all kinds of gear on it. When I tried to lift myself over the edge of the boulder, the vest caught. My foothold began to slip and my hands dug into the moss covering on the rock. I don't remember getting past the top, but I definitely remember hooking the bottom edge of my ballistic vest over the edge of the rock. Somehow I did it... though, to this day, my fingerprints remain in the raw rock on the canyonside.

We made an announcement on the public address system trying to negotiate the suspect out. No dice. The entry team and gas members composed a search plan, and all buildings, trailers and tents were gassed with CS teargas on the way into the campground. It was not a quiet time.

Chris, an entry team member, was prone in the campground and suddenly found his view blocked. There was a pair of feet and legs belonging to a captain in front of him. The captain was completely unaware of the team member's presence. A startling "excuse me" from Chris made the captain retreat from the area. Cap realized that if the SWAT member had been the suspect, he would have been cold meat and he needed time to clean out his underwear.

The area was almost secured, leaving only the suspect's tent. I could see the flashlights of the team when they switched them on and left them lying on the ground to light up the area. In the lights, I could see the form of a young woman lying with her head back over the edge of an unused fire pit. I could see no movement through the 3x9 telescopic sight, but a bullet wound in her right cheek was very obvious. Team members worked their way forward and confirmed that she was dead and cleared the tent.

Nothing to do now but wait for daylight. The team members talked and waited for dawn. About 5:30 a.m. we got a camera and took pictures of two Administrators sleeping in their cars. Who knew when these might come in handy?

At 5:45 a.m. we were bored. The only thing more dangerous than a bored SWAT team is a scared SWAT team. The Undersheriff was an okay guy and we knew he was on our side. We could trust him and he had a sense of humor.

One team member knew the Undersheriff would only respond to high-minded stimuli. "Yo, Chief! We found some hard-core porn books over here!" True to form, the Chief came on the run entering the camper where we had planted a Playboy from one of the other camps.

When the Chief was well inside, two team members reached inside the camper and began beating on the cloth cushions. The teargas boiled out of the cushions and filled the tiny camper in seconds. The Chief came out choking, nose running, and eyes streaming. He managed to croak, "You bastards are gonna pay for this!" When his eyes cleared, he looked around quickly and asked, "Where's the Sheriff? Can we gas him next?" "Naw...No sense of humor."

We searched for the suspect high and low all morning and into the afternoon, climbing several mountains in the process. We found the suspect's trail through the area I had been in the night before. He had climbed out before our arrival, and was behind us before we arrived.

Early that night, the suspect pulled up to a roadblock as a passenger in a car. He told the astounded deputy, "I think you're looking for me? I shot my daughter last night." Come to find out, the suspect sat on the mountain behind me all night long watching our every move.

In later questioning, he also said after he realized that his daughter was dead, he went back inside the tent, set his back against the ridgepole and prepared to kill anyone entering the campground. When he heard the assault team members moving, but couldn't see them, he got scared, slipped out of the tent and swam the river. He had sat on top of the mountain watching the teams' every move and was behind me and my partner all the time. Sometimes, it's just not our time to go.

At the door of life, by the gate of breath,
there are worse things waiting for men than death.

Algernon Charles Swinburne
1866

MOVE LEFT DAMMIT!

The call was a domestic violence, and officers Mitch and Bobby were responding to help. The suspect was named Billy and both officers were aware Billy was a convicted felon. They approached the front door of the house with caution, but it wasn't enough. The door whipped open and Billy was perched just inside with the cavernous mouth of a sawed-off shotgun pointed at Bobby's waist.

The only thing Billy said was, "Get off my property or I'll blow you in half!" Mitch scrambled and got behind a car, while Bobby remained frozen where he was. Mitch leveled his side-arm toward Billy then quickly pulled the weapon up and away. He couldn't get a sight picture. Bobby was standing in his way.

Negotiations began in earnest between Bobby, Billy, and Mitch. Bobby's trump card was Mitch hiding behind the car. "Look Billy, you haven't done anything yet that's not fixable. I'm not going to lie to you. You're going to have to go with us. But if you shoot me, you lose your kids and maybe your life. Put down the gun."

Billy screamed threats and the officers countered with calm reason. "You hurt me, and Mitch hurts you. Nobody benefits from that Billy. Give it up. There's cops from all over on their way, and you won't win. Especially if you pull that trigger."

Bobby was caught in the open, and all Mitch could think about was, "Move left Bobby dammit, move left! Give me a chance to get a clear line." Billy finally lowered the gun and gave it up.

Officers get caught with their drawers down on occasion. It's part of the nature of the beast.

In 1983, two officers responding to a fight call, walked to the door of a home in a very affluent neighborhood. It seems the local kids had been riding their bicycles and just being children. An older gentleman had taken exception to the noise and threatened them.

Again the door swung open before the officers knocked. The elderly gentleman was standing in the door dressed in slacks, shirt, comfortable shoes and a .38 snub-nosed revolver pointed at the mid-section of one deputy. The suspect threatened to blow a hole in the deputy unless they "got the fuck off his property."

The partner, who had taken a position on one side of the door, reached around the door jamb and placed the muzzle of his sidearm against the left temple of the suspect. A warning was given, even though it wasn't really necessary under the circumstances. The suspect lowered the gun and was taken into custody. It could have easily ended differently.

Talking may be necessary in some situations, in others action may be necessary. We all hope that we never find it necessary for our partner to be behind us, silently screaming..."Move left dammit, move left!"

Habit: noun - A shackle for the free.

Ambrose Bierce

SHOTS FIRED

The Special Enforcement Team is not called out on the average call, nor are their tactics average. They have slaved over training and tactics. They go up against the worst of the worst. They risk their lives. Not once in a while...but *every* time.

This particular call-out was nervous-making to the extreme. A parolee was back on drugs. It was known that he was an enemy of, and actively hunted by, a suspect whom he had burned on a drug deal. Our parolee had armed himself.

Pretty straightforward situation, right? Now throw in the kicker. There was at least one woman and a small baby in the home, along with others unknown. The plans were made, diversions planned, options discussed, and the team went out again. Our team has been formally in existence since 1980, and we have yet to lose a member nor have we lost a situation. That possibility looms around the corner, so our people are dedicated, and they train...HARD!

The house was surrounded, entry made, and diversion begun. The SWAT members screamed their identification as police officers throughout entry. This house was a hodge-podge like no building inspector had ever seen, and no house cleaner had been there for quite a while. The team members found themselves with more than they bargained for.

Jeff saw a woman come out of a bedroom on the west side of the house. The scantily clad woman took one look at the camouflage attired SET team members and fled into the bedroom with Jeff in hot pursuit. In SWAT teams the motto is, 'You catch 'em, you clean 'em." This means the officer who sees a suspect during a raid situation deals with that suspect with the appropriate level of force, *now*...no waiting, no hesitation. Jeff went after the woman and went through the west bedroom door just as all hell broke loose.

The parolee had awakened and was armed with a 16 gauge shotgun. He proceeded to fire two rounds through the west door of his bedroom and one more for good measure into the ceiling. Wood, drywall, dust and smoke filled the entryway by the front door of the house as the muffled shotgun blasts sounded from the bedroom.

One of the diversionary team members outside the house felt a pellet from the shotgun strike him on the right side of the forehead. He knelt in place and told his partner, "I think I'm hit!" He was evacuated by his partner and another member secured the door. Adapt and improvise.

Jeff was inside the west bedroom doing his best to get down as well as get the woman down. She, in turn, was struggling and screaming. A very common reaction but it wasn't until later Jeff realized she was screaming about her baby in a nearby crib. The child remained unhurt and Jeff succeeded in hand-cuffing and calming the incoherent woman.

It took some talking, but the suspect was finally convinced to surrender. The rounds the suspect fired had gone through the walls, and the round that hit the ceiling had penetrated the door outside. The nearly spent pellet which was a ricochet had hit the diversionary team member merely dimpling the skin on his forehead. No one in the house was hurt and no rounds were fired by police. A remarkable piece of restraint on behalf of all team members.

The parolee was taken into custody and returned to his former lodgings in state prison.

If you know the enemy and know yourself,
you need not fear the result of a hundred battles.

Sun Tzu
600 B.C.

NEGOTIATION TOOLS

Negotiation tools are many and varied. During the time I was on the Special Enforcement Team we used quite a few. In one call we scrambled to secure a scene in the Sierra Nevada Foothills outside the small town of Colfax. A convicted murderer who had escaped during a conjugal visit with his wife, had been found holed up in a trailer on the outskirts of town.

When Howard, a police officer, and his sergeant, John, arrived at the trailer, the suspect confronted them with a rifle at the door. The officers bailed off the front porch, looked at the open field around the trailer, and decided discretion was the better part of valor. They took refuge underneath the trailer. One of the officers injured his back in the bail-out and couldn't move quickly. A nasty situation.

There were many patrol officers under cover on the outer perimeter. Our team rolled up and moved to the inner perimeter. The outer perimeter was put on "defensive only" upon our arrival. The hostage negotiator was outside with a bullhorn. It was confirmed there was no one else inside the trailer. We negotiated that the suspect would come out if we delivered food and drinks to the house.

This advisement went out… "The suspect is going to break a window. This is not a hostile act! Team members are instructed to hold their fire unless fired upon." The suspect stood up and broke out the window of the trailer. He stood up directly in the cross-hairs of my scoped rifle and I saw he had an M-1 carbine with a 30 round clip. There was no doubt about the firepower he had at his disposal. I told the tactical team leader what I saw, and the delivery of the food was made through the broken window.

The suspect failed to respond to any other calls or attempts at negotiation. I moved to a position on higher ground putting most of the east side of the trailer under observation. The hostage negotiator was below me by about 40 yards, using a flimsy barn as a bit of concealment. He would have little protection if the suspect cut loose with that rifle.

The freeway noises continued for another 20 minutes or so as the hostage negotiator called intermittently without results. Then, at our request, the California Highway Patrol shut down the freeway. The silence was eerie. The hostage negotiator then told the suspect, "Listen, we are going to shoot out one of the street lights. DON'T FIRE ON OUR OFFICERS. If you fire, you will be fired upon." The instruction was repeated several times with no response from the suspect. Deputies were told to take good cover and the streetlight was shot out. Still no response from the suspect.

The tactical team leader let the situation go on for quite awhile. The officers had been evacuated from under the trailer, but we were getting nowhere with the suspect. The hostage negotiator came back on the bullhorn and told the suspect that time was up, reminding him he had agreed to come out if we provided food and drink, which had been done. He explained it was out of his hands now, and he was being told by others what was going to happen. This was true. The tactical team leader had taken control.

My radio mike crackled in my ear and the tac leader said there would be more gunfire...a burst of three rounds which was NOT hostile fire. The stillness was then shattered by the automatic weapon fire which was directed into the air and into the canyon by the tac leader.

Quick results! The suspect began shouting at the hostage negotiator. The negotiator began talking with him again and 10 minutes later the suspect exited the house with his hands raised in the air. The suspect walked to the front of the trailer and knelt down upon demand.

When the hostage negotiator walked near him, the suspect grabbed him around the knees and hugged him. Our primitive "negotiation tools" had worked well. The suspect went back to jail, then back to prison where he belonged.

The advocacy of "prisoners rights" seems to be useless to me. These people are many times convicted felons for the most part. They are responsible for the crimes for which they were caught, as well as those that were plea bargained away. In some instances they are also responsible for crimes which were never reported (sex crimes are frequently not reported due to victim shame or inability to face the trauma of a trial) as well as those the felon committed which were never detected.

Incarcerated felons have proven they cannot and will not concede to their victims "right to life, liberty, or pursuit of happiness." How are prisoners entitled to stereos, TV's, VCR's, microwave ovens, movies, free medical and dental care at our expense, a high calorie diet along with weight machines and exercise yards? This only allows them to come out "with arms built by prison," in better physical condition, stronger than ever and, therefore, more dangerous.

If all that wasn't enough, these convicted felons have "conjugal visits?" Our tax money allows them a place to meet and have sex with their wives. In my opinion, these convicted felons have proven that their heredity is NOT desirable in the general gene pool. Society also has to support most of the offspring from these conjugal visits through the welfare system. Furthermore, what did they do to deserve the pleasure of conjugal visits?

PRISONS WERE NEVER SUPPOSED TO BE A PLEASANT PLACE! Prisoners rights laws seem to be useless, designed only to allow attorneys to siphon off public funds, and give convicted felons the life, liberty and happiness they were only too ready to deny their victims.

Useless laws weaken the necessary laws.

Charles De Secondat-Baron
1748

IN THE CROSSHAIRS

I was on top of a ridge above the cabin. The position sloped downhill radically, and about 75 yards away, I could see the clapboard cabin's front door. I was there as part of my department's SWAT Team, and one of three elements. The first element was to take the cabin itself; the second element, would take a small camp in the woods 50 yards from the cabin; and I was element three, the countersniper.

I was responsible for overall team security. If anyone became unfriendly down there, it was my job to see they didn't hurt one of my teammates. It was also my job to direct lethal force to a specific point upon orders from my SWAT commander. That last one didn't worry me too badly. If I received the order to use lethal force, I would know why, and have time to set up the shot. The surprise situation was the one I disliked, and watched for most carefully.

"In the cabin, this is the Sheriff's Department. Come out one at a time with your hands empty and on top of your head. In the cabin, this is the Sheriff's Department." The bullhorn helped bounce the commands back and forth over the canyon walls. I heard voices down at the cabin and I zeroed in on the front door. My rifle was nested solidly and the crosshairs rested on the top of the front door frame. The cabin was cantilevered out from the road over the canyon wall, so there was no back door to the house unless they had a trap door and ladder or rope in the cabin floor.

After some normal voice negotiations which I couldn't hear clearly, the front door opened and the major suspect, Gary, walked to the door. He was wearing blue jeans and no shirt, and despite being told to have his hands empty, he had a freshly lit cigarette clamped in his fingers. He was directed to the ground away from the cabin and told to lie on his belly.

Another suspect dressed much like the first appeared in the doorway and complied with directions, lying face down on the ground in front of the cabin door. The next male suspect appeared wrapped in a blanket, Indian fashion. I watched him carefully with the scope dialed down for widest field of view possible.

The suspect was told to drop the blanket, which he did, standing there stark naked. He was told to turn slowly, which he did, ordered to move away from the blanket and lie on the ground. It was a brisk morning. His stupidity was not using the time between the call and the exit of the other two suspects to get dressed...this would cause him some goose-flesh and discomfort.

More people came out of the cabin and were proned out. Women and children were also present. The women were cleared of weapons and were allowed to sit with the children under the guard of a team member.

I looked down on the crowded scene. The main suspect, Gary, had finished his cigarette and now stubbed it out. I watched the five men lying within the field of view of my scope and kept the crosshairs on the ground between the people. Gary slowly looked around and raised up slightly. He moved his hand under his body and towards his belt line. I clicked the safety off the rifle, shifted the crosshairs of the scope onto the top of his head and radioed in, "Somebody better tell that guy to get his hand out from under him."

"You, on the ground, freeze! Don't move. Slowly bring your empty hand out from under you. The hand had better be empty!" Gary complied with our instructions and I again moved the crosshairs of the scope over to neutral ground between the suspects. The suspects were ordered to their feet and moved to a pair of SWAT team members for handcuffing.

The second SWAT element made their announcement to the camp. The call was put out repeatedly, but no amount of challenge made anyone in the tent acknowledge or comply with their directions. A rumpled sleeping bag could be seen...we waited and wondered. Finally, the SWAT leader came over the radio and ordered the use of CS gas to empty the tent. The CS gas was contained in plastic slugs called "ferret rounds" fired by a 12 gauge shotgun. The report of the shotgun bounced back and forth over the area. No response from the tent. The second round was put in a little too close. A puff of white down erupting from the foot of a sleeping bag was clearly visible to the SWAT members. The tent was cleared and no one was there. The situation was secured and I was told to come down out of my eagle's nest.

It took me quite a while to work my way down to the scene, but when I broke out of the brush with my scoped rifle, the suspect's eyes were round. One team member stepped over to

Gary, "You don't know how close you came. Reaching back under your body was slightly stupid." Gary mumbled a half-hearted epithet at the cop, but his eyes never left mine.

Six stolen cars were recovered from the area near the cabin, as well as many poached deer hides, and other miscellaneous stolen property. According to neighbors who lived in the area, Gary and his crew had a nasty habit of kicking in cabin doors and taking whatever they wanted. If that included a woman in the house, Gary's guns and a sound pistol whipping would convince them not to fight.

Everyone in the area was afraid to testify against the gang. They were released on bail within a couple of days. Counting gang members who were not there that morning, there were more of them than there were SWAT members. This would not be our last encounter with this crew. Just the first in a series.

The Lacedemonians are not wont to ask
how many the enemy are,
but where they are.

Agis
5th Century B.C.

A PARTICLE OF EVIDENCE

The local police officer looked at me and said, "I've got a missing person report that is really a weird one." The missing person, a 19 year old woman, had been in the Colfax area with friends at a party the night before. She left to take a Greyhound bus back home, 30 miles away, and never arrived. I didn't think much about the report until later that afternoon.

The radio blared out, "Meet the California Highway Patrol officer near Weimar Crossroads for found property." I went, wondering what kind of strange item had been found now. When I arrived, I got a real bad feeling about this one. The CHP officer met me and said, "We've either got a rape, a homicide, or both." Looking at the articles along the highway, I knew he was right. Lacy underwear, a skirt, and other clothing were on the ground alongside a blanket. I used my baton to turn a corner of the blanket and exposed a large blood stain. I called for detectives. The lead homicide investigator came on the radio coder, and told me to photograph and carefully collect the items for evidence.

I took photographs, walked the area immediately around the property, then carefully collected and folded the items, placing them atop my car for another photo. I then placed the items separately atop the patrol car trunk box for transport to Auburn, where I put them direcly into the hands of the lead homicide detective.

Later that afternoon, my Sheriff's Department began assisting Colfax Police with their investigation of the missing person. The next morning, the victim's purse and additional articles were found along the railroad right-of-way. Friends of the missing person were interviewed thoroughly over the next few days and a search and rescue team made a complete search of the area where the clothing and purse were found.

During the search and rescue, the California Highway Patrol Helicopter was called in to assist and was doing low-level operations in the surrounding area. David, one of the "friends" of the missing person was driving in the area during the search.

He turned a corner while looking up at the helicopter and hit a parked California Highway Patrol car. According to David, he was just wondering how the search was going.

Two months later, the body of a 15 year old girl was found 20 miles away. She had been hitch-hiking in the area, had called her parents from a pay phone telling them she was with "Dave" and would be home in an hour or so. She never made it. The body was badly decomposed and had been there for some time.

Detectives continued the investigation and checked David's car. They took fiber and particle samples from the car's interior upholstery. The results of the fiber and particle samples were sent to the California Department of Justice for analysis. The missing person's clothing had already been submitted. The head homicide investigator's name was Jeff, and I don't think I've ever met a smarter man. Jeff got the results from the Department of Justice which tied the clothing I recovered to David's car. Our missing person had been there. David lied and his lies would trip him up.

David had moved to Carson City, Nevada where he was working construction. Jeff obtained an arrest warrant for David for homicide. David was arrested without problem and brought back to California. During the ride down the Sierra Nevada Mountains, David confessed to our missing person's murder, a murder found two months later along Interstate 80 in Loomis, and another murder along the Sacramento River Levee. All victims were female, ranging in age from 15 to mid-30's. During the trip, they stopped where David had hit the CHP car and David showed them where the missing person's body was located.

During the time between arrest and trial, I received a report of a woman standing in an upstairs window nude, exposing herself to passing high school students. When I arrived, I found it was David's mother who was supposed to be the "suspect." I looked at the full-foliage trees, the road, exit to and from the high school, and decided it was patently impossible for anyone to see a person standing in the upper floor window. I wondered which member of David's defense team had called in the complaint. Nah! My suspicious mind!

David went to trial. I thought his defense was a novel one. According to his lawyers, he had been twisted by his "exhibitionist" mother who had exposed herself to him. He also said he did not rape the women he killed. He killed them first, *and only then had sex with them!* I didn't know how that was supposed to benefit him, but it was a dodge the defense tried.

The District Attorney brought me to testify about the collection of evidence. The defense tried to get me to testify that David's mother was an exhibitionist. I told them the reasons why I believed the report was bogus. They quickly dismissed me from the witness stand.

The verdict was read..."We find the defendant ... guilty on all counts." The penalty phase of the trial began and the jurors heard evidence about David they were not privy to before. Evidence that would have been "too prejudicial."

At an unrelated trial after David's conviction, I stood talking with the defense counsel who had defended David. He looked at me quizzically and said, "You know, I have to prepare for the very real eventuality that David will get the death penalty." I told him I didn't see a problem with David being sentenced to death. The attorney looked at me with an open sneer. "I suppose you're for the death penalty." I told him that was a really silly question to ask someone who carries a gun for a living. The defense attorney looked at me and tried to play his trump card. "I supposed you'd pull the switch." I smiled and put my right hand out, slapping the palm with my off-hand and playing the higher card, replied, "Put that switch right there." The defense attorney left in a huff.

I see no conflict here. I am sworn to the preservation of public safety. If a court sentences David to death, they have found he is the ultimate danger to society. Were I to be the one to pull the switch on the gas chamber, I would not be thinking about David. I would be thinking about the stolen lives of Kerrie, Lancie Ann, and an unnamed woman in Sacramento. Plus two more in Florida which we can't prove, but for which the modus operandi was similar, and David was in the area at the time of occurrence.

I don't believe in coincidence...five times over.

I could pull that switch.

For a deadly blow,
Let him pay with a deadly blow.
It is for him who has done a deed to suffer.

Aeschylus
456 B.C.

241

THE GREAT BANANA CAPER

It was not spring yet and there was still a chill in the air. At night in my jurisdiction, it gets downright cold. As I went by the intersection of Rippey Road and Taylor Road, I saw an elderly Oriental lady squatting on the side of the road talking into her coat sleeve. Okay...that's the first time I've seen that today.

Thirty minutes later, I got a report of an elderly Oriental woman cursing at pedestrians, including children. I went back to the intersection and found the woman still holding down her spot alongside the roadway. I approached the woman who remained in her squat position. She rendered her Social Security card while hardly moving and still talking quietly into her coat sleeve. She cussed me out a little when I didn't immediately understand her verbal rendition of her date of birth. I wrote the date on the back of the Social Security card. No warrants, local, state, or national.

I asked her if she had any money. When she didn't answer, I asked if she understood English. She erupted with some accented English, indicating she clearly knew the first words everyone learns in a new language. Of the words she knew, most began with "mother" followed by a word generally used as an action verb.

The woman was probably in her 70's and emaciated. It was cold enough at night that she could easily freeze to death. She had two paper grocery sacks with a handful of bananas in each one. I asked dispatch if there was a named victim on this complaint. The complainant wanted to remain anonymous and would not sign a complaint. Well, nothing I could do. No victim, no crime.

Other units in the area said she had been around for about three days. She had been transported to Mental Health once and that illustrious agency decided she didn't need mental health evaluation or housing. She was obviously destitute and they decided that talking into her coat sleeve and hallucinating wasn't good enough to qualify. From bitter experience, I

243

knew if she had medical insurance to cover her costs, it would have been an entirely different matter.

I asked her to move from the intersection. She picked up her bags and began shuffling slowly down the road. Well, nothing more to do here. I left for another 20 minutes and made another round through my patrol area. When I went past the old lady again, I saw she had moved all of 200 yards and was now squatting next to a church parking lot across from a high school. No improvement there.

As I went by, I saw a bunch of bananas lying on the shoulder of the road about 50 feet from the old lady. I slowed and opened my driver's door scooping up the bananas on the move. I stopped about 20 feet from the lady and got out of my car. This woman looked horrible. I've seen pictures of survivors of Auschwitz and Dachau. I suppose they looked somewhat like this in person. The woman was so bad off if she didn't get some kind of help, we were going to be taking a coroner's case on her soon. I walked up and set the bunch of bananas in the first open paper sack near her.

The woman exploded into motion and speech. "You mudha fucka! You sonabitch! You don't fuck wi' me! I kill you!" She reached for the bag, grabbed the handful of bananas and threw them at my head. Young reflexes took over and my upper body swiveled to take my head out of the path of the airborne yellow projectiles.

I looked at the old lady who was still spouting gutter verbiage. I would bet that if left on her own, the coroner's case was no more than two to three weeks away. Well, let's do something about this! I grabbed the old woman's arm as it swept down in follow-through from the pitch. I thought she was possibly the Dennis Eckersly of the Orient. A full wind-up, fast pitch, and a complete follow-through. I got her hand-cuffed and put her kicking, cussing, and struggling 70 pound figure in the car. I picked up her bags of clothing and bananas and put them in the trunk.

A woman came out of the church nearby and screamed at me, asking what I was doing. I told her that the old lady was under arrest. The woman demanded that I release the old lady. Ms. Christian said I could not arrest her because she had just brought some food for my prisoner. I told her I could not stay to argue, the old lady was going to jail for assault on an officer. I made a thorough report and went into detail on the Oriental woman's condition. I didn't know it at the time, but I had just stepped into a hornets nest.

I got a call from a local judge about the lady and I answered his questions. Seems the judge had our Oriental lady in court previously and wanted to adjudicate her incompetent. Mental Health fought him, citing expenses to the county, denying any affliction of mental problems, then denying jurisdiction; in short, refusing the judge's order. The judge wanted to toss the Director of Mental Health into jail for contempt of court so bad his teeth hurt. At that time, there wasn't any criteria in the case that clearly said the old lady was a danger to herself or others. Talking into your coat sleeve wasn't enough.

Then along came my case. Judge Hizzoner promised that he was going to rearrange the Mental Health agencies attitude or someone from that agency was risking joining her in her cell. The judge ended his call by thanking and congratulating me for a "creative solution" (his words) to the problem.

Ms. Christian complained loud and long to my department and wrote a scathing letter to the editor of the local newspaper. She said I had acted rudely and was insensitive to the homeless. The editor of the newspaper got hold of my report and put a post script on Ms. Christian's letter. The editor pointed out Ms. Christian was only going to feed the Oriental lady *one* meal. At the time, our lady had been in jail for several days receiving medical care, *three* meals a day, sleeping on a soft bed, in a place where she was in no danger of freezing to death.

Mental Health suddenly decided that they wished to re-evaluate the case and were full of helpful and creative solutions. Judge Hizzonner at work, I presume. In all fairness, Mental Health has improved greatly in the past few years.

My co-workers were merciless. The Great Banana Caper was a daily serenade for the next few weeks. I'd find bananas in the damndest places! Nice guys.

The world breaks everyone and afterward many are
strong at the broken places.
But those that it will not break, it kills.
It kills the very good, and the very gentle,
and the very brave impartially.
If you are none of those,
you can be sure that it will kill you too;
but there will be no special hurry.

Ernest Hemingway

BODYSITTING

The three young men were devastated. There *had* been four of them. They had been playing around on the Foresthill Bridge, a 740 foot tall span over the American River, by the light of a full moon night. One young man had been trying to reach the girders in the center of the bridge. He thought he might make it if he hung down off the inside railing and dropped onto the girders which were about two feet wide and 20 feet below him. The 19 year old hung down on the inside railing, then let go. His friends heard him hit the girder, then heard nothing for a long time. Finally, they heard a distant splash.

The next morning when myself and another dive team member were recovering the young man's body, I was standing under the middle of the bridge in freezing water up to my waist waiting for my partner to come back with some equipment. When I looked up I saw all these folks leaning over the outside rail of the bridge looking at us under the *inside* of the bridge. My partner looked up and remarked that if anyone fell, we should be reasonably safe, but we would have extra work to do before we left.

I've recovered several bodies from below that bridge, one accidental, the rest suicides. All were badly used by the sudden stop at the end of the 740 foot acceleration.

I've gone on dive calls for drowned swimmers, boats that disintegrated on the water, coroner's cases of cars going too fast, sleepy drivers, drunk drivers and their victims, fires, plane crashes, electrocutions, industrial and farm accidents, homicides, you name it.

Recently I responded to a medical aid call for a fall victim. The location was in the American River Canyon and I knew the area to be very remote, rugged, and steep. Firefighters had already started in with a stokes litter to carry the victim out if possible. It wasn't possible. When California Highway Patrol Helicopter H-20 arrived, he reported it appeared that CPR was in progress on our victim. Shortly thereafter, the paramedic from the helicopter pronounced our victim deceased.

In talking with the hike leader, I found he was a member of a large activist environmental group. A small group had gone on a "wildflower" hike into the canyon. Did they have extra food? "No." Extra water? "No." Warm clothing? "No." Ropes? "No." With each consecutive "no" answer to my questions, I found myself becoming more angry. For being "naturalists and conservationists" these folks didn't know much about preparing to hike the area into which they were going.

The American River Canyon is mostly on-edge. At the bottom, the temperature can vary by forty or fifty degrees from afternoon to early morning. The canyon and its river can, and does, kill people every year. We have bears and mountain lions in our area, as well as bobcat, possum, fox, coyote, feral cats and dogs, and river rats that all prefer to be carnivorous whenever possible. My sergeant wanted to get someone in to guard the body against predators. After my partner and I were equipped to stay the night, we were helicoptered in to within 100 yards of the body.

The deceased, a 68 year old woman, had been walking atop a ridge about 75 feet above the river. The group had been walking for about 2-1/2 miles looking at the flowers. The trail was so primitive as to be non-existent and the hardest climb was ahead of them. The decedent was tired. She slipped and her feet hit a 70 degree pitch that was covered with moss. She never had a chance. She fell about 45 feet and slammed into a rock bench about 30 feet above the river.

My partner and I put a vinyl bag around the body to help contain the scent. We alternated staying up watching for large and small predators. I brought a shotgun with buckshot and rifled slugs. If bears might be expected and my partner and I were required to annoy them, I wanted something that would prevent annoyance from becoming aggression. You can't negotiate non-aggression treaties, mutual trade, and disarmament pacts with a black bear or cougar. I wanted something that would make Mister Predator lay down and be a rug.

We brought in food, water, warm clothing, blankets, and pads to insulate ourselves from the cold ground, in addition to lights, and materials to start a fire. Even so, it was a cold, rough night.

The next morning, dive team members brought down a river raft and equipment. We put the deceased and ourselves in the river raft and floated down the river through bad whitewater to the next bridge. We were carefully calculating and took only minimal risks, and only those risks we were equipped to meet.

There is a point here. Water, snow, high-speed winds, great heights, fire, and other natural conditions *do not recognize your "right" to life.* "Right to life" is a man-made and man-maintained concept which can be lost. "Nature" does not acknowledge man's right to life. Once gravity grabs you, it doesn't let go. Seas and rivers don't hear your pleading and stop their motion. Snow won't stop being cold, avalanches don't stop on request, and tornados and hurricanes don't take orders.

Those who face "fake danger," the thrill-seekers who place themselves in jeopardy intentionally, assume the risk on their own. Their antics are self-imposed and if they seek them out, neither they nor their loved ones should be surprised when their pastime kills them. Nor should they be allowed to sue anyone. Their actions started the situation that lead to their death. They are, and should be, held accountable for their actions. If death is the result of their actions, well...that's the ultimate accountability.

Those facing real dangers from the elements need to calculate, prepare for, and reduce the threat of danger as much as possible. Never, never, go into a situation unprepared to deal with the conditions.

Natural laws have no pity.

Dr. Robert Heinlein

IT'S NO BIG THING

My partner was a new Reserve Officer in training. We were working a beat in a freeway service business district, and one of the more active beats. Bar fights were somewhat common and thieves were active in the area. Gerry and his female reserve partner were working the same area in another patrol car.

Our portable radios didn't work worth a damn and the patrol captain and sergeants were death on getting out of the car without letting the office know where you were. Bathroom breaks and other comfort breaks would promptly be charged against your break time. It was crap and we all found dodges to get around the directives. The easiest one to outwit was the bathroom break.

Atop "Beacon Hill" not one minute from the lights of the business district was a deserted spot. We often spotted couples smooching up there, drug deals being made, and burglars meeting at what they thought was an "out of the way spot." Our most common use for the spot was as an informal urinal. I'd pull the car up, back into the bushes and step out to the roadside. The police radio could still be heard and no "personal break" time was used.

Tonight I backed the car into the bushes and killed the headlights. I opened the driver's door and my trainee got out of the passenger side. We were both nearly to the mid-stream sigh when a patrol car burst over the rim of the hill, turned on headlights, spotlights, and overhead emergency lights all at once. It was Gerry and his female partner!

I turned away in school-boy reflex and hurriedly zipped my pants while cussing at the top of my lungs. My partner did the same on the opposite side of the car. Gerry turned and went down the hill leaving smoking tire tread on the roadway.

Just as I got back in the car, the radio crackled. Gerry was calling me. When I answered, I was tight-jawed. Gerry came over with my call sign and advised me, "It's okay. My partner says *it's no big thing*!" I sat stunned for a second or two feeling my hands form into claws that would fit nicely around Gerry's neck. Then it struck me and my partner funny at the same time. We both sat and roared with laughter.

Nice going Gerry! Such a simple gag. And so damned effective. A real work of art!

Come to think of it...I still owe him for that one!

Never miss a chance to eat, sleep or pee...
You never know when the chance will come again.

Dr. Robert Heinlein

TRACK STARS AND FOOT PURSUITS

People who think they are track stars sometimes miscalculate badly. One night we received a call about an extremely large juvenile party being held in a field in the Rocklin area. We headed in that direction, as another training car arrived on the scene. They walked into the field and spent several minutes listening to the chatter of the kids, watching to see if anyone was using drugs, and watching beer being tapped out of kegs. They shouted notice to all the juveniles to drop their beer. Pandemonium broke loose! Beer cans and bottles flew through the air. People scattered through the field like a covey of quail.

As my partner and I arrived, a burly young man ran up over a bank and to the passenger door of a parked Chevy. He put his key in the door as my partner lit him with a spotlight. The young man took one look at the marked county police cruiser and ran. "Go get him," my training officer shouted. I was out of the car and running, with the suspect about twenty yards ahead.

We went through a field, into some thin brush, then into water reeds. I heard a squeal as the suspect fell, then scrambled up quickly and clambered over an unseen object. I climbed the partially downed wire fence, flashlight in one hand, baton in the other. We continued into the field on the other side of the fence. The kid was doing his best. Despite the ballistic vest and gear, I settled into a fast pace and kept shouting for the kid to stop. I was gaining on him, slow but sure.

The kid looked over his shoulder and saw me closing in at about 10 yards. He knew I was going to catch him. He turned around, threw both hands over his head and fell backwards like a felled pine tree. Stiff as a board, he hit the ground. I came alongside him and told him to turn over. My partner and I handcuffed him.

As we were heading to the patrol car, Kent, our training officer approached us. He told our prisoner, "You know, you're really an unlucky guy. You picked the only two people in the department who could have caught you. See the guy in green? He's our department's champion sprinter. The other guy in grey? He runs marathons!"

This was the first either one of us had heard about our status as departmental champions. The kid looked up, "Aw shit! What woulda happened if I hadn't run!" Kent asked the young man if he saw anyone else in handcuffs. The juvenile looked around and all he could see were his friends loading into cars and practicing the better part of valor...being elsewhere.

His parents picked him up. Charges: drunk in public and possession of a small amount of marijuana. Because he got stupid and ran, our young man went home to mommy and daddy. After talking to the parents, I think the punishment they meted out was probably more than he would have received from any court in the land.

I discovered several things that night:

1) Make verbal identification repeatedly and loudly. "Police, stop!" or "Sheriff, stop!" The suspect will hear it and so will anyone else standing around in the area. The suspect can't say, "I didn't know they were cops."

2) Follow your suspect exactly. Step in his footsteps. Take the same route.

3) Let your suspect find the hazards first. Clotheslines, a hose across the path, landscape wires, treacherous footing, and hazards of all kinds.

4) Put on a burst of speed to keep the suspect in sight, then settle into a pace that allows you to sustain the run for as long as necessary. Don't burn out.

5) Your suspect will most likely be checking over his shoulder frequently. Every time he does, he loses up to half a step. The more he checks, the faster you catch up.

6) Beware of the suspect stopping suddenly and running back to confront you. If he stops and runs back, you're suddenly closing at twice the speed you are running.

7) Should the suspect reverse field and come toward you, get ready for a nasty surprise. It's a cinch he's not coming back to give you a friendly greeting.

8) Unless lethal force is indicated, don't run with your sidearm in your hand. Several officers have ended up fighting with suspects over their sidearm. The suspect reverses field and grabs the officer's drawn gun before the officer knows what's up.

9) The second officer can follow on foot at a more leisurely pace. When the pursuit concludes, he will be better able to perform physical control of the suspect. In nature, many successful large animals hunt by using the "relay system." This is useful for police as well.

One must therefore be a fox to recognize traps,
And a lion to frighten wolves.

Machiavelli

A MOONLIGHT JOG

In the early 80's, we had a bar in the Auburn area called The North Fork Dry Diggin's, which was the scene of frequent fights and problems. On routine patrol one night, another deputy from my office, Tony, saw a fight in the bar parking lot. When he arrived at the lot, the suspect took one look and decided to take "leg bail." Of all the people to run from, Tony was definitely the wrong one. Tony was a SWAT team member and well versed in martial arts to boot. In short, the first person to look for, and the last one to mess with.

The suspect took off across a field. Tony went to the edge of the parking lot and warned him to stop. The suspect kept running. Tony shouted, "If I have to chase you, you're going to regret it!" The suspect kept going, opening a large lead across the deserted field.

Tony finally shouted, "Okay, you want to run, go ahead and run, but when I catch you, you're not going to like it." He broke into a run. They both traveled through the field with Tony identifying himself as a peace officer and shouting for him to stop. The suspect should have taken the hint, because our man, weighted down with plenty of equipment, wasn't even breathing hard. Tony was having no trouble keeping up.

Tony changed verbal tactics. The suspect knew he was a cop and had been warned to stop. "You better run faster, I'm catching up," Tony shouted. "Oh boy, I'm getting closer!" "This is gonna be fun!"

These and other pleasantries were shouted several times over the next mile and a half. At the end of that mile and a half, the suspect's head was thrown back and he was sucking air with every fiber of his being. His legs were pumping furiously to out distance the recurrent nightmare behind him which was steadily gaining ground.

Between running and shouting repeatedly at the suspect, Tony found time to radio in a complete running commentary (lousy pun) of his foot pursuit. Other deputies had gone to the bar parking lot and learned the suspect Tony was chasing had attacked a woman and her boyfriend in the lot. Tony reported back he didn't think this guy was running for the exercise. This was no normal moonlight jog.

From the suspect's point of view, he *knew* why he was running...sheer panic! This cop was gaining even more after one and a half miles. The California Highway Patrol car 100 yards ahead must have seemed like a water mirage to a man dying of thirst. If he could make it there, the Highway Patrol officer would take him to jail and he wouldn't have to face this steady breathing engine relentlessly gaining on him.

The suspect angled his run toward the patrol car and the waiting arms of the CHP officer. Tony shouted, "Let him go, he's mine!" The CHP officer had been listening to the entire foot pursuit over the radio and must have thought Tony deserved this one. He got in his car and drove away!

No marooned sailor seeing a ship disappear over the horizon had ever felt more hopeless than our suspect. He physically collapsed. Tony began to approach the suspect who was lying on his back and probably felt he was seeing the last stars of his life. Tony said, "Hello. Don't you hear well? I've been talking to you for the last couple of miles. I asked you to stop and you didn't. I told you to stop and you didn't. I was sure you would stop sometime. Well, here we are! Now don't you feel stupid?" Tony approached and took a control hold, rolling our vomiting suspect over. The handcuffs went on with several clicks and Tony calmly called a patrol unit from the bar parking lot to come pick him up with his prisoner.

We believe man as a weapon is here to stay.
(Was there ever any doubt?)

Major General James Gavin
(paraphrased)

MINDING MY OWN BUSINESS

Recently I was listening to a radio broadcast with a sergeant from my department. The transmission was from one of the more active patrolmen in our agency who was in pursuit of a burglar. His second burglar in the last couple of days. The sergeant looked at me with a half-smile, "That guy is a shit magnet! He gets into the damndest situations." I laughed, knowing he had probably referred to me by that term (and worse) over the years. For instance...

Early in my career I was off duty, minding my own business, walking down a street in Auburn with my six month old German Shepherd pup. I saw a pickup turn into a local parking lot and heard three young men inside shout something. I couldn't hear what was said, but I watched them carefully as they entered the street and passed me.

The pickup had an out-of-state license and I memorized the number as they went slowly by. The truck stopped and a young man got out of the passenger side making his way to the sidewalk in front of me. I saw two elderly ladies walking toward a signal light at the corner. I began walking faster wondering about the possibility of the young man stealing a purse.

The young man walked past the women and stopped on the corner as if waiting for the light. Nah! Just my suspicious mind. I slowed down, still 30 yards away. The young man turned and grabbed the cane and purse of the oldest woman and yanked. Both women began screaming. The young suspect yanked on the purse twice more as I dropped my dog's leash and began to run.

The suspect succeeded in knocking both women to the ground and freeing the purse. He left the screaming, crying victims where they fell and began running down the sidewalk toward the pickup idling in the traffic lane 40 yards away. The center passenger looked back over his right shoulder and opened the right hand passenger door for the fleeing suspect to get in "on the fly" while the truck began accelerating.

I came within the width of the curb from jumping into the back of the pickup. I re-confirmed and committed to memory the license number of the pickup. I looked at the suspect over gunsights. The kid who had committed the strong arm robbery looked young. Firing at him would not stop the truck. I could recognize them on sight. I had the license. Let it go at that. We would find them later.

I went back to the elderly ladies and identified myself as a peace officer. I told them to stay where they were and I would call an ambulance and police. The eldest victim's legs were shredded from hitting the pavement. She was 82 years old. The other woman who had tried to support her and keep her from being pulled to the pavement was her 62 year old daughter. I went into a store and made the call to the local police department. A general broadcast was issued for the suspects and their vehicle.

I went back outside to the victims to see if I could give any help. The eldest victim, Vernie, was repeating over and over, "When I left the house. I wondered if I should take that10 dollar bill. I'm so glad I left it home. I'm just so glad I left it home." The thieves took a little over four dollars and change. What was both heartbreaking and revealing was the fact the 10 dollar bill meant so much to the woman. It said much about her and her situation.

Later that evening I was called to positively identify the suspect and their vehicle. They were arrested and I went along to help with the booking paperwork. I was dressed in Levi cutoffs, a football jersey, and sneakers, just as I had been earlier in the day. When I asked the suspect a paperwork question, he sneered, "Who the fuck are you!" The Auburn police officer leaned across the booking counter and said, "This man is a policeman. He was there when you robbed that lady today. He chased you, he got your license number, he's going to identify you in court. In short, you and your friends are in deep shit!" The suspect didn't say much after that.

I went to court after a full midnight shift. The court day wore on...and on...and on. I waited...and waited...and waited. At 4:30 p.m. the district attorney told me I would be next on the stand. After being up for over 30 hours, I testified to what I had seen and done.

The D.A. charged the two suspects with Strong Arm Robbery and Conspiracy. The suspect who had done the grab from our victim got up on the stand and testified in his own behalf. He had quite clearly been coached, since he testified only to things which would include Grand Theft Person; stealing something from the direct control of a person, instead of Strong Arm Robbery, a heavier felony.

The main suspect reported on his date for sentencing...and went to jail for a year. The middle passenger who opened the door for him failed to show for his sentencing...and went to prison.

An optimist sees a glass as half full;
A pessimist as half empty.

Author Unknown

Realists know,
If they stick around long enough,
They'll have to wash the damn glass!

(I've never heard this addition anywhere else,
so I'm claiming it.)

Rocky Warren
1991

A GOOD NIGHT'S SLEEP

The doorbell was ringing, fast, strident, and persistent. The man outside was shouting, "Help! Help! They're trying to kill me!" I came fully awake and catapulted out of bed. Dressed in my robe and service sidearm, I went toward the front door of my house and flipped on the front porch light. In the light, I could see a shadow against the panes of glass near the door. I shouted at the man outside to move away from the door. I saw the shadow retreat from the glass.

I knelt beside the door, cross-handed the door lock and knob and opened the door. The muzzle of my weapon was leveled at the young man's navel from the instant I opened the door. The young man was dressed in Levi's, shoes, and no shirt. His upper body was a mass of welts and brush cuts. I had seen similar markings on many people I had chased throughout my career. My orders to him were instantaneous, "Get down on the ground on your face. Do it NOW!"

The man complied. I shouted at my wife to call the Sheriff's Department. She shouted back that she already had. I told the young man that no one was going to hurt him now. If anyone tried, it would be a mistake, but he was definitely not to move.

As the situation developed, I learned this young man had earlier attended a party at a house not far from mine. He left the party but returned later, breaking into the ground floor of the house. The homeowner's son had come downstairs and confronted the suspect. The suspect had grabbed a kitchen knife. The two young men fought, and the homeowner's son had beaten the tar out of the suspect.

The two young men had been standing in the back yard of the house arguing and considering whether to fight some more, when the first police unit arrived. The suspect fled into the brush. Two hours of foot pursuit followed, during which the suspect lost the officers in the heavily wooded area, only to emerge from the brush and beat on front doors. My house was the fifth and last one he tried.

Our patrol deputy, Tracy, was frustrated from the long drawn out situation when he received a radio call. Dispatch came over saying the suspect was now at 725's home. My radio call sign is 725. There was a long pause over the radio then Tracy came back over the air, "Uh, bad decision!" Dispatch gave directions to my house and I soon saw the headlights of the patrol unit pull into my drive. This was followed by the shifting beam of a spotlight focused on the suspect.

I crouched behind my door frame with my sidearm and heard Tracy approach from the side of the entryway. Tracy's booming voice rang out, "Hi! I've been looking for you!" Tracy handcuffed and lead away the 20 year old suspect.

I had just been assigned to the Investigation Division and received my neighbor's burglary case the next day. I also received the clearance for the arrest. The victim later refused to proecute.

An armed man is a citizen,
An unarmed man is a subject.

Author Unknown

A MIDNIGHT CALLER

I was on patrol as a single man unit. I preferred it that way. I looked where I wanted, and contacted who I wanted. I did things my way. I think it made me a better cop because working single forced me to rely on myself, gave me no false sense of security, and taught me to expect the unexpected, and think ahead. My butt was on the line and I had to be able to handle, or get away from, anything I poked my nose into.

The radio call came over, "Burglary in progress at Brady Lane. One suspect held at gunpoint." I took off with lights and sirens, arriving in very short order. The nearest units were some distance away and I knew I was definitely on my own. I pulled up in front of the driveway and flashed the spotlight over the front windows.

A woman in a bathrobe came to the front door and waved at me. I got out and she told me her husband, Mr. Brady, had a man held at gunpoint at the back door of their home. I asked Mrs. Brady if they knew the suspect, she replied they did not. As she led me through the house, she continued to explain the events of the evening. She and her husband had been asleep when they heard noises outside the house. Mr. Brady got up, grabbed a handgun, and was holding the suspect.

I peered around the corner into the laundry room where the back door was located. A large male suspect was standing six feet inside the door. I pointed my handgun at the the suspect and then I noticed a second door across the room at which a bathrobed man stood pointing a two inch barreled revolver at the suspect.

I looked across the room and asked, "Mr. Brady, I presume?" The armed man nodded and asked politely, "Would you mind getting this garbage out of my house?" I warned the suspect not to move and holstered my sidearm while moving into the room. "Mr. Brady, please cover him." Mr. Brady said, "Don't worry son, I will."

I moved to the suspect's left arm and took a wrist lock in one motion then handcuffed him. The suspect was drunk, but he was definitely not stupid. He didn't want to push Mr. Brady. I began searching the suspect for weapons. In an aside over my shoulder, I told Mr. Brady, "It'd make me feel a lot better if you would put the weapon away, sir." He said he already had as soon as the suspect had been handcuffed. The suspect went to jail for burglary.

Even after all these years, I still get an occasional call or visit from Mr. Brady.

It is circumstance and proper timing
that give an action it's character,
and make it either good or bad.

Agesilaus
400 B.C.

DROP YOUR PANTS SONNY!

The elderly security guard called us from a phone inside the lumber mill. He was actually a fire guard placed there by the company to protect against fire danger. It was about 3:00 a.m. and during his rounds he had seen a man backing out of the mill office carrying one end of an office desk. The guard walked over to his car, which was parked inside the mill, and retrieved a small semi-auto pistol.

Taking a position behind a wood pillar, the guard pointed the gun and shouted, "Hold it right there." As one suspect fled out the side office door, Lawrence, the remaining suspect, took one look over his shoulder at the guard with leveled gun and froze in place.

The guard later told me he had been in Europe during World War II. He never forgot what a sergeant told him. He and his squad had learned some extra German. They were able to say, "If you move I will shoot you in the stomach." At that time, and level of medical technology, a particularly messy way to go for the "shootee." More intimidation in favor of the shooter.

The guard had told the thief the statement given him by dear old Sarge so many years ago, made him drop his pants around his ankles, effectively hobbling the criminal, then made him lay down. It worked. The suspect was still there, proned out in all his glory when we got there. I moved in and hand-cuffed the crook.

The security guard moved over to his car and indicated the handgun he had dropped on the seat when we arrived. I took the weapon from the seat. There was no magazine in it. When I popped the slide back, no round of ammunition came out. EMPTY! I looked at the old man and his face was crinkled up in a smile.

"It was a war souvenir, son. I've never had any bullets for it. Wouldn't want to hurt anyone." I looked at the man's huge grin. He had confronted the suspect with an unloaded gun. The old man's hoarse laugh bounced around through the huge mill building as I led the criminal away to the car. Our crook had a long history of burglary, drugs, and other crimes. He was headed back to prison.

The next time a criminal faces an armed citizen, they've got to ask themselves, " Is it unloaded or not?" The chances are in favor of it being loaded. The criminal then has to decide whether they're willing to stake their life on the answer.

Why do you suppose the creeps of the world
have declared open season on Americans?
Are we not the posterity of Patrick Henry,
George Washington, Nathan Hale, Buck Travis,
Teddy Roosevelt, and George Patton?
How do they dare?

Colonel Jeff Cooper

CRASH AND BURN

Tracy was planning on having a couple cups of coffee and headed toward the front door of a local restaurant. A young man came bursting through the door, took one look at the uniformed officer and cut a hard right, running to the side of the building. The restaurant manager ran out the door shouting, "He didn't pay!" Tracy had walked into a "dine and dash" situation.

Tracy kicked it into high gear, running around the west side of the restaurant. There were low juniper bushes planted between the restaurant and the freeway. Tracy and the young criminal both went through the landscaping giving a good imitation of track and field hurdlers. One more juniper bush to jump for Tracy. He raised his right foot to jump...and his heel caught on the juniper bush. Head over heels was the order of the next couple of seconds as Tracy crashed and burned over the shrubbery and into the landscape gravel. Tracy shouted, "Ouch! Dammit! This isn't worth it! It's over! I quit!"

The suspect stopped and looked back. Tracy slowly got to his feet and looked at the kid. "Nice race, kid! You run pretty good. You won this one. My name is Tracy." As he said this, Tracy walked slowly forward and extended his right hand. The kid stayed put with a smile on his face, knowing he'd won, and extended his right hand to shake Tracy's hand. Tracy reached past the extended hand, grabbed his right wrist and completed a step-under to a twist-lock. The kid was taken into custody, and with the ashes of defeat wrested from the jaws of victory, he loudly let it be known, "You didn't play fair!"

Madam Montholon having asked what troops
he thought the best
"Those who are victorious," replied the emperor.

Napoleon Bonaparte

JUVENILE ESCAPEE AT...

I received a radio call on a pair of juvenile escapees who were at a market in Meadow Vista. Another officer, Rich, and I arrived at the store at the same time. I was familiar with one of the juveniles, having chased him the previous summer. This juvenile, Ryan, would run, fight, or both. We had information that Ryan had been in possession of a handgun last night, but had supposedly been talked out of it by his mother. Mommy had not called us, a store employee who knew the suspect had.

I went into the store with Rich at my heels. He went to the manager of the store. I spotted our escapees. The manager had been prepared and closed and locked the back door for us. There was nowhere for the kids to go except through us.

I walked down the aisle and saw Ryan with his back to me. The other young man I didn't know, dropped his head and said nothing, probably hoping I wouldn't notice him or that he could disappear into the floor. I walked up behind Ryan and took a light grasp on his left arm. I said, "Hello. How are you guys today?" Ryan looked over his shoulder and saw two uniformed police. His arm muscle tightened under his jacket. I quickly said, "Ryan, you don't want to resist. Drop what you have in your hands." Ryan relaxed then tensed again and tried to run. I encircled his neck with an arm and pressed him to the ground in a sitting position. My knees landed on the floor on either side of his body. I closed my arm around his neck, completing a carotid control hold, and put the pressure on. I told him, "You didn't learn anything last time, did you? Knock it off or I'm going to put you to sleep." Ryan relaxed and I flipped him over onto his stomach, directly into a prone control hold.

I was joined by the store manager who held Ryan's right hand while I handcuffed the left. The manager helped greatly in controlling the mildly thrashing juvenile. Rich had much less trouble with his young escapee. I think he saw how things were going with Ryan, took one look at Rich, and decided not to chance it. The whole conflict took no more than 15 seconds.

In handcuffs, both were ready for booking at juvenile hall.

I'd like to make a point here. There have been instances where I've been on the ground fighting with a suspect and citizens have stepped around us or passed by while looking out their car windows. In other instances, I've had folks come up, dig right in, and give me a hand. There have been instances where officers were saved by citizens, and I've certainly had my carcass pulled out of the fire by citizens more than once. I thank and appreciate them, and always try to make sure they receive recognition for their efforts and the risk they went through.

There is no greater weapon than knowledge and familiarity.

Chinese Proverb

A COMPARISON

As a result of an earlier scuffle with a suspect, I had damaged a wrist and was put on light duty, working in the jail for 10 days. The first night there, two drunks came into the jail. The first one wouldn't cooperate and was shut away in a cell to sleep it off without preliminary. The second suspect remained calm...too calm.

I walked into the booking room and saw one of the deputies pick up a jacket and ask the suspect if it was his. The suspect went ape! He balled up his fists and swung. Three deputies, two males and one female, pinned the suspect's arms partially. The sergeant went toward the fight and I saw the suspect swing at her and connect before everybody went crashing onto the concrete floor. Shit!

I reached into the tangled mess of arms and legs and came up with the suspect's right arm. I took a prone control on the arm and took up the slack. The suspect quit fighting, intent on the hold I had applied. I let the other deputies untangle from our suspect and disengage from the close encounter.

From that point, it was a simple matter of explanation, persuasion, and playing on the suspect's pride. "Listen sport. I'm giving you one chance to get up and walk like a man to a cell. You're going to do exactly as I say. If you still want to fight, you're going to hit the ground hard and it's going to hurt. I'm going to turn you to your left and let you get up. Remember, you only get one chance. Don't do anything stupid."

The statements I made were not idle talk. This guy had tried to hit other deputies and connected with my sergeant. I wasn't going to have his violent temper hurt any of my co-workers. He had demonstrated his violence adequately for justification of escalation of force if he wanted to continue the fight.

I turned the suspect, got him to his feet, turning the prone control into a twistlock. We walked into a detox cell and I directed our suspect into a prone position using pain compliance when he became resistive and wouldn't do it. Belt and shoes were taken so our suspect couldn't damage himself. When the other deputies were done getting objectionable articles off him, I walked to the door shutting it behind me.

This incident and the one in "Juvenile Escapee At..." are recent. Throughout this book, you will find incidents of use of force. In most instances, they will concern impact weapon or physical control. Contrast those earlier incidents of tackles that hurt me, but did not hurt the suspect, with these two incidents. The difference is the level of training I have now, versus my training then. Training is not easy, nor is it inexpensive. Yet training is always one of the first items cut from police budgets.

In these recent incidents, physical control was used which was the right level of force. The suspect breaking loose and fighting would have justified impact force. Producing a weapon could justify lethal force. The call is the officer's at the time.

The training each officer gets is crucial to his decision making. Training is the difference. Good, active training will add more "tools" to the officer's "tactical tool chest."

In this encounter, none of the deputies were hurt, the suspect was not hurt, and I was not hurt. A successful conclusion, but not always possible.

By the data to date there is only one animal
dangerous to man;
Man himself.
He must supply his own indispensable competition;
He has no enemy to help him.

Dr. Robert Heinlein

MAN AND WEAPONS

A couple hundred thousand years ago Og, the caveman, picked up a knotted, gnarled branch and swung it experimentally. Finding it improved his reach distance and provided him more leverage and power than his soft-skinned body could create alone, he kept it and learned to use it through trial and error.

My trainee and I were in a local park and were joined by another training officer and his trainee during our stop and interview of four suspects. My trainee decided he wanted to do a frisk of one of the suspects. The suspect was mildly resistive and my trainee handled it well, taking a low key control-hold and frisking the suspect. Suddenly all hell broke loose.

"Gun!" my trainee shouted, raised a chrome semi-auto handgun into the air, backed off and let the control hold go. He had taken the gun from the back pocket of the suspect's Levi's. I slid forward quickly and pulled the gun toting suspect into a twist-lock control hold. I pulled the suspect off to one side and completed handcuffing post-haste. The trainees fanned out to take two other suspects, the training officer taking the third.

After the excitement died down, the training officer and I took the trainees off to one side to make some training points. We both began by complimenting the trainees for functioning well under a tense situation. I then told them the following for consideration and possible future use.

When a weapon is found on your suspect, it's removed quickly under most normal circumstances. This is only common sense. The point I wanted to make to the trainees was the same as that illustrated above by our friend Og - namely that the weapon is not the problem. The person using it is. The person, their training, effectiveness, and willingness to use the weapon, dictate whether the weapon is an object or a lethal threat. The tree branch was a piece of forest debris until our caveman pal picked it up and swung it.

When our trainees backed off, they gained distance from the suspect, but they lost control of the initiative and opened up the situation for the suspect to seize control. If we immobilize the person holding the weapon, the weapon is useless. In this situation, a twist-lock and handcuffing was all that was required to control things.

In a traffic stop early in my career, I saw a driver make some movements as if he were placing something under his seat while coming to a stop. I walked up cautiously and made contact, and saw the grips of a revolver poking out from under the front seat. I gave no hint that I had seen the gun, went back to my car carefully, and got back-up before calling the citizen out.

Because I was alone, being prepared to take defensive action, retreat, take cover, remain behind the suspect, and keep the suspect in his car, were my best options and the best way to immobilize him. Once back-up arrived, I took the initiative and ordered him out of the car using high-risk stop procedures. When I handcuffed the suspect and searched him, I found a second gun, a small derringer, in a front pants pocket.

The weapons were not the problem. As long as I could keep the advantage over our suspect, there was minimal danger. I made the point to our trainees that they need to look at both situations. Four cops and four suspects on an even footing in a park setting. Cops and suspects have roughly equal mobility. Which is better, backing off and allowing the suspect or a companion to use a weapon with a clear field, or remaining close and taking control of the suspect? It's their decision dictated by the circumstance and it's something they should consider ahead of time.

Our modern day policeman is loaded down with items of armor and hardware which may make him the equivalent of a squad of infantry of past conflicts. If the point comes where our police officer is too burdened with technology, we'll know it. Someone armed much more simply, say our caveman friend, Og, with his primitive club, will sneak up behind our officer and bash his head while he's trying to read his computer screen. Training and ability. These need to be the police officer's strongest suit. With or without weapons.

A person is no more armed because he buys a gun
Than he is a musician because he buys a violin.

Jeff Cooper
(roughly paraphrased)

GUILT AND REMORSE: A DEFENSE ATTORNEY'S TOOLS

Defense attorneys will use whatever they can against cops. If you allow them to use your own emotions to discredit your motives or actions, they figure they're ahead of the game.

I had been in an on-duty, officer-involved shooting. The judge was in place with the jury sitting in the box. The defendant was at counsel table staring at me trying to elicit some reaction. Defense counsel was doing exactly as I'd been told he would. In short, he was giving me the royal once-over.

"Officer, we all know that someone who shoots another person, and does not feel remorse, would have to be a sociopath. Officer...(dramatic pause) are you sorry you shot my client? Looking back at the defense attorney, I waited to see if there would be an objection then replied, "I wish the situation hadn't happened counselor, but your client chose actions that made it necessary to shoot him."

The defense attorney pressed on, "Do you feel sorry about shooting him?" "Maybe a little guilty that you shot him?" I replied, "Your client shot at me and my officers, making my actions necessary."

The defense attorney danced around trying to get me to take any kind of responsibility, blame, sorrow, guilt, or remorse. Avoiding what this attorney was trying to do will save you untold grief in a police career.

Officers need feel no sorrow, guilt, remorse, nor culpability for their justifiable actions during the course of police duties. These emotions are felt by those who do something wrong! Any admission by an officer that they feel these emotions in regard to their own motivations or actions, will make an attorney glow with satisfaction and start counting up his chances of acquittal. The attorney will also examine the possibility of buying another Mercedes from a suit against you and your department.

When you admit any of these things, the defense attorney gets up in closing arguments and says, "Ladies and Gentlemen of the jury, you have heard the officer during testimony admit he did something he was sorry for. The officer admitted he felt guilt and remorse, and he would not feel these emotions unless he mishandled this case! You heard the officer. His admission of remorse indicates, *he knows he did wrong.*"

Don't be flip or emotionless during your testimony either. This allows a defense attorney to stand and say, "Ladies and Gentlemen of the jury, you heard the officer during testimony. He feels nothing. Essentially, the officer's statements and actions in this case reflect the fact the officer is "stone cold," a "borderline sociopath" and feels no compassion whatsoever for his fellow man."

Wishing it hadn't happened, placing the initiation of the action back on the suspect, and refusing to take responsibility, blame or feel sorrow, guilt or remorse gives the defense attorney less to hang his hat on. The officer has stated he is of good conscience, duty-bound, and justified in his actions.

Criminal defendants have nothing better to do than try this tactic inside or outside the courtroom. I recently searched a prisoner in jail with a twist-lock control hold. The suspect said I was hurting him and later filed a grievance. I did another search, with the same method, on the same prisoner a week later. The suspect said, "I forgive you for hurting me last week and again just now." I didn't buy it, replying, "The search procedure allows me to stay safe and doesn't hurt you. I've had the same hold applied to me thousands of times without injury. I won't ever apologize for doing my job the right way. I don't need, nor accept your forgiveness. There's nothing to forgive."

The prisoner's attempt to forgive me, or any admission that I felt sorrow or guilt, would have validated the prisoner's contention that I did something wrong. Whether in the custody setting or on the street, you need feel no remorse for doing that which is moral, legal, right, justifiable, and part of your duties. Keep this in mind. If your career is an active one, it will save you loads of grief.

Thou shouldst not mourn.
Likewise having regard for thine own duty,
Thou shouldst not tremble.
For another, better thing than a fight required of duty
exists not for a warrior.

Bhagavad Gita

WRITE IT DOWN, DAMMIT!

I know report writing is not one of the "sexy subjects," but we are all intent on keeping ourselves from being unjustifiably sued...so prepare your use of force and all other reports the right way.

Myself and several partners were standing around a prone, handcuffed suspect, breathing hard, and occasionally cussing. "Damn! That was a hell of a fight! Glad we don't have to do that a couple times a night." There were minor dings and scratches on all of us. We took the suspect to jail for Assault with a Deadly Weapon and assorted other crimes. When I read the report after the lead officer wrote it, I was dismayed. I handed in my Supplemental Report setting out the circumstances of the fight in much more detail and better protecting us all.

What I found in the lead officer's report was in essence: "The suspect resisted, was subdued and handcuffed, transported and booked into jail." There was no mention of the suspect's closed fists, his crouching into a fighter's stance, his statement that he was perfectly willing to kick our asses...nothing.

Let's hypothesize for a moment here. I never looked at the report nor added my Supplement to it. One year down the road, we receive notification of a lawsuit. You can't add anything to your report now. There's a plaintiff's attorney out there licking his chops waiting for you to do something that stupid. You have to go into court with the documentation you have. You get on the witness stand and the plaintiff's attorney approaches and begins questioning. "You testify you saw the suspect, crouch, ball up his fists, say he was going to kick your ass...exactly as it happened, right?"

At this point, the attorney is very likely to turn to the officer, "Officer, why were you so deficient in your reporting and documentation?" When you stutter and stammer that you were too busy to set out all the details in your report, you're going to look foolish or negligent to jurors who have never pulled a duty shift in their life.

What you may not hear after you leave the courtroom is the plaintiff's attorney in summation: "Ladies and Gentlemen of the jury, what was the officer trying to hide? Why did he not completely document his use of force? Why are these reports so deficient? *Because the officer did wrong!*" At this point the plaintiff's attorney can go ahead and allege nearly anything. You're not in court to refute him, no one can interrupt his closing argument without extremely good cause, and it's the plaintiff's attorney's time to howl, brandishing your copy of a weak report.

The suspect's actions which justified our use of force, our attempts at verbal control, the suspect's failure to comply, the suspect's resistive actions, and any stated intentions to resist, the officers failed control methods, the officer's successful control methods, follow up medical treatment...all these things need to go into the report in detail.

When you go into court, you have all the justifications and actions down...everything is in a row and you have nothing to fear. A plaintiff's attorney has much less to hang his hat on.

The path of nature and of truth is narrow
But it is simple and direct;
The devious paths are numerous and spacious
But they all lead to error and destruction.

Robert Jackson
Circa 1804

PROFESSIONALS...A TEAM

Curtis was my partner. We were patrolling the base at Fort Benning, Georgia and a cold wind was whipping through the jeep's canvas sides. I hated it when we had the sides on the jeep because it cut visibility down to near nothing. Curtis was a senior military policeman, an experienced, smart cop and very sharp in his appearance. He was one of my first training officers when I arrived on base and was patient with my mistakes, youth, occasional stupidity, and inexperience. I learned a lot of techniques for dealing with people from Curt. He was very even-handed with people and treated everyone as a human until they messed with him. Then he took care of business immediately and efficiently. I owe him a lot. I also owe him my life.

The call of a domestic violence came out to us. We went to the sergeant's housing area in Sand Hill and walked to the door of a set of quarters (apartments) belonging to our fighting couple. There was a little switch in store for us. The apartment door opened to a large black woman who was hugely pissed. "That fuck! He stayed out all night!" Her husband, a slightly built black man, was sitting at the kitchen table bleeding from a cut on his head. Wifey had tried to level the top of her husband's head with a frying pan.

The apartment was warm and seemed humid as all get out after the cold of the night. I looked over at the woman and Curtis moved in close to her as the husband broke out with his side of the story, "She hit me with the damn frying pan. She's been threatening to cut me up for more than an hour."

Curtis was staying near the woman and I stayed near the male half of this tag team. Right now, he had been tagged "it." I didn't want him to try to even the score. The woman was screaming at both her husband and us. Curtis was trying to reason with her. The woman began to move toward a large steaming, boiling tub on the stove.

The woman shouted again asking what we were doing in her house and what we intended to do there. I replied if what we heard so far was true, she would have to come with us to the Provost Marshal's Office. The woman looked at me and said, "You paddy mother-fucker, I'll scald and skin you like a hog first!" I was shocked to see a large butcher knife next to the steaming, scalding pot. I'd missed it when I first looked, and now the woman was closer to the stove and knife than either Curt or I. Curtis looked at the woman and told her, "You're not gonna do anything." The woman looked at Curtis and said, "What are you gonna do about it?" Curtis looked the woman in the eye and told her, "If you try to throw that water, I'm going to shoot your ass."

This woman had a good gutter vocabulary and she roundly cursed at both Curt and I all the way to the Provost Marshal's Office. She saved most of her bile for me. Being a young, inexperienced Military Policeman, I was in awe of the woman's references by way of threats, sexual innuendo, marital status of parents, intelligence, preference, biases, etc. Some of the mildest terms the woman used on Curtis were "Uncle Tom" and "Boy." Curtis happened to be black and she saw it as an insult that Curt would stand up for me when I was "just a honkey." Curt was professional all the way through. We both wore the same uniform and did the same job. That was good enough for both of us.

Being young and dumb, I'm not sure I even thanked Curt after he saved me from being flayed by scalding water. I'd like to thank him now, even though it's 20 years late.

No one has been barred because of his race
from fighting or dying for America...
There are no "white" or "colored" signs on the
foxholes or graveyards of battle.

President John Kennedy

HAZARDOUS MATERIALS - EVERY TIME

Dave Rose and I were teaching an expandable/collapsible baton course. We were giving the "fun" part of the class. We were both in F.I.S.T. gear and students were hitting our amply padded frames with ASP and CASCO expandable/collapsible full street batons. The extended shaft and Yawara-type strikes were flying. We made students miss strikes, and complimented them for good, hard strikes. We verbally cautioned them about targeting accuracy, power, and grabbed batons that were left extended too long after strikes. In short, we were acting like teachers as well as suspects for our students' impact force.

After the class was over, Dave and I posed for a photograph. My left forearm and Dave's right forearm had been hit with full-shaft extended strikes. There was swelling on both of our arms, a small cut on top of the bone on my arm, and a small amount of dried blood present. No permanent injury, no missed work time, but this raises a question.

An officer goes into a street arrest situation and the suspect resists. If bio-hazards weren't present when we started, and force is used, they are probably present when we get done. Do we wear safety glasses on the street? Defense attorneys don't have such a great argument against sunglasses any more. They protect our eyes from blood-borne pathogens spilled or thrown into the air. The eyes, nose, and to a lesser degree, the mouth, are all mucous membranes or pathways into the body. Suspects are prone to throw obnoxious substances on cops. We cannot tolerate this.

In this age of Hepatitis B, Human Immune Deficiency Virus (HIV), Adult Immune Deficiency Syndrome (AIDS), strains of Tuberculosis that no antibiotic can kill, and contagions of all types, police should not be forced to tolerate this type of insidious attack.

Bio-Hazard protection is necessary and throwing of blood or blood-bearing material is occasion for impact force to gain quick control. If the suspect is deliberately throwing blood or blood-bearing material and screams he's got AIDS, we need to assess the threat, react to avoid or prevent the throw, control the thrower, or retreat post-haste.

Do we have leather gloves on? Leather is somewhat better for several reasons. Leather absorbs perspiration from our hands and so is more comfortable to wear over long periods of time. The leather outer shell absorbs blood-borne pathogens and doesn't allow them to run off onto your wrists and forearms under most circumstances. Leather gloves may also have Kevlar inserts and are much more puncture resistant than latex. After a blood or airborne pathogen exposure it may be necessary to take protective measures for three to six months. It is best to have some puncture resistance protection against needles, razors, and "sharps" of all kinds. Surely we need to have a method to disinfect the gloves between candidates whenever circumstances allow. Consider this - frequently when we use defensive tactics or impact weapons, and every time we use lethal force, we create a bio-hazard zone. We need to make sure we protect ourselves.

Wear your ballistic vest. It may prevent or partially block a thrust with a contaminated blade or needle. Pulling the attacking hand into your vest gives you a somewhat "safe" zone on your body for maneuvering, and for a leverage point in disarming. If the suspect is using a blade, it's a threat of lethal force. The attacked officer breaking an arm or leg to stop the suspect is not out of line. Use of lethal force is not out of line either. If a needle is used, impact force is imminently justifiable. Officers need to use the fastest and most certain way to stop the threat.

This brings me to another point. When you survive your shift and arrive home, you know you have been exposed to blood or airborne pathogens. So what do you do? You'd best protect your spouse, and children. Your family and loved ones are your support system. It's critical you support them. Law enforcement is a high-risk occupation. As such, we need to protect ourselves and our family *first*. Worry about the general population next. Be careful for yourself, your family, and loved ones. You need each other healthy.

May the Gods grant you all thingswhich your heart
desires, And may they give you a hearth and a home
and gracious concord. For there is nothing greater and
better than this; When a husband and wife keep a house-
hold in oneness of mind, a great woe to their enemies,
a joy to their friends, And win high renown.
Homer

REPLACEMENT VALUE

I heard this story when I was in the military. I told it to a friend of mine and he says it dates back to the Korean War. I don't know where it originates, but it helps to prove my point so I'm going to relate it here just as I heard it.

There was a young serviceman who was trying to get "compassionate leave" since his father was sick in a stateside hospital. The young man tried and tried to find any "freedom bird" heading back to the U.S. No luck. The Air Force Military Airlift Command sergeant couldn't find any connecting flights that would get the serviceman back to the USA to be with his father.

Desperate, the young man saw an F-4 fighter plane land, taxi, and tie down on the flight line. While the sleek airplane was being serviced, the soldier asked about catching a ride on the fighter. The MAC transport sergeant promptly sawed him off at the knees for even asking. The man pleaded to get home to his ill father. Even MAC transport sergeants must have some heart (though personally I never saw any evidence of this). The young soldier found himself talking to the fighter pilot, a major, about his transportation problem. The soldier showed a copy of his telegraph and orders to the pilot who told him not to eat anything and to be there at 0500 sharp.

When the major arrived on the flight line he found the serviceman waiting for him and tossed the soldier a flight-suit and helmet. After outfitting, the major and the serviceman walked out to the sleek airplane. The serviceman was going to make it home after all, and in style at that. This was a once-in-a-lifetime thing.

Cautioning the soldier, the pilot helped the man into the seat of the aircraft and told him, "Don't touch anything! If you screw up, you could put us both into the ground. But there's one exception to this. If you hear me say EJECT, pull the ejection handles hard. If I say eject, and you ask, What? ... You're talking to yourself!" That pilot knew physical things can be replaced. No one's life is worth a $10 million airplane.

When the airplane ceases to be of benefit and begins to be harmful, get rid of it, now! How does this tie into police service?

Policemen use their hands for holding plenty of things. Steering wheels, notebooks, pens, radios, flashlights, impact tools, and firearms. Is it possible that an officer will have something valuable in his hands when he gets into a confrontation? If you have an active career, I can almost guarantee it. Whether it's your $2,000.00 personal notebook computer, or your agencies $1,800.00 portable radio, *no matter how expensive, you need to drop it without hesitation!* You can replace the dropped item. You can't stop the attack if you're burdened with a non-tactical item in your hand. Better yet, throw the object at your suspect! If you throw something at your suspect's head, he generally flinches away and tries to defend. This may give you a break and let you make up reaction time.

The one thing that cannot be replaced is the unique bundle of heritage, experience, and personality that comprises *you.* Those observations, emotions, personality traits, and the unique folds in each person's brain that make us individuals are not reproducible. Use or throw whatever you have in your hands and respond to any threat now...immediately!

Train this way so when it happens on the street, you won't think, "Jeez, I never thought about this! What do I do now?"

Weapons are an important factor in war,
But not the decisive one;
It is man and not materials that counts.

Mao Tse-Tung
1938

FIGHT AND SURVIVE

The person sitting in my kitchen was a large man, comfortable with himself in a way that brought assurance to those around him. He had a glint in his remaining right eye, the left eye was missing. I asked if he minded being interviewed about his shooting and he gladly consented.

In March 1982, Wyoming State Patrolman, Steve, received a report of a bank robbery at the Alpine Savings and Loan in Craig, Colorado. The physical description of the suspect was very vague; white male, 5'6" to 6" tall, 150 to 200 lbs., brown hair. This area is very remote and traffic extremely light. A fish and game officer had seen a red sports car with Oregon license plates near the area of the robbery. The driver of the sports car matched the suspect's description. When the license number of the sports car was run, it returned stolen out of Oregon with the driver wanted in connection with sex crimes in that jurisdiction. All officers assumed the sports car was responsible for the robbery.

Steve was patrolling a very remote area of Wyoming, when he saw a brown Plymouth Champ go by. Steve decided to stop the Plymouth to ask if the driver had seen the red sports car. When Steve turned on his emergency lights, the driver applied the emergency brake and exited his vehicle shooting. The first bullet penetrated the windshield, Steve's sunglasses, and his left eye. The bullet came to rest at the rear of the eye socket along with glass fragments from the windshield and his sunglasses. Steve slumped over in the seat and radioed for help.

When he next looked up, the suspect was three feet from his open driver's window. The suspect shot Steve four times in the left lower back,then reached in and began ripping the radar gun off the dash thinking he was disabling the radio. Steve swung at the suspect with a fist, then kicked the door open into him.

The suspect threw away the radar gun and ran to his car. Steve got out and fired at the suspect six times, putting four · bullets in the driver's seat headrest. The remaining two bullets hit the driver's seat back. One of the rounds hit the metal post of the headrest, and the copper jacket separated striking the suspect in the top of the shoulder. The wound was superficial, but bled heavily. The suspect drove away. Three miles away, another highway patrolman caught the suspect and took him into custody. The suspect is now serving a life sentence in a Wyoming state prison.

If you are hit, regardless of the type of weapon, keep going. Fight back. You can take effective action. With one eye shot out, and four bullets in the back, Steve survived and was able to be astonishingly accurate with his sidearm.

Steve not only survived, but is flourishing. When he first got his false eye, wearing it created an allergic reaction. Since then, medical advances and a new space-age coating technology have stopped the allergy. Steve wanted to return to work as a peace officer. Because of his vision, he wouldn't be able to work patrol, but with a twinkle in his right eye, Steve told me, "You know me, Rocky. I'll find a way to get back on the street." With his guts, drive, and determination, I don't doubt it at all.

I am indebted to Steve for his permission to use these events so other officer's can benefit from his experience.

Bravery is the capacity to perform properly even when scared half to death.

Omar Bradley
US Army General

P.S. I heard from Steve not too long ago...he made it!

NOW YOU SEE IT...
NOW YOU DON'T

It was New Years Eve and things were not quiet. I had just finished taking my umpteenth report of the night due to revelers, fights, and party-goers. I saw a green, poor condition station wagon pull out of a side street and when the rear swung into line there were no tail-lights on the car. There were three large male subjects aboard the car. I radioed in the stop and the driver pulled off near a major intersection without street lighting. I came up to the car and got the driver's license and registration. After my approach I saw that two of the three men had white shirts on with blue jeans. There was a black leather jacket in the rear seat. Uh-Oh!

The people in the car couldn't know it, but my heart was pounding and my mouth was dry. The description of two of the suspects matched a pair of armed robbers from the Roseville area. I carefully backed to my car and called for assistance..and please make it fast! A Rocklin police officer came to back me up and, using the patrol car's public address speaker, I asked the driver to get out of the car. He did as asked and complied with my directions. I backed him up using verbal commands until I was able to put a control hold on him.

During the search, I moved the right hand side of the driver's jacket. I clamped my hand down on the mass of a holster on his belt. The only thing more un-nerving than a full weapon holster on a man's belt, is an empty one. This one was empty with two suspects still left in the car. I jerked the driver back behind the patrol car's lights and hollered, "WHERE'S THE GUN?" The sound of my back-up officer's sidearm coming out of his holster was reassuring.

When all was said and done, a different gun was found rolled into a coat on the back floorboard of the suspect's car. The gun I seized was a revolver. The holster on the driver's belt was for a semi-auto pistol. I never located the semi-auto though the car was searched thoroughly. Investigation proved the suspects were not the ones who committed the Roseville armed robbery. Lucky me!

■ ■ ■ ■ ■ ■ ■ ■ ■ ■ ■ ■ ■ ■ ■ ■ ■

On a cold September night George was patrolling the back side of a sparsely populated housing area in the county. He found an El Camino pickup idling in the roadway with its lights out. A male form came out of the brush and trees on the roadside, nearly scaring the water out of George. The male suspect was belligerent and said that George had, "no right to hassle him." George pointed out this was a very unusual area to be hanging around at 4:00 a.m. The male suspect, Patrick, didn't seem to think so. He admitted he didn't live near there, but refused to account for his actions.

Because Patrick was verbally belligerent, a back-up officer, Dennis, started toward the stop. George didn't know why he felt so suspicious, but some sixth sense warned him if he got too near this man something disastrous could happen. He chose to wait and talk to the man, engaging him in a simple conversation about the cold night and conditions.

Dennis arrived and both he and George accompanied the suspect/driver to his car. Dennis took a look inside the El Camino and saw a box of .45 caliber handgun ammunition on the front seat. He noticed the way the suspect was standing with his shoulders hunched and hands inside the pockets of his Army field jacket. Dennis' response was immediate and his service sidearm came out of his holster and levelled at Patrick. "DON'T MOVE! You move and I'll shoot you!" George, with his previous suspicions, was not surprised by Dennis' sudden actions. He helped cover Patrick, then worked his way in and took him under control.

What George found made him thank his Lord for another day of breathing. Patrick had a cocked, loaded, .45 caliber semi-auto pistol tucked into the front of his waistband.

Probably the best indicator of the suspect's state of mind was the fact that when George took the gun away, he found that THE GUN WAS COCKED AND LOADED WITH THE SAFETY OFF. In addition, there were TWO FULL MAGAZINES OF SPARE AMMUNITION IN PATRICK'S JACKET POCKETS.

You can't come much closer to being in a firefight without having shots fired. Patrick's method of carry indicated he wanted the gun ready for instant use. He wanted to be able to sweep the gun from his waistband and use it within a second. It also made Patrick a candidate for what has been called an "explosive vasectomy." That would be a better outcome than injuring or killing George or Dennis.

George's sixth sense saved his life. I'm convinced that he saw things that made him uneasy which were not enough to excite the "reasonable cause" that courts and attorneys require. Gut hunches are not admissible in court. But I think George would encourage you to listen to the hunch that will save your life.

Dennis and George both have plenty of training and experience. The way the suspect's shoulders were hunched, and the fact his stance just didn't look right, set off alarm bells for both of them. When Dennis saw the ammunition, that clinched it.

Patrick went to jail for possession of a concealed weapon. He was a semi-truck driver and there were two large Peter-Bilt trucks parked near where he was found. George believed that Patrick was there to rip off the trucks. If the owners had discovered him at it, they were at risk of being killed.

The bottom line here is that George and Dennis are still working. They survived.

Courage is the complement of fear.
A man who is fearless cannot be courageous.
(He is also a fool.)

Dr. Robert Heinlein

YOU WANT TO WALK... DON'T YOU!

"Boy 90, S-7, report of a suicidal suspect. His doctor is calling and states the suspect has a terminal heart condition. Suspect has only six months to live and intends to kill any responding officers." Dispatch continued, "The suspect is at the Foothills Motel and his wife and infant daughter are with him. Doctor is concerned that suspect will harm them. Suspect is drunk and known to have numerous firearms."

I picked up the radio microphone and transmitted, "Charlie 25, I'll back-up on that call." Don also answered and volunteered to provide back-up since this sounded like a bad call. I arrived at the motel and pulled to the back side of the lot. From there I could see the front door of our suspect's room. As my Sergeant, Keven, walked around the side of the building accompanied by Randy and Don, the suspect opened the door and stepped out lighting a cigarette. Bad heart and obviously a health nut smoking like that. I called on the radio to let the approaching officers know our suspect was up and mobile.

When Keven and his entourage came around the building, the suspect swung around, widened his stance, and leaned his weight on his forward leg. The suspect then made small palm to palm circular hand motions. I recognized these motions as "kata" movements or martial arts moves, and decided I should get up there. I crossed the 50 yards of lawn while watching our suspect's movements. He was standing with his back to me and had no idea I was there. My duty gear does not rattle with keys or metal. As I walked up behind the suspect, I caught Don's eye and pantomimed a take-down maneuver. Don nodded. The suspect was leaning further forward and his speech, though slurred, was very threatening. He was threatening three armed officers with attack.

The suspect suddenly became aware of my presence and began to turn his head. Now or never! I used a hair pull take-down which put his feet where his head had been and vice-versa. He went limp on the grass. I handcuffed him and checked his vital signs; heartbeat strong and steady, breathing okay.

He began to struggle and I took a control hold, getting him to his feet, even though he didn't want to walk.

As I led him off, he collapsed and took the falling impact on his left shoulder. As he hit the ground, I ended up straddling his body, and he threw his right knee up toward my groin. I moved toward his head to move above the arc of his striking knee. This time when I brought him back to his feet, I used a bio-mechanical hold with pain-compliance and made sure he *wanted* to stay on his feet.

We confiscated eight rifles and handguns, as well as two samurai swords from his motel room. Steve, the suspect, threatened to kill everybody - officers, medical people, and anyone who came into contact with him - he wasn't particular. He said several times he had nothing to lose, he was going to die soon anyway. The judge's verdict was, "No jail time. It's not appropriate." Last I knew, Steve was still out there, dangerous to the public, himself, and even more so to his wife and child.

A long way to go for this story. But the point is not a minor one. Police carry plenty of gear. When I was young and weighed 175 pounds, out of curiosity I weighed myself with all my duty gear...weapon, belt, boots, ballistic vest, uniform, baton, radio, flashlight, notebook, and all pocket paraphernalia...I weighed in at a whopping 207 pounds.

It's a fact of life that some criminal may, with intent, set out to injure or kill cops. More officers die from traffic accidents than are killed in hostile actions with armed criminals. But the loss of an officer to a deliberate act is hard to understand. More commonly we are struck by heart disease from unresolved stress, lousy hours, erratic sleep habits, crummy eating habits, and lack of exercise. However, one of the most frequent causes of police disability is back trouble. Partially from lousy car seats, partially because of the equipment we have to carry, and all too frequently because we have to pick up somebody who throws a little kid tantrum and won't walk on their own.

We're carrying around a good size pack load and we're expected to jump tall fences in a single bound while burdened like a pack mule. How many times have you seen someone reach down and pick up a limp suspect by bodily force and try to carry the suspect's full body weight? Why do we do this?

We must realize that non-compliance is a form of resistance. We want to encourage this person to walk without damage to us or the suspect. We do that by employing pain-compliance holds. This is safer than lifting the suspect bodily.

Safer for us and for the suspect. We should not take the very real risk of a career-ending back injury.

Employing pain-compliance holds to make a suspect walk eliminates the risk to the suspect of either being dropped, or of a shoulder injury due to the suspect being muscled off the ground by their arms. The officer should explain the procedure to the suspect first. Then the suspect can't say, "I didn't know what was going on." The officer has told him what is expected of him. The suspect is levered to a sitting position, with his legs in front of him. The pain-compliance hold is taken and the suspect is pushed forward until he or she rises under their own power. If they collapse, pressure is exerted on the hold until the suspect wants to walk. If the suspect complies and walks, the pain-compliance hold is relaxed until control is there, but the suspect has no pain. If pain persists after control is gained, the suspect will eventually fight. We ease off the pain-compliance - we want control, not resistance.

This doesn't work well with a PCP suspect, nor anyone with a massive chemical impairment. However, there are a variety of nerve stimulations, control, and bio-mechanical holds that may prove effective. Train in all methods, otherwise the officer may well apply the hold too vigorously under the adrenaline of the situation.

Pain-compliance. Inhumane? No. Inhumane is dropping suspects from a three foot height flat on their face when they can't catch themselves with their hands. Inhumane is a career-ending back injury to a young officer when it is unnecessary. Inhumane is when a suspect is inadequately controlled and the officer is injured. Inhumane is when quality training could have prevented the injury to the officer and it has not been given.

Nothing is easy in war.
Mistakes are always paid for in casualties...
and troops are quick to sense any blunder
made by their commanders.

Dwight D. Eisenhower

OH, HE'S NO PROBLEM!

I had a new trainee in the car. As usual, I want the busiest beat and hopefully the primo calls. A trainee needs experience and this is how to get it. "Alpha 25, drunk suspect creating a disturbance...Rock Creek Plaza." Fortunately we were on the other side of the shopping complex at the time, so response was just a matter of seconds.

As I drove the car toward McDonalds, we saw our drunk suspect, seemingly walking in defiance of gravity. My trainee said, "Oh! I've dealt with him at the jail. He's no problem." I didn't say anything. I hoped the trainee was right. This guy was really plastered drunk and a fairly good-sized man.

The trainee approached calmly and called the suspect by name. The drunk turned around like a turret, his body swiveling and arms flapping loosely. The trainee talked with him for a moment then asked him to go into a position from which he could be handcuffed. My trainee clasped the suspect's hands, which were behind his head. The suspect's cowboy hat was jiggled during the handcuffing procedures. He broke one hand loose from my trainee's hold, picked the hat off his head and threw it down on the ground. In the throwing motion, the suspect's open hand slapped my trainee's outer right thigh. I stepped forward and grabbed the suspect's upper arm. He turned his head to watch me. While I dominated the arrestee's attention, my trainee completed the handcuffing. We took the drunk to jail and went through the booking process.

Once we cleared the jail, I turned to my trainee, "Okay, let's dissect that last arrest. You did plenty right. Number 1, you took the suspect under verbal control. Number 2, you made the verbal control firm and exerted command presence. Your positioning for handcuffing was good. After that, things went to hell." The trainee was startled. "How do you figure things went to hell?"

My trainee and I went to a remote location and I had him get out of the car. We both unloaded, checked and rechecked both our service sidearms, then removed all ammunition from our persons. I had the trainee take me into the control-hold used to begin handcuffing. When the hold was applied, I showed the trainee how simply the downward motion of the suspect slapping his leg could be turned into a disarm. Before the trainee could move or respond, I had his sidearm, and pulled off three clicks of the hammer beside his body in a safe direction behind us.

I turned and looked at a white-faced trainee. "The other mistake you made was you had a preconceived idea this person was no problem. Don't pre-judge a situation." Then we went over alternative handcuffing positions and weapon retention. When I demonstrated the alternatives, the trainee was eager to learn and did well.

The basic problem was not the trainee's inexperience nor the handcuffing method used. The problem was that too many people in the police and military service have never been in a fight before. It is nearly impossible for them to realize that *one and one-half seconds is enough time for two attempts to kill an officer.* One of those attempts may be successful. Especially if the officer doesn't react and stop the motion!

Police and the military better understand that someone who moves undirected, or in an undesired direction, is *not* complying with your order nor submitting to your authority. In a failure to comply, the officer is in danger of physical assault or losing his life depending on the aggressiveness or violence level of the suspect. Suspects in a hands-on situation who continue to move despite direction by a policeman or soldier need to be brought under control. Right now!

In a felony arrest or high-risk vehicle stop, it is common for some people, especially former prison convicts, to simply refuse to comply with verbal directions. If you are trying to take that person into custody for a felony and they fail to comply with your direction, is it appropriate to use impact force on them? Absolutely! This felony suspect is showing non-compliance. Non-compliance to your *lawful* arrest is...(let's say it all together)...*resistance!* So we may *stimulate* our felony suspect with impact force to comply with our lawful authority and lawful attempt to take him into custody.

Control may be as simple as a compliance-hold, bio-mechanical leverage, or take down. It may be necessary to use impact force or lethal force. In a high-risk situation, the officer's most neglected option is *retreat!* This option is under-used. The soldier or officer must make the necessary decision within a second. Not an easy task.

To be successful...
what you must know is how man reacts.
Weapons change, but man, who uses them,
changes not at all.
To win battles you do not beat weapons.
You beat the soul of man...

George S. Patton

VERBAL TRAPS

I was sitting on the witness stand recounting the arrest of a burglary suspect..."the suspect slid open the sliding glass door and I heard him run across the back yard. I heard him jump up on the fence and saw him straddle the top of the board fence." The district attorney said, "And then what happened?" I continued, "I ran up to the suspect, pointed at him with my finger and told him, 'Sheriff's Department, Andy! Come down. If you make me chase you, you're gonna get hurt!'

The district attorney looked at me and said, "What did the suspect say, if anything?" I looked steadily at the D.A. and replied, "The suspect said, 'Aw fuck!' then came down from the fence." The D.A. grinned, the judge smiled, and the court spectators broke out in laughter.

■ ■ ■ ■ ■ ■ ■ ■ ■ ■ ■ ■ ■ ■ ■ ■ ■ ■ ■ ■

Jerry is testifying in federal court about one of his large narcotics arrests. The suspect was looking at major time in a cell at federal prison. The defense attorney was really trying to rake Jerry over the coals. Jerry set out the facts which led him to a search. The defense attorney kept hammering on it. For the third time the defense attorney asked the question, "Officer why did you search the defendant's car?" Jerry looked at the defense attorney then deliberately and slowly said, "Because I can! The law allows me to!"

There was a stunned silence in the courtroom for a few seconds. The defense attorney rapidly moved to strike the answer. The judge had a twinkle in his eye when he refused to strike Jerry's reply. "You asked the question counselor, the officer only answered it."

Later in the court hallway, after the conclusion of the case, the judge saw Jerry and told him, "You know, I get so sick of legal jargon, evasive or flowered-up answers. Your answer to that question was so true and simple, it was refreshing. A good job, deputy."

■ ■

"Your Honor, move to strike as unresponsive." "The witness is admonished to confine himself to the question." "Your Honor, I would ask this court to have the witness answer in an affirmative fashion." "Just answer the question, yes or no." You have just witnessed some prime danger signals. If the judge agrees with the questioning counsel, you should have alarm bells going off in your head.

If you, as a witness, are confined to a yes or no answer, it can be a trap. To use an extreme example (and not a subtle one):

QUESTION: Just answer yes or no, officer. Has your relative stopped working as a prostitute?

If you answer yes to this example question, you are admitting a relative *was* working as a prostitute. If you answer no, you are stating the relative *is* still working as a prostitute. An unscrupulous attorney can use this method in a much more subtle fashion to make questioning a living hell. Attorneys want nothing more than to rattle you, scare you, shake your confidence, and try to make you appear incompetent in front of a jury. **So don't let them.**

Listen carefully to each question. Above all, be truthful. Don't be afraid to ask for the lawyer to repeat or re-phrase the question. Don't be afraid to admit it if you don't understand the question. Don't be afraid to say, "That question can't be answered with a simple yes or no." Pause for a second before you answer questions from both the D.A. and defense. This gives the D.A. or your attorney time to raise an objection to the question. Don't allow the attorney to rapid-fire questions at you. They can change questioning in mid-stream and your fast answer may trap you into an incorrect or careless answer.

Expect the defense attorney to attack the witness on any major case. They do this to insinuate bias on the officer's or witnesses part. What it should indicate to the judge and jury is that the defense has no other means of defense. They don't dare attack the other case witnesses or evidence because they are too strong. They can only attack the credibility of the officer and hope to discover something of benefit. We don't need to make it any easier for our opponents. Incidents of previous bias are only going to help tear us apart. Think your personal enemies, former arrests, ex-spouse or some unwitting friend won't tell them? Think again.

If the judge confines you to a yes or no answer, it's because you are ducking and dodging what seems to be a telling point of the case. *Don't commit this error!* Testify truthfully, clearly, and to the point on all your cases. Don't be afraid to testify to something which the defense may depict as favorable to their case. Defense attorneys are very obliging at picking a minor point, or one that draws attention away from their client's guilt, and trying to distract a jury with it.

Testify to the case cleanly and honestly, then let the prosecutor get your points back on re-direct examination. If you follow this method of testimony, the jury will see that (1) you are telling the truth, (2) you are not harboring a "grudge" against the defendant, and (3) you are doing your job in a professional manner.

The truth is found,
when men are free to pursue it.

Franklin D. Roosevelt

LIGHT AS A WEAPON

It was our usual Friday night shift. "Paul 31...report of a large juvenile party with approximately 50 people, loud music and alcohol." The broadcast continued with an address and particulars. Myself and several other officers decided to invite ourselves to the party.

We parked near the house, the walls of which were flexing outward in time to the beat of the hard rock music. I got out of the patrol car, and accompanied by the other officers, came up the walk toward the driveway. The owner of the house, a responsible older citizen, came out to the driveway and said they were holding a party for the football team and it had just gotten a little out of hand. He spoke with his son, who dashed back inside the house and the volume of the music immediately dropped drastically. The party-goers were sleeping there overnight and everyone had parental permission to be there.

About this time, I heard an aggressive male voice behind the side yard board fence. "Where's them fucking cops. We oughta kick their asses. They got no fucking right here!" The side gate opened and a teenager stepped out. As he hit the side walkway, I took the 30,000 candlepower flashlight and directed a short burst of light into his eyes. The effect was immediate. The young man's head recoiled as if slapped, his hands snapped out in front of him, and he stopped immediately, effectively and temporarily blinded. Coming from the darkened interior of the house, into the darkness outside, and then into the blazing flashlight beam, the young man was dazzled, and stood fixed while I walked up to him and took a control hold. He had no warrants, wasn't drunk, and had no drug indications. Just a case of juvenile bravado...letting his alligator mouth overload his tweety-bird ass.

Some years later I was teaching a training class on high-risk felony stops. "Put your high beams on in your car, turn your side spotlights on, and put the overhead lights on. Now...step out in front of the car and look back. You see a curtain of light, and that's all."

It's important for police to realize the lights they carry on their person and on their car can be a weapon of sorts. Make the suspect squint and look hard to find you.

Here's the flip-side of light as a weapon. The suspect can use it against you. The patrol car that pulls up behind you at night with its headlights on, is back-lighting and silhouetting you for the suspect's evil intentions. If this happens we need to have a pointed discussion with our co-worker about back-lighting us.

On occasions at low-speed, we can use the parking lights on our car and drive while using the front unit's headlights. All this has to be done with safety uppermost in our minds. If we have to walk down a hallway with a light behind us, it might make good sense to unscrew the light bulb or turn off the light.

If you're caught on the bad side of light control, overwhelm the suspect's light with a brighter one, move and take cover, or make yourself scarce in any way you can. Military people know that back-lighting themselves is not a good idea. Police sometimes forget this. Patrol settings tend to lure us into the idea that tactical "light control" is unnecessary.

Nothing could be further from the truth.

We are not weak if we make a proper use
of those means which the god of nature has placed
in our power. The battle sir, is not to the strong alone;
it is to the vigilant, the active, the brave.

Patrick Henry

BAD PEOPLE - EVERY WORK DAY

Jail briefing. This prisoner is causing a problem. These prisoners had a fight today. This prisoner can't be put with this one. These are co-defendants...no contact. I look around the table and see some officers paying strict attention. Others are not. The officers who aren't paying strict attention seem to be the ones who generally consider the jail a "controlled environment." It is to a certain extent. That is its danger point.

The concentration of criminal suspects is 100% in a jail setting, and becomes 100% criminals in any prison setting. The "controlled environment" statement means that help will be there on the floor with you in 20 to 30 seconds. Usually not over a minute. In previous stories we've established that this is enough time to make 15 or 20 serious attempts to stop your breathing permanently, or ruin your health and well-being. We cannot go into a jail or prison setting with the mind-set that we will certainly "go home that night." It just ain't so.

Recently we had an officer-involved fight in our jail. It's not unusual and happens daily or nearly hourly in some jurisdictions. What made it unusual was that there were three officers in this housing area. I was working with 70 plus of the highest risk inmates in my counties' jail. The call came out of an officer-involved fight and the two other officers scrambled to get out of the housing area. I couldn't leave. By orders, I was assigned to this place and had to stay in the cell-block area.

Some time later, I checked with the control center and made sure that our officers were okay. They were. The suspect was restrained quickly. One of the inmates came up and asked me, "What happened a little while ago?" I told the inmate the situation had been handled. The former prison inmate, now enroute back to his illustrious former home looked at me steadily. "I hope that prisoner got his own back before you guys took him down." I looked back evenly and smiled slightly, "He's going to the infirmary to get checked, that should tell you something. My officers are okay. "The inmate scowled as he turned away, "You guys will win eventually here, but we can always get some of our own back."

This is a very revealing statement. The prisoner goes into the fight with the mind-set that he doesn't care about win, lose, hurt, or dead. All he wants to do is hurt you before he gets restrained. In the jail or on the street, the police of this country cannot be paranoid, but must be able to "gear up" their mind-set and physical capabilities IN A FRACTION OF A SECOND. Some people would say that this ability would give us a split-personality. "Other duties as required" does cover a lot of ground, and part of that ground is being able to be efficient and effective with physical or lethal force control on short or nearly no notice.

Figuring that we work in a "controlled setting" leads us to complacency. Leads us to drop our awareness. Lets us relax. That's something we can't afford too much of. When the prisoner or arrestee gets physically or lethally violent, we need to "up the ante" and make it too expensive or hellishly difficult to hurt or kill the people who wear the badge and uniform.

The first blow is half the battle.

Oliver Goldsmith
1775

"MINDSET"
(And A Political Commentary ...
(Definitely Not Apolitical Commentary)

The Criminal Mindset

From where I sit, the true mechanism to halt the crime problem is criminal control through deterrence. Crime is not society's fault, nor has our proven willingness to throw money at every real or imagined inequality solved it. The crime problem is not some real or imagined blame placed on society by the suspect or his attorney. The crime problem does not stem from the weapon, but from the warped, twisted mind and motive of the criminal.

The criminal's lack of respect for others stems from a failure to recognize another individual as a person. The victim is an abstract "object" or "thing." A means to gratification, not a person.

The rapist actually relishes and craves the degradation and control they exert on the victim. Gang members enjoy the intimidation and fear they instill as a group. Criminals and terrorists do not consider their victims "people." They seek gratification, reward, or feedback from the victim, but don't regard them as alive or feeling.

The less worthy of respect the criminal or gang member is, the more they will demand respect from their victims. Failure to give that respect may evoke a violent reaction. They are fearful their internal insecurity will be revealed. Thus their need for bragging, posturing, displays, and combativeness when odds favor them.

This also explains their necessity to overwhelm by numbers, physical dominance through attacking a smaller or weaker person, or necessity to arm themselves. They dare not tackle anyone or anything on even terms, and are incompetent to do so. They are afraid to appear less able, or "inferior" to anyone or anything.

It is a very bad sign when a criminal seeks to de-humanize his victim. When suspects refuse to acknowledge you as a person, they blindfold, hood, force to the floor, or tie down victims. Terrorists and criminals cover the eyes so they can kill an "object," not a person. They restrict movement or put victims face down on the floor to make control of the "object" easier and render them helpless for execution.

The criminal also knows he or she need not fear their victims for the most part. They do not fear the police since arrest is the usual result, and their "rights" are strictly observed during and after arrest. The possibility of death for the suspect at the hands of the legal process is so unlikely as to be negligible. Incarceration is half to three-quarters of the time to which they are sentenced, is not uncomfortable, and affords them status among other prisoners.

The problem here is not the weapon. It is the deviate mind and actions of the criminal or terrorist. The weapon is an inanimate object. The criminal gives it impetus, motion, and animus. Control or deter the criminal and any weapon they can devise becomes impotent.

The Citizen Mindset

The citizen is a thinking, rational, skilled human being. Citizens are secure within themselves and may have never known victimization. For the most part, citizens feel peace and harmony with those around them. They make their own way in the world and pay for themselves. Citizens are the productive members of society. A citizen is able to rationally think through a situation and resolve conflict by compromise. Victimization seems very far away.

However, the ability to skillfully work through the problems of everyday life may become a handicap. The citizen may very well regard their state of mind, and way of dealing with things, as "universal." Their inability to see that a criminal or terrorist does not hold their views, abilities, or goals, may prevent them from reacting to the threat by placing them in a state of denial. "This can't be happening" is most often heard.

The citizen may not believe the criminal will hurt or kill them for little or no reason at all. Citizens have been killed in our larger cities for making eye contact with gangsters. Why do we tolerate criminals who will kill at a glance? Such depravity must be deterred by swift, harsh, and certain punishment.

The Defensive Mindset

The person who has a defensive mindset takes a considered, thinking, realistic approach to life. They are skilled in dealing with the situations, and compromises, of modern life, with one added dimension: they have considered the "what if's..." in life. They do not ignore the actions of criminal predators. They do not believe, "it won't happen to me." Their options have been thought out or visualized ahead of time. They have been self-taught to respond to external threat. They will have a wider selection of responses because they will have thought out, discussed, and/or trained possible courses of action.

They are more likely to be armed than the average citizen, and are more likely to be effective with their weapons. They know criminals seek gratification *now*, are violent, and do not care about hurting or killing people. This realistic view allows the defensively oriented person to think ahead and be somewhat more cognizant of potential hazards.

The defensive mindset was graphically illustrated when armed terrorists hijacked an Air Liberia flight. The unarmed passengers promptly beat the terrorists to death and left them collected in a corner. A later hijacking of an Aeroflot Russian airliner netted each terrorist a bullet. Terrorists no longer attack these flights.

American transport is another matter...

The Achille Lauro hijacking occurred in the Mediterranean Sea. A cruise liner was taken over and a wheelchair-bound American passenger was executed and thrown overboard as an example.

The hijacking of a mid-east flight and the execution of an American serviceman on the tarmac of a Syrian airport further illustrates the problem. The victim was selected from among passengers of many other nationalities, primarily because he was American.

Pan Am 103 was bombed out of the sky over Lockerbie, Scotland in a terrorist act. We still have not caught, nor punished those ultimately responsible.

As a society, Americans have become used to staying in their homes at night, not walking in parks, having their children victimized, and having rape and murder be an everyday headline news item.

The incredible thing is the American public tolerates it. Americans have not brought more stringent sentences and laws to bear on felons through political pressure. Americans have somewhat lost the defensive mindset and are considered targets by terrorists and criminals. Americans as individuals, and collectively, need to get back the defensive mindset. It is sorely needed!

Political Mindset

Politicians are currently verbalizing about the "crime problem" in this country. Instead of endorsing the tough solution, the popular politician wants to legislate against firearms. This is an inexpensive, and ineffective solution to the crime problem for the popular politician and allows him to point to a supposed "anti-crime" record. Rubbish!

The popular politician refuses to acknowledge the crime problem lies in the actions of the criminal. That would be too difficult to solve. Effective crime reform would be hard, expensive, and unpopular with liberal factions. The death penalty would need to be made a reality and expanded to include more crimes.

Acknowledgment would have to be given that sex-offenders and violent offenders are repeat offenders. Eighty-five percent of released sex offenders re-offend and are re-incarcerated within two years of release leaving more victims in their wake. Life without parole would have to be considered, legislated, and enacted.

Prisons would have to be made less agreeable. Why are convicted felons allowed "conjugal visits" to have sex with their wives? They have proven through their own actions that their heredity cannot be afforded, and should not be tolerated in our society. Felons in prison are allowed to inherit property (which probably should rightfully go to their victims as reparation) marry, own real property, and file lawsuits against the state. Some prisons have motorcycles inside the walls for "occupational therapy." They have microwave ovens in cells, personal TV's and VCR's, free medical and dental care, free exercise equipment, nutritious diets, and leave to file lawsuits against the state for the "inhumane conditions" under which they live. Oh, we also have to pay for legal counsel to represent the prisoner against this "unfair society" which convicted and placed him in this "inhumane system."

Popular politicians want to blame an inanimate object rather than the person who gives it impetus. They are lying, to themselves and to you. This approach will not reduce crime, it just makes the popular politician's head rest somewhat easier knowing they can falsely say, "Well, I tried!"

Myself, I think popular politicians simply believe in the following quote. Not that they'd admit it to anyone.

To win the hearts and minds of the people,
First disarm them.

Mao Tse-Tung

A POLICEMAN'S PRAYER

Teach me that sixty minutes make an hour,
sixteen ounces a pound
and one hundred cents a dollar.

Help me so to live that I can lie down at night
with a clear conscience,
without a gun under my pillow,
and unhaunted by the face of those
to whom I have brought pain.

Grant that I may earn my meal ticket on the square,
and in earning it, I may do unto others
as I would have others do unto me.

Deafen me to the jingle of tainted money
and to the rustle of unholy skirts.

Blind me to the faults of the other fellow,
but reveal to me my own.

Guide me so that each night
when I look across the dinner table at my wife,
who has been a blessing to me,
I shall have nothing to conceal.

Keep me young enough to laugh with little children,
and sympathetic enough
to be considerate of old age.

And when comes the day of darkening shades
and the smell of flowers,
the tread of soft footsteps,
and the crunching of wheels in the yard,

Make the ceremony short and the epitaph simple
"Here lies a man"

Author unknown

ROCKY WARREN

AN IRISH TOAST

Here's to your coffin.
May it be made of 100 year old oak.

The coffin made from the tree
I shall plant tomorrow.

ABOUT THE AUTHOR

Rocky Warren is a Sergeant for the Placer County Sheriff's Department in Northern California. He has done patrol work as a deputy for the majority of his 19 years with Placer. Rocky has held assignments in Patrol, SWAT, Dive-Rescue, Detectives, Field Training, Agency Training Manager and is currently a Jail Supervisor. He is a Firearms, Defensive Tactics, and Impact Weapons Instructor who has testified in court as an expert in firearms, suppressers, and physical holds. He also teaches part-time on the staff of Los Rios Community College/Public Safety Center, Sacramento, and Chabot/Los Positos College, Livermore (Alameda Training Center). He currently holds two Bronze Medals of Valor for Police Service.

Rocky lives in the Sierra Nevada Foothills of Northern California with his wife and family. Hobbies include fishing, shooting, reading, writing, teaching, and traveling.

The Placer Sheriff's Department jurisdiction extends from just north of Sacramento to the North Shore of Lake Tahoe. The Department has 260 sworn personnel, over 70 corrections officers and more than 200 civilian personnel. Placer county is one of the fastest growing population areas in the country and has approximately 215,000 total population. Terrain in Placer varies from the agricultural area of the Sacramento Valley (200 ft. elevation) to the high Sierra Nevada Mountains (9,000 plus elevation). Snow skiing is close and accessible in winter, and hunting, fishing, and water skiing are favorite summer pastimes.

San Francisco is 100 miles away from the Placer County seat of Auburn. Reno, Nevada is a nearly equal distance eastbound on Interstate Highway 80. For further information about Placer County Sheriff's Department visit our web-site at: http://www.iwn.com/pcso/pcso.htm.